# Women, Patronage, and Self-Representation in Islamic Societies

# Women, Patronage, and Self-Representation in Islamic Societies

EDITED BY
D. Fairchild Ruggles

STATE UNIVERSITY OF NEW YORK PRESS

Published by
State University of New York Press, Albany



Printed in the United States of America



For information, address State University of New York Press,
State University Plaza, Albany, N.Y., 12246

Production by Cathleen Collins
Marketing by Fran Keneston

**Library of Congress Cataloging in Publication Data**

Women, patronage, and self-representation in Islamic societies / edited by D. Fairchild Ruggles.

p. cm.

Includes bibliographical references and index.

ISBN 0-7914-4469-4 (alk. paper) — ISBN 0-7914-4470-8 (pbk. : alk. paper)

1. Arts, Islamic. 2. Muslim women in art. 3. Muslim women—Art patronage.
I. Ruggles, D. Fairchild.
NX688.A4 R84 2000
700′.82′0917671—dc21

99-054125

10 9 8 7 6 5 4 3 2 1

# Contents

# Illustrations

# Preface

This book grew from a session of papers at the College Art Association's 1996 meeting in Boston. That session, "Gender, Patronage, and Society in Islamic Art," was sponsored by the North American Historians of Islamic Art (since renamed as the Historians of Islamic Art), whose president at the time was Nancy Micklewright. As the five participants worked closely together on the session, we began to recognize that we were making a significant new contribution to feminist Islamic studies and to think about the various available venues for committing our ideas to print. We also rued the fact that there was no book extant for historians and art historians to use in university courses on gender and Islamic visual studies, despite the fact that many such courses are now being taught. And so, partly to provide a source book for our own courses, as well as to provide a supplementary text for gender courses taught in other departments such as women's studies and Middle East programs, I decided to steer this book into publication.

One of my aims in transforming the conference session into a book was to invite the participation of authors whose work would expand the geographic and temporal scope of the initial project: hence the book addresses contemporary art by a Muslim woman and stretches beyond the "Islamic" parameter to discuss patronage by non-Muslim women in comparison with their Muslim counterparts or descendants. That the book's historical frame does not include Islamic material prior to the twelfth century (the non-Muslim material begins in the first century B.C.E.) or include the vast populations of Southeast Asia is an omission that, I hope, will be rectified by other scholars in the future. We read with interest the slim eighty-eight-page issue of *Asian Art* devoted to female patronage in Islamic art that appeared six years ago (in fact one of the authors in this book contributed to that issue). Whereas the mission of that issue was to demonstrate that such patronage existed, our goal was to pose questions, such as why and how "matronage" occurred and whether or not it differed from the patronage of men. The authors of the present volume were variously provoked and inspired by earlier research, of which there was little, in any case. Soon after I submitted this collection of essays for publication, Gavin Hambly's edited volume, *Women in the Medieval Islamic World: Power, Patronage, Piety,* appeared in print. One of the many strengths of Hambly's collection is the broad range of issues pertaining to women. Our volume focusses more specifically on the question of how women have historically represented themselves, or appeared to do so. That two such books on the subject of women and public space (and the question of gender and visibility) have appeared almost simultaneously is a welcome sign that this area of Islamic studies has captured the interest of scholars. I hope that *Women, Patronage, and Self-Representation in Islamic Societies* will stimulate further research and stand not as a set of conclusions but a point of departure for new studies on Muslim women, matronage, and representation.

I would like to thank all the authors for their ideas and suggestions regarding the scope of the project, and in particular Leslie Peirce and Elizabeth Frierson for their critical reading of the introduction. The authors and editor together must thank the anonymous reviewers of the State University of New York Press for their insightful comments and advice regarding revisions.

## A Note on Transliterations

All attempts have been made to achieve consistency among the essays of this volume. However, many languages are used in transliteration, including Arabic, Persian, Turkish, and Sanskrit, and the author of each essay has chosen the extent and form of diacritics used.

—D. Fairchild Ruggles

# 1

# Vision and Power

## An Introduction

*D. Fairchild Ruggles*

When lecturing about Islamic architectural history, teachers often use images that show historic buildings in contemporary use: ablutions prior to prayer in a congregational mosque in Morocco, or Muslim students gathered around a professor in a *madrasa* (traditional college). Because they demonstrate how people interact with spaces and buildings, these images counteract the emptiness of other architectural slides in college collections that attempt to capture historic monuments in an unpeopled, timeless state, free of the clutter of fruit stalls and political posters blocking the facades and decorative details that are of primary interest to an architectural historian. The pictures of buildings with people contextualize the spaces, and for many students, particularly those in the West who are unfamiliar with Islam and the Middle East, they bring the architecture to life. But there is still an emptiness in many of these images. Some students are quick to notice it and will ask, "Where are the women?" An excellent question—but it is really two questions. The first is, "Where are the women in Islamic society and architectural space?" The second is, "Where are the women in these *representations* of Islamic society and architectural space?" The issue is one of presence in society and absence in representation.

The history of women in Islamic societies has been explored by a number of scholars in the late nineteenth and twentieth centuries. Even as early as the 1860s, there was an active discourse regarding social reform in Islamic countries that focused on the status and rights of women, and a reaction to it that sought to place women more firmly within conservative

Muslim traditions. In the last quarter of the century a few women from elite ranks of society began to publish on these topics in Egypt and Turkey, and by the 1890s, a new class of professional educators and journalists, both male and female, emerged in significant numbers across the Islamic world whose writings on women in a burgeoning popular press served to create a new female subject.[1] As the essays by Elizabeth Frierson and Nancy Micklewright in this volume show, the "woman question" in rapidly modernizing Islamic countries was inextricably linked to larger questions of national identity, colonialism, class, modernity, and social and economic advancement. Studies of women in Islam have accelerated internationally in the past decades, in part due to the rise of women's studies in the West. But both Muslim and non-Muslim scholars have wisely pointed out that one cannot take a methodological approach developed for western studies and blindly translate it to the Middle East. Hence Middle Eastern gender studies may respond to, but are in no way a mirror of western gender studies.

Given the wealth of recent research on individual Muslim women, and on class structure and gender, economics, political leadership, and legal status as it pertains to them, it is surprising that so few studies have emerged from the field of visual culture. This book rectifies that omission, bringing together a variety of in-depth studies on Muslim women (and in Ellison Banks Findly's paper, Buddhist and Jain women) in the Middle East and South Asia at various periods in Islamic history. Its premise is that the issues of self-representation and empowerment are best addressed by juxtaposing and comparing the artistic patronage and production of women during the various dynastic periods of Islam and the contemporary era. The political or feminist agendas that drive our various directions of research are undoubtedly a reflection of modern ideological assumptions—the contemporary interest in gender and the history of power relations certainly had no meaning for premodern Muslim women—but it is a given that no historian researches with the same motives that led the object of study to produce.

In this book we examine the artistic and literary production of women in order to shed light on an area of representation that has been overlooked by other historians. Adopting the view that the challenges and deviations from the norm sometimes reveal significant consistencies in the cultural production of the majority, the authors of this volume have looked for instances where women have initiated or been invoked in production processes, examining the reasons for and results of their participation and—equally important—the limits imposed on them. Some of the papers combine gender theory with visual theory, exploring the relationship between subject and object as determined by a socially constructed visual field. Typically, this line of questioning addresses the relationship between the viewer and the viewed, understanding those positions to be implicitly gendered. The argument, to state it simply, is this: artists and architects have historically been male; men have traditionally controlled and generated the gaze; women are the objects of that gaze; and thus vision is a socially constructed tool that gives men power and denies it to women. In contrast, the papers in this volume explore instances where women have exercised control over representation either as patrons of architecture, consumers of clothing, participants in mass print culture, or artists in their own right. In Lucienne Thys-Şenocak's paper, the author concludes that a major public mosque complex was designed specifically to accommodate a female gaze and that the result was a building that was typologically quite different from its contemporaries. Earlier historians who had looked for a reflection of a canonical linear typology in the mosque were confused by its unusual layout, but when analyzed from this new perspective of gender and vision, its logic emerges.

Critical theory and gender studies have been largely the domain of scholars in nineteenth- and twentieth-century fields. There is no intellectual reason why such methodological approaches should be limited to the modern period, but in Islamic studies, and especially Islamic visual studies where so many of us work on earlier periods, we have almost no models to follow and are compelled to reinvent and adapt. The quantity of visual analysis is particularly small in contrast with the ever-increasing historical, literary, sociological, and anthropological studies on women of the modern era. Nonetheless, the contributions of art historians and other scholars dealing with the literary and visual genres are important since these will provide an answer to that second big question regarding the representation of women: where are the women in Islamic art? Visual studies are no longer—if indeed they ever were—the exclusive domain of art historians; hence the interdisciplinary collaboration among scholars in this book has been especially fruitful.

## Vision and Visibility

Two overarching themes emerge from the papers offered here. One is the theme of power, under the heading of which we can include the power, motivations, and means of patronage that comes from family or dynastic ties; I shall return to this shortly. The other is the theme of visibility and representation. Many of the essays in this volume address the question of vision and the "visibility" of women as writers, architectural patrons, consumers, and charitable donors of services in Islamic society. In focusing on patronage and consumption where women are usually the agents of their own representation, we have avoided having to rely on information on women in contemporary paintings and illustrations. As Micklewright has pointed out elsewhere, women neither painted nor commissioned those representations. In her words, "The women who appear in Ottoman painting were placed there by male artists for male viewers and can be understood as functioning in the ideal manner envisioned by the male."[2] Such images tell us less about women than about what men think of them. In the absence of other forms of documentation, the images are useful, but primarily in telling us about women's limited visibility in the world of men. Of course, no representation is ever unmediated and objective, and thus none represents the absolute "truth"; rather, each representation is the product of an author, architect, patron (and perhaps also a reader, as discussed below) whose preconceptions shape the final image. Therefore, with regards to women, it is essential not to rely exclusively on men as authors when their interests with regard to social, political, and personal power are, at key points, in competition with those of the women they purport to represent.

The question of who controls the representation is critically important. In the buildings commissioned and paid for by women, often bearing their names, representation is to some degree controlled by the patronness. But there are two caveats to this assumption. First, the taste of the patron, whether male or female, was largely the product of a cultural milieu. Even the most wealthy and powerful of male patrons did not reinvent architecture with each new project. Building, painting, sculpting, and writing are always negotiated processes that depend to varying degrees on the patron, the artist, regional and historical techniques and concepts of style, and finally on the audience and its readiness to receive, understand, and legitimate a work of art or literature. Second, we cannot assume that women, when they wrote, built, or commissioned works of art, adopted a voice that was different from their male counterparts. Countless examples of women's production and patronage in the East and West indicate that they generally used the vocabulary of the prevalent mode of expression, which invariably reflected male values.[3] Ethel Sara Wolper's contribution to the volume argues, further, that the women may have been minimally involved, if at all, in certain Seljuk-period buildings, and that the inclusion of their names in inscriptions simply served as emblems of regional dynastic alliances achieved through marriage. But, on the other hand, Islamic architectural history affords numerous glimpses of intense female architectural involvement and creativity, such as the inventive decorative repertoire in the tombs of the female-dominated funerary complex Shah-i Zindeh (1360–1436) at Samarkand, that suggest that women patrons felt perfectly at ease commissioning buildings that were highly individualistic and on the cutting edge of fashion. One of the important lines of questioning pursued by the papers in this volume, thus, is the extent to which the hand of the patroness is evident in the works she sponsored, how she was identified in inscriptions, and how she was seen or not seen in social spaces.

A term employed by several of the authors is "invisibility." The papers by Leslie Peirce and Thys-Şenocak make a distinction between the "invisibility" of charitable acts, such as endowing a mosque with funds to feed the poor, and the "visibility" of the building itself. This suggests that the performance of good works and the social institutions themselves have less noticeable or permanent impact than the buildings that contain them, or, as indicated in the paper by Yasser Tabbaa, that buildings and their inscriptions work to keep the memory of the charitable act alive. I suggest that this is because buildings, being large, space-occupying objects, are not only literally present themselves but also denote a *representational* "presence." That is, the buildings stand, in the sense of synecdoche, in place of their donors, and enjoy a public profile denied to the woman herself. Perhaps it is also because charitable acts, although witnessed by society, are recorded in those centuries in texts written by men, so that women may appear to have no agency and are therefore "absent."

Instead of regarding this as a conspiracy on the part of men, it is useful to understand the omission as the natural result of a written genre that was more concerned with the act—charity—than with the actor, who happened to be a woman. We cannot apply modern expectations regarding feminism, which carries with it the relatively recent western notion of individualism, to a genre that privileged institutional agency over individual will. Written texts that may be essential research tools for modern scholars were almost never written for the purposes to which we put them. However, textual silences regarding women's charitable activities may direct us toward another more informative record of women's activities: works that were commissioned or made directly by them.

These sources and the analyses presented in the following essays amply demonstrate that women patronized the arts and had wealth and positions of power in the premodern era: one needs to think only of Shajar al-Durr, Gawhar Shad, and Nur Jahan for outstanding examples of Muslim queens who had the status and means to become significant arts patrons. As the journalist Hind Nawfal wrote in 1892, "[H]ennaed hands have held the reigns of kingdoms."[4] But it was largely in the late nineteenth century that the expectations for women in a rapidly transforming society began to change and that the definition of her role was debated publically with women taking an active part in the discourse. In journals such as *The Ladies' Own Gazette* and sections devoted to women in mainstream journals in Turkey, Egypt, and many other countries, women began to voice their opinions regarding the education and training of women, their economic status, their roles as wives and mothers, and their contributions as workers and breadwinners.[5] In the ways that they represent themselves in these writings, as well as in changes in dress that signaled modernity and western notions of female behavior, it is clear that women recognized the profound transformations that they were undergoing and understood precisely what was at stake both for women and the Muslim societies in which they lived.

## Power

Power is a significant theme that arises in all of the papers. In dealing with the question of uses, sources, and expressions of power, most of us are to some extent grappling with issues explored earlier by social historians who sought to explain the meanings of objects within larger social and political contexts. A number of art historians in recent decades have specifically taken up the question of how power is manifest in the patronage of precious objects and the appropriation of urban space.[6] The present volume of studies looks at the material expressions of power from a new and different angle, exposing a fundamental contradiction: women, traditionally viewed as outside the circle of power in Islamic history, have nevertheless built major charitable institutions and tombs, and owned and sponsored luxury goods such as finely crafted textiles, furniture, books, ivories, and jewelry. On the one hand, we can deduce from this that women were not so weak as earlier historians supposed. On the other, the paradox between political disempowerment and women's patronage asks that we explore more critically the term "power" and what it means.

When we speak of power, are we talking about a strictly public force that is expressed in the act of setting governmental policy, negotiating treaties, appointing high-ranking administrative officials, and creating institutions and buildings to house them? Are we speaking of wealth and the economic means to purchase land, goods, and services? Are we speaking about legal codes that guarantee certain personal rights such as inheritance, owning property, bringing lawsuits, and divorce? Finally, are we talking about an even more individual form of empowerment: the benefits conferred by marriage, motherhood, or celibacy? It is not enough simply to state that women wrote, spoke, and commissioned objects, buildings, and garments and therefore had power. We must ask far-reaching questions about the nature and exercise of power and avoid the trap of defining it as a male prerogative to which sequestered women only occasionally had access. Both men and women in the royal courts could be sequestered, and in neither case did the presence of walls (or absence of sexual activity) prevent access to political control. The essays in this collection do not suggest that power is something obtained solely on those rare instances when a women stepped out from behind the veil or harem walls to participate in public life, as if that alone were proof that Muslim women participated actively in society; they look instead at how women shaped the world (both masculine and feminine, public and private, walled and open) they lived in, and how, why, and where they did so.

Once again, the issue of visibility arises. Because the interior of harems—meaning both the royal institution and the private quarters of ordinary households—were not seen or described by public (generally male) eyes, they have been discounted by historians as marginal to mainstream public life. Some scholars have dismissed harems as places of feminine idleness and sexual license, regarding the women's quarters as seething with intrigues and factionalism but ultimately invisible and therefore without serious political impact. These observers of Islamic culture mistakenly defined the harem as a walled and gendered place rather than a sacred concept and assumed that the walls that kept outsiders from looking in also prevented women from affecting the world beyond the walls.[7] But agency is not so much dependent upon visibility as on the ability to see, as Thys-Şenocak shows in her study of the plan and sight lines of the Yeni Valide Mosque complex in Istanbul. Walls, screens, and veils that kept strangers from looking in did not necessarily prevent women from gazing out. As modern studies on a range of topics such as French prisons, eighteenth-century English landscape, and cinematography have shown, vision is a form of power, and seeing implies possession.[8]

What endowed a Muslim woman with power in the eighth through nineteenth centuries? The essays in this volume propose six critical categories of empowerment: financial independence, sons, natal family, celibacy, education, and finally voice (which may be the outcome of the above categories). Money and property are the most obvious sources of power; without them, neither men nor women can build large monuments, donate to public charities, make influential gifts, and buy loyalty, service, and information. There is ample evidence to suggest that plenty of women at various periods in Islamic history possessed abundant financial resources. Although the women in the studies in this volume belong mostly to an elite, rich, ruling class, it can be assumed that wealth gave women and men equally the economic power to build, donate, and endow. Here it is useful to remember, as Peirce cautions at the end of her paper, that "female" is not an essentializing category: the possibilities for women differed markedly depending on a myriad of factors, such as where and when they lived, their legal status, race, ethnicity, and the social class to which they belonged. Money was only one of many factors contributing to empowerment.

Relatively few women spent money as conspicuously as the women described in the studies presented here, but both elite and ordinary women acquired land, goods, and money in five fundamental ways. First, according to the Qur'an (4:7–12, 176), they had a right to an apportionment of their deceased relatives' wealth. Second, they retained ownership of the goods and properties settled on them as dower at the time of their marriage. Third, they could be appointed as the trustees to a *waqf* endowment, established by a parent, other relative, or even themselves, and might draw an annual salary in that capacity. Fourth, they could receive gifts from parents, husband or other family member that, unlike inheritance, were not subject to the apportionment dictated by Islamic law, and unlike certain types of dowries, did not have to be ceded in divorce proceedings initiated by the woman. Under this category also should be considered the formalized stipends from the state that elite women of the Ottoman and Mughal courts received, as well as extra money and land they not uncommonly acquired from the treasury in order to found charitable establishments.[9] Finally, women accumulated wealth in the form of profits from the management of estates and businesses. Findly's comparison of Jain, Buddhist, and Muslim women in India shows that in all three cases women gave generously to the religious establishments of their choice, dipping into their own resources to do so and without seeking permission from their spouses. The scenario suggests that women had considerable resources and knew about contractual negotiations and the management of money.

As Tabbaa, Thys-Şenocak, and Peirce demonstrate, the birth of a son was a source of power for most women and, particularly in the case of the ruling family, changed a women's status from mere royal consort (whether wife or concubine) to a mother with dynastic investment. A child born to the slave concubine of a free Muslim was born free and earned eventual manumission for the mother. Among ordinary free women, in a society that assigned the role of provider and head of household to the male and that sent the daughters away to live in the house of her husband's family, the production of sons was of critical importance. Sons were a guarantee of future security for the entire family and the continuity of the patriarchal line. Among royal consorts, the production of a male heir was even more significant because it ensured the survival of the dynasty on which the fortunes of the entire state depended. When a son inherited the father's throne, the mother rose to the preeminent rank of queen-mother; therefore, a good mother dedicated her energies to promoting her son's political and military career in hopes of securing for him the reins of state. The mother of the ruler not only presided over the harem, and thus the residential portion of the court, she also could wield considerable influence in affairs of state. Additionally, there are cases of queen-mothers serving as regents, or choosing the regents for sons (or more rarely grandsons) who were too young to rule, such as the Ayyubid Dayfa Khatun and the Ottoman Kösem Sultan.

The genealogy of a woman's natal family could be a source of power or prestige, as Kishwar Rizvi, Wolper, and Tabbaa demonstrate. Free-born brides brought their own bloodlines into royal marriages and their marital unions cemented alliances or pacified foes. In personal terms, these women, even though married and living among their husband's people, enjoyed the protection of their fathers and could call upon that support in times of need. Whereas concubines had no home to return to, no patriarchal support to invoke, and no competing bloodlines of their own (which Peirce suggests was largely their attraction for the Ottomans), free-born wives were entitled to all the respect and honors due to their father's house and brought, as part of their marriage portion, a distinguished genealogy. Findly states that in the Hindu context women were identified almost exclusively by their family roles as wife, mother, daughter, niece, and so on. Other sources indicate that patriarchal support operated even in the cases of Muslim women who became scholars and religious leaders, since often the way toward their unusual achievement was opened by mentoring fathers.

While the empowerment of women through family ties has been studied in recent years, no research has been directed toward the intriguing question of female celibacy as an alternative to a life devoted to household service and child-rearing.[10] The idea of nunneries and celibacy as a deliberate choice was frowned on in Islam, which regarded the protection of women as a male responsibility. A woman was protected first by her father, and then by her husband and son; if these guardians died or failed to provide, she could, in concept, fall back on her brothers, her father's brothers, or other members of the extended family. Indeed, the common practice of marriage between first cousins (not unusual even today) intensified the familial binds that supported her.

Nonetheless, celibacy was occasionally possible for women as an alternative to the domestic life of household management and child-rearing. Throughout the Islamic world, from Spain to India, there are cases of Sufi women who did not marry, rejected worldly preoccupations, and devoted themselves to learning and Sufi devotions.[11] Some of them became influential Sufi leaders and saints, earning the respect of their communities and the veneration of succeeding generations. There were *ribat*s (convents) and *zawiyas* (Sufi centers) for women in Cairo, Aleppo, Baghdad, and other cities, but as to whether this constituted a significant means of greater empowerment and independence—defined economically, legally, and in public acts such as teaching, preaching, or building—remains to be seen. Sufism and sexual abstinence may have provided an acceptable alternative to the expected female social roles for some women, but one cannot interpret this at face value as constituting a climate favorable to women and their greater independence. In Sufism there was considerable ambivalence toward women who could represent either extreme faith and piety or the distractions of worldly life.[12] Whether or not celibacy became a more common option for women under the aegis of Sufism is a rich topic for future study.

However, among the Safavids of Iran there is ample indication that some high-ranking women in court eschewed marriage. Rizvi cites the case of Shah Tahmasb's sister and political advisor, Mahin Banu, who was ritually betrothed to a deceased religious figure so as to prevent her marriage and removal from his court. These unmarried Safavid women dedicated themselves to the career interests of their brothers and fathers, undistracted by marital obligations and loyalties. This leads us to the fifth category of empowerment for women: education. One of the reasons that Safavid women so often served capably as trusted political advisors to their male family members was that they were taught, like their brothers, reading, writing, calligraphy, and religion as well as archery and horseback riding.[13]

The education of royal women was particularly emphasized among the Safavids, but it was quite usual for Muslim women of even modest means to be able to read and recite the Qur'an. Women patrons funded the establishment of schools and *madrasas* and, as *waqf* trustees, women could serve as managing supervisors.[14] However, they did not formally enroll in these institutions, receiving their education instead at home, tutored by a well-lettered male relative or perhaps a privately hired teacher, and occasionally reaching an level of expertise admired even by male chroniclers who were usually suspicious of women's learning.[15] Clearly women in prosperous households had more time and better access to tutors and thus were more likely to acquire advanced learning. For this reason, education was tied to class and economic status as well as the existence of a favorable social climate (as in the Safavid court). When nineteenth-century educational reforms established state education for girls in some countries, these class limits began to disintegrate and education was tied, instead, to imperial and later nationalist loyalties.

Finally, we arrive at the issue of voice, which arises as the result of the late nineteenth century's increasing concern with individual autonomy. Houria Niati's subversion of orientalist modes of representation, as described by Salah Hassan, is possible only because she is able to demand an audience and to be heard in a way that Algerian women of earlier generations could not. Frierson's essay explores the initial stirrings of a new feminist (in the sense of its time) moral and public authority, in which women used the written word to rewrite the gendered assumptions of previously male public institutions. Although the essays in this volume show that there were numerous previous acts of agency on the part of an influential *valide sultan,* regent queen, or other politically strong women, one can surmise that while women may have felt the need to survive and triumph within the confines of the prevailing order, they did not challenge its underlying premises or the fact that it was scripted by men. With the rise of self-conscious feminism and the increasing politicization of women around the world, however, women became active participants in the discourse, both written and visual, defining women and their place in society, and they began to insist on having a role in shaping the public institutions that govern the private lives of both women and men.

The questions of visibility and power examined here in essays ranging from the twelfth century to the present and from India to the Maghreb are important not only for the study of Muslim women, but for the fields of visual and Middle Eastern studies in general. Indeed, recent research on women is reinvigorating the historiography of Islamic studies in significant ways. Beginning with familiar sources and paradigms, we are generating an entirely new and highly productive set of questions regarding Muslim society, representation, and gender of the past and present. These questions then direct us to new textual sources—*waqfiyya*s (endowment deeds), Qurʾanic law and legal judgments, chronicles, memoires, biographical dictionaries. and the explosion of print culture that hit most areas of the Islamic world in the nineteenth century—as well as material sources such as personal objects and architectural space that increase our ability to think, write, and teach more comprehensively and reflectively about gender and the Islamic world as a whole. As Frierson and Micklewright demonstrate, the perception and status of women in Turkey and Egypt, as indexed in newspaper columns and fashion design, reveal how thoroughly the "woman question" inflected a broad range of social concerns and political ideologies. In the earlier periods, the roles of women reflected deep-seated social preoccupations: as aristocratic spouses they symbolized the integration of competing political groups, and as the mothers or sisters of sultans and royal heirs, they protected dynastic interests. Later, women—their bodies, dress, voices, and social roles—were intrinsic to the greater (and overlapping) debates of westernization, colonialism, modernization, and competition in world markets and political spheres.

Women, traditionally ignored as actors in the creative process, are examined here both as patrons and artists. To adapt a well-known statement by Linda Nochlin, perhaps there have been no great women architects and artists in Islam prior to the twentieth century, but one way to reintegrate women into the history of art is to broaden the definition of the creative act to include the patrons.[16] In the Islamic world, where women could and did possess great wealth, one need not look for long to find examples of female patrons building mosques, schools, hospitals, tombs. soup kitchens, and caravanserais. In so doing, we begin to acknowledge, also, the dynamic presence of the viewer/audience; for while patrons may participate in the generation of art, they are also to some extent the receivers of it. For example, Hassan has interviewed the artist Houria Niati about the making of her own art as well as her response to the Orientalist works she addresses. In a different manner, Peirce deals with the public reaction to women who assumed powerful roles, such as the queen mother Safiye who overstepped the limits of political acceptibility and was almost expelled from Istanbul as a result.

Poststructuralist methodology that addresses the artwork's contemporary audience and implicates the present audience—ourselves—in our own subjective interpretations is more widely embraced in the modern period and in western studies but can and should condition the work of scholars in non-western and premodern areas. Each of us is implicated in the construction of meaning of the material and textual works that figure in the essays presented here. Art, or a text, does not simply fossilize at the moment of creation to be excavated intact by later researchers like ourselves; rather the attribution of meaning is an interactive process that is constantly negotiated as we frame new questions and form new interpretations of these monuments, objects, and writings. Often those changes in meaning are reflected in material changes made to the body of the object, as a building is redecorated or expanded, or a text revised and adapted. Ultimately, the process is not simply about reenvisioning society with the women present (the question with which this introduction began); nor is it simply the acknowledgment that representation (no matter who is the artist and who is the object of the view) is never neutral. The act of interpretation—occurring now while I write and while you read—is a dynamic and reactive operation that is open to the very same kinds of inquisition that we have applied to the objects themselves. It is most fruitful when it concedes that the writers and readers do not have common goals, historically or contemporaneously; hence this book presents a collection of essays from scholars of different academic disciplines and backgrounds who adopt a diversity of approaches to the history of women and representation, and to the analysis of Islamic society as a whole.

## NOTES

1. Margot Badran and Miriam Cooke, eds., *Opening the Gates: A Century of Arab Feminist Writing* (Bloomington: Indiana University Press, 1990); Leila Ahmed, *Women and Gender in Islam* (New Haven: Yale University Press, 1992), 140–42; Elizabeth Frierson, "Unimagined Communities: Women and Education in the Late Ottoman Empire, 1876–1909," *Critical Matrix* 9.2 (1995): 55–90.

2. Nancy Micklewright, paper delivered at Middle East Studies Association annual conference (Washington, D.C., 1995), unpublished.

3. This question of the gendering of voice and gaze is a subject of considerable debate in contemporary scholarship. Laura Mulvey, a film critic and theorist, has argued that the positions of object and subject are gendered so that "the

woman is image; man is viewer," and that even when women adopt the stance of the viewer, their gaze (which is socially rather than individually constructed) reflects the male unconscious; see *Visual and Other Pleasures* (Bloomington: Indiana University Press, 1989). John W. Baldwin, examining the question of sex in medieval European discursive traditions, states that the women writers in his study did not differ noticeably from the men; *The Language of Sex: Five Voices from Northern France around 1200* (Chicago: The University of Chicago Press, 1994). In contrast, Griselda Pollack argues that a feminine gaze is possible, citing works by Mary Cassat and Barbara Kruger as examples, "Rebuilding Art History: Vision, Place and Power," in *Vision and Textuality,* ed. Stephen Melville and Bill Readings (London: Macmillan, 1995), 38–66.

4. Hind Nawfal, "The Dawn of the Arabic Women's Press," trans. B. Baron, in *Opening the Gates,* ed. Badran and Cooke, 217–19. See also Fatima Mernissi, *The Forgotten Queens of Baghdad,* trans. M. J. Lakeland (Minneapolis: University of Minnesota Press, 1993).

5. Frierson, "Unimagined Communities," 71.

6. Oleg Grabar in his doctoral dissertation of 1954 and again in his 1973 work, *The Formation of Islamic Art,* framed the essential questions of Islamic art history in the context of social history, demanding that artistic production be understood as a deep-seated expression of ideological values. In his interpretation of the Dome of the Rock in Jerusalem (completed c. 692), for example, he stated that the monument's site, decoration, and inscriptions asserted the power and victory of the new faith and the Islamic state (2nd ed., p. 63). Many of his students have likewise pursued the theme of power via the social contextualization of objects and architecture.

7. For a discussion of the harem both as a concept and a space, see Leslie Peirce, *The Imperial Harem: Women and Sovereignty in the Ottoman Empire* (New York: Oxford University Press, 1993), 3–6.

8. For relevant studies on vision and power in diverse fields: Kaja Silverman, "Fassbinder and Lacan: A Reconsideration of Gaze, Look, and Image," *Camera Obscura* 19 (1989): 54–84; Michel Foucault, *Discipline and Punish,* trans. Alan Sheridan (New York: Pantheon, 1977), and "The Eye of Power," in *Power/Knowledge,* ed. Colin Gordon (New York: Pantheon Books, 1980), as well as commentaries on his work such as Martin Jay, "In the Empire of the Gaze: Foucault and the Denigration of Vision in Twentieth-Century French Thought," in *Foucault: A Critical Reader,* ed. David C. Hoy (London: Basil Blackwell, 1986). My own work in Islamic architecture and landscape has centered on the issue of sovereign power, space, and the view: Ruggles, "Humayun's Tomb and Garden: Typologies and Visual Order," in *Gardens in the Time of the Great Muslim Empires* (Muqarnas Supplements 7), ed. Attilio Petruccioli (Leiden: E. J. Brill, 1997), 173–86; Ruggles, *Gardens, Landscape and Vision in the Palaces of Islamic Spain* (University Park: Pennsylvania State University Press, 2000).

9. Peirce, *Imperial Harem,* 122; Ellison Banks Findly, "Women's Wealth and Style of Giving," chapter six in this volume.

10. The term celibacy here means not having procreative sex. In a culture that permitted homoeroticism and to some extent homosexual relations among men, it is not unreasonable to expect that some women may have engaged in sexual activity with other women. Indeed, the need to prevent such fraternization—or "consorority"—by means of night-time illumination and elderly female guardians in the dormitories of the Girl's Palace at the Topkapı suggests that lesbian relations did occur. See Ottaviano Bon, "Descrizione del Serraglio del Gransignore fatta dal Bailo Ottaviano Bon [1608]," in *Le Relazioni degli Stati Europei lette al senato degli ambasciatori Veneziani del secolo decimosettimo, Turchia,* ed. Nicolò Barozzi and Guglielmo Berchet (Venice, 1871), 71, cited in Gülru Necipoğlu, *Architecture, Ceremonial, and Power* (Cambridge: MIT Press, 1991), 179 and note 113.

11. See Jamal Elias, "Female and Feminine in Islamic Mysticism," *The Muslim World* 77 (1988): 209–24; Julia Clancy Smith, "The House of Zainab: Female Authority and Saintly Succession in Colonial Algieria," in *Women in Middle Eastern History,* ed. N. Keddie and B. Baron (New Haven: Yale University Press, 1991), 254–74.

12. Annemarie Schimmel, *Mystical Dimensions of Islam* (Chapel Hill: University of North Carolina Press, 1975), 426–35. I am grateful to Sara Wolper for directing me to this chapter, "The Feminine Element in Sufism."

13. Maria Szuppe, "La Participation des femmes de la famille royal à l'exercice du pouvoir en Iran Safavide au XVIe siècle," *Studia Iranica* 23 (1994): 242.

14. Jonathan Berkey, *The Transmission of Knowledge in Medieval Cairo* (Princeton: Princeton University Press, 1992), see especially chapter 6, "Women and Education."

15. Berkey (*Transmission of Knowledge,* 169–70) suggests that women could also listen to lectures in *madrasa*s as well as more open learning environments, such as mosques.

16. Linda Nochlin, "Why Have There Been No Great Women Artists?" *Art News* 69 (1971): 21–46, reprinted in Nochlin, *Women, Art, and Power and Other Essays* (New York: Harper & Row, 1988). For a recent critique of approaches to feminist art history, see Karen Edis-Barzman, "Beyond the Canon: Feminists, Postmodernism, and the History of Art," *The Journal of Aesthetics and Art Criticism* 52 (1994): 327–39.

2

# Ḍayfa Khātūn, Regent Queen and Architectural Patron

*Yasser Tabbaa*

The study of women of high status in the Islamic world has generally focused on the modern and contemporary periods, where ample documentation and stark contrasts have generated complete portraits of these women as individuals and in terms of gender and class. Much less has been done to define the personalities of influential women in medieval Islam and to highlight the areas in which they chose to exercise their authority and patronage. The otherwise excellent recent studies by Mernissi, Ahmed, and others have attempted to deal comprehensively with the social history of women in different periods but have generally failed to say anything new about medieval women.[1] As is often the case with such diachronically ambitious projects, the middle Islamic period seems to get lost between the theoretical underpinnings of early Islam and the archival richness of later periods. At the very best, women of the middle period are assumed to have behaved and acted in a manner similar to women of the Umayyad and Abbasid courts.

More focused studies by Williams, Humphreys, Atıl, and others have contributed a much needed perspective about the architectural and artistic patronage of women in the middle Islamic period.[2] Despite these innovative works, however, the study of the patronage of women in medieval Islam remains very underdeveloped, particularly when compared to similar studies for the Ottoman Empire or medieval Europe. This state of research and, more specifically, the absence of any published work on Ḍayfa Khātūn will help formulate the questions and shape the discourse for this paper.

The questions I ask are both general and specific, initially addressing the status and patronage of some women of the Ayyubid court (1174–1260) before focusing on the regency and architectural patronage of Ḍayfa Khātūn in Aleppo in the 1230s. I will look first at the general patronage of monuments by court women and then more carefully at Ḍayfa Khātūn's commissions built within the context of her powerful but gendered position in a world of men. Although Ḍayfa achieved an unprecedented measure of autonomous political influence, becoming the first regent queen of her time, the paper will argue that her elevated status and prodigious architectural patronage were at least equally linked to the fact that she was wife, mother, and grandmother of successive Ayyubid sultans. Furthermore, the paper will demonstrate that Ḍayfa Khātūn, while operating within the Ayyubid system of architectural patronage, exhibited strong preferrence for foundations that catered to the needs of the Sufi mystics, some of whom were women.

Two anecdotes from contemporary observers underline the power enjoyed by women of the court and the high regard in which they were held. The first is from the late-twelfth century Andalusian traveler Ibn Jubayr, whose vivid and awestruck observations are seen through the lens of a more conservative Muslim culture. Recounting his encounter in 1184 with three royal women, or *khātūns* as he called them, during the pilgrimage to Mecca, he said:

> Among the strange affairs that are discussed and listened to by men we witnessed the following. One of the aforementioned khātūns, the daughter of prince Mas'ūd, . . . came to the Mosque of the Apostle of God—may God bless and preserve him—on the evening of Thursday, the sixth of Muḥarram, the fourth day of our arrival at Medina, riding in her litter (*qubbah*), surrounded by the litters of her ladies and handmaidens and led by Koran-readers, while pages and eunuch-slaves, bearing iron rods, moved around her driving the people from her path until she arrived at the venerated Mosque. Wrapped in an ample cloak, she descended and advanced to salute the Prophet—may God bless and preserve him—her servants going before her and the officials of the Mosque raising their voices in prayer for her and extolling her fame. She came to the small *rawḍah* between the venerated tomb and the pulpit, and prayed there wrapped in her cloak while the people who thronged around her were kept back by the rods. She then prayed in the *ḥawḍ* beside the minbar, and moving thence to the west wall of the venerated *rawḍah,* sat in the place where it is said that the Angel Gabriel—peace be upon him—came down. The curtain was then lowered on her, and her pages, slaves, and chamberlains remained behind the curtain

> receiving her commands. She had brought with her to the mosque two loads of provisions as alms for the poor, and stayed in her place until night had fallen.[3]

A second account by Ibn Wāṣil, contemporary with Ḍayfa Khātūn, describes a journey from Cairo to Aleppo taken by al-Malik al-Kāmil with two of his daughters.

> In the year 629/1232 the sultan al-Malik al-Kāmil left Egypt in order to claim Amida [Diyarbakr] from its owner, accompanied by the "Elevated Veil" Fāṭima Khātūn, wife of al-Malik al-ʿAzīz of Aleppo; Ghāziya Khātūn, wife of al-Malik al-Muẓaffar of Hamāh; and also the judge Bahāʾ al-Dīn Ibn Shaddād. The companion [al-Ṣāḥiba] Ghāziya Khātūn, mother of our lord the sultan al-Malik al-Manṣūr—may God bless his soul—arrived in Hama in great spectacle and ceremony. She embellished Hama by her arrival.

Meanwhile, Fāṭima Khātūn, accompanied by the judge Bahāʾ al-Dīn Ibn Shaddād and other dignitaries, continued toward Aleppo. On her way there, her caravan was ceremoniously received at several prearranged spots: the first in Hama; the second in Tell al-Sulṭān, where she was received by her aunt Ḍayfa Khātūn; and the third just outside of Aleppo, where al-Malik al-ʿAzīz Muḥammad, sultan of Aleppo, came out to meet her. They rode back to the citadel of Aleppo together, "with row upon row of soldiers flanking them."[4]

These anecdotes attest to the wealth of medieval Islamic court women, their independence, penchant for ceremony, and proclivity toward charitable acts. Whether in public processions or in private moments of worship, these princesses of the Zengid and Ayyubid dynasties of Upper Mesopotamia, Syria, and Egypt commanded a great deal of respect and a royal status rarely accorded to court women before them. While this does not indicate anything of their political power or legal status as independent agents, it does indicate that they enjoyed a "public" profile and notable presence. Indeed, they form the first group of women who are named on the inscriptions of their own monuments and in the contemporary texts. Although their person was hidden from view by veils, cloaks, and curtains, their actions were highly visible.

There are perhaps three factors that might have contributed to this situation and might explain its exceptional nature within the medieval Islamic world. The first is that these were princesses not concubines; that is, they were free women of noble origin rather than merely slaves in a harem. Concubines and harems undoubtedly existed in this period, although they do not seem to have been as common as they had been under the Abbasids[5] or as they would be later under the Ottomans.[6] The small size and relatively limited means of the ruling dynasties of this period—most of whom ruled over quasi-autonomous city states—may have stood in the way of such accumulation. But it is equally possible that the austerity and militarism that characterized these dynasties, including the Ayyubids, would have also mitigated against such open display of luxury and consumption. Finally, one has to consider the severely limited space within which these dynasts lived: huge harems were simply inconceivable within the cramped quarters of citadels.

Second, although free status was no guarantee for social promotion, Ayyubid princesses also enhanced their prestige by means of political marriages.[7] This age-old institution was especially valued under the Ayyubids, who ruled over Egypt and Syria as a large family confederacy consisting of quasi-autonomous provinces.[8] Marriages within this confederacy were often arranged in order to initiate, foster, or seal alliances among different members of the royal household. It follows then that court women, through marriage to their male counterparts, elevated their own status and fostered a sense of unity in the larger Ayyubid family tree. Simultaneously linked to two royal branches, these women enjoyed the protection of their natal families and the prestige associated with their spousal families. Leaving their father's house and living with their husbands, often in a faraway land, they acted as diplomatic representatives and as agents of good will.

The third factor, the ultimate seal of status, was giving birth to a male child, a future prince or even ruler. Procreation was obviously central to the survival of the dynasty, but it also guaranteed the continued well-being and prestige of the princess, whose status was now that of *umm* or *wālidah,* mother of a sultan or even queen mother. This was such an important status that it was adopted by Ḍayfa and other princesses as an epithet designating elevated status as well as protection.[9]

This is precisely the path that was laid out for Ḍayfa Khātūn, the favorite daughter of al-Malik al-ʿĀdil, who had succeeded his brother Saladin as sultan of the Ayyubid dynasty. Al-ʿĀdil could claim control to most of Saladin's possessions with the exception of Aleppo, the only province that Saladin granted to one of his sons, al-Ẓāhir Ghāzī. As a result of this divide, there was considerable tension between Ghāzī and al-ʿĀdil, and it threatened to dismantle the Ayyubid confederacy. To resolve the tension Ghāzī asked his uncle al-ʿĀdil for his daughter's hand in marriage. With the marriage approved, Ḍayfa Khātūn was dispatched to Ghāzī in Aleppo in 1212 at the head of a great retinue that was received amidst great festivities. According to Ibn Wāṣil:

> The *khātūn* arrived in Aleppo in great ceremony. She was received by al-Malik al-Ẓāhir along with the emirs of Aleppo, its turbaned [scholars], and its notables. Her entry into the citadel was a famous day. She had with her textiles, furnishings, and diverse jewelry that required fifty mules, 100 Bactrian camels, and 300 dromedaries to carry. . . . It is also mentioned that she had in her retinue 100 slave girls, all singers who played different instruments; and another 100 slave girls who could make various wonderful crafts. . . . When she entered the court of al-Malik al-Ẓāhir, he arose and took several steps towards her and showed her great respect.[10]

This was probably the most important marriage in the history of the Ayyubids, for it helped remedy the seriously threatening rift between Ghāzī and al-ʿĀdil. Ḍayfa was therefore instrumental in the maintenance of the unity of the Ayyubid house, a destiny shared by several other women of her standing. Ḍayfa's status changed considerably in the following year when she gave birth to the male heir that Ghāzī had desired, the son who later became sultan al-ʿAzīz Muḥammad. As wife and then mother, Ḍayfa was little more than a passive vehicle, and any other daughter of her father's house would have served equally well. However, destiny ultimately called her to step out of the traditional female role and to distinguish herself in the pages of history as a regent queen.

Little is reported about Ḍayfa during the remainder of Ghāzī's reign, who died in 1216, or that of their son, al-ʿAzīz Muḥammad, who died in 1236 at the age of twenty-four.[11] Muḥammad's son and successor (the later Salāḥ al-Dīn II) was, however, only seven years old at the time of his father's death, a situation that necessitated the creation of a regency council. This council consisted of the two emirs Shams al-Dīn Luʾuʾ al-Amīnī and ʿIzz al-Dīn ʿUmar b. Majallī, the vizier Jamāl al-Dīn al-Qifṭī, and Ḍayfa Khātūn's own slave Jamāl al-Dawla Iqbāl al-Ẓāhirī al-Khātūnī. The latter acted as Ḍayfa Khātūn's secretary and deputy at the regency council, whose decisions she herself ratified as regent queen in the name of her grandson. Thus, she in effect ruled Aleppo from 1236 until her death in 640/1243.[12] She was the first woman to govern an Islamic dynasty, predating by about fifteen years the far more notorious queen Shajar al-Durr, who ruled Egypt from 1250 to 1257 before being ignominiously killed.[13]

Though the actual sovereign of an Islamic state, Ḍayfa Khātūn seems to have exercised considerable restraint and discretion in keeping her voice, her person, and her regnal symbols hidden from view. The secretary Iqbāl was her mouthpiece to the regency council and to the public alike,[14] and she was herself an embodiment of her titulature which described her as the "elevated curtain and impregnable veil," metaphors for virtue and chastity. Furthermore Ḍayfa abstained from claiming for herself the classical emblems of Islamic rulership, namely demanding that coins be struck in her name and the Friday *khutbah* (sermon) be pronounced in her name. Keenly aware of the limits of female power and the boundaries of acceptable behavior, she walked a fine line between her *de facto* sovereignty and her *de juris* position as simply the grandmother and advisor to the future sultan.[15] Symbolically, the line of male succession in the Ayyubid dynasty of Aleppo continued uninterrupted despite her regency.[16] Rather than threatening this lineage, her regency protected it, which may explain the public's tolerance of her rule.

Ḍayfa Khātūn's seven-year reign was militarily uneventful, making it possible for her to dedicate her efforts to civic affairs and the patronage of scholars and mystics, for whom she created several important institutions. Ibn Wāṣil wrote: "She was just to her subjects, very charitable and loving towards them. She removed various taxes in all the regions of Aleppo. She favored jurists, ascetics, scholars and people of religion, and extended to them many charities."[17] This testimony is confirmed by Ḍayfa's architectural patronage, which focused on *khānqāh*s (Sufi convents) and mausoleums.

Ḍayfa's involvement in architectural patronage was the rule rather than the exception among Ayyubid court women. In a recent study, Humphreys has estimated that about one fifth of all religious structures and one fourth of *madrasa*s (colleges) built by the Ayyubids of Damascus were founded by women.[18] Although court women under the earlier Fatimids and later Mamluks also commissioned pious foundations, their relative number falls below those founded under the Ayyubids.[19] First in Damascus and then in Aleppo, court women of the Zengid and Ayyubid dynasties founded mausoleums, *madrasa*s, and *khānqāh*s in order to promote religious learning and as a means for enhancing their prestige and commemorating their names. Sitt al-Shām (Lady of Damascus), wife of Saladin, for example, founded the *madrasa* al-Shāmiyya in 1185, initiating a type of family mausoleum not previously known in Damascus.[20] Akhshu Khātūn and Khadīja Khātūn, respectively wife and daughter of the Ayyubid sultan al-Muʿaẓẓam ʿIsa, built two *madrasa*s of some note in Damascus:

al-Māridāniyya in 1227 and al-Ṣāḥibiyya before 1245.[21] All three *madrasas* are fairly small, consisting of little more than a mosque with an attached mausoleum, and lacking the residential cells present in larger educational foundations.[22]

In Ayyubid Aleppo, women's patronage seems to have found an outlet primarily in the building of *khānqāhs*, of which six are mentioned by Ibn Shaddād, the thirteenth-century topographer of Syria and Upper Mesopotamia.[23] Interestingly, each of these *khānqāhs* was also intended for women ascetics, a fact that underlines the centrality of Sufism in female piety. Indeed Sufism, which did not require the same kind of knowledge and erudition as jurisprudence, was somewhat more open for women's participation and even leadership. Schimmel, for example, proposes that "sufism, more than stern orthodoxy, offered women a certain amount of possibilities to participate actively in the religious and social life."[24] In a study specifically dealing with education in Mamluk Cairo, Berkey concludes that "formal Sufism and the broader forms of Muslim mysticism may have been an important route by which learned women could acquire standing in the religio-academic world."[25] The emphasis on a direct and personal path to the Divine, the prominence of emotional and ecstatic practices, and perhaps even the possibility of celibacy may have conjoined to make Sufism especially attractive to medieval Muslim women.

It is also quite likely that some of these convents served as hospices for unmarried or widowed women without families to shelter them, who would have found in them protection as well as spiritual fulfillment. Although this important feature is not noted for any of the Ayyubid *khānqāhs* in Aleppo, Berkey discusses several instances in which *ribāts* (nearly synonymous with *khānqāhs*) were specifically intended as "places of residence for elderly, divorced, or widowed women who had no other place of abode, until their death or remarriage."[26] This was most likely the case with the *khānqāh* al-Farafra.

The two structures founded by Ḍayfa in Aleppo are the *khānqāh* al-Farafra located beneath the citadel (*taḥt al-qalʿah*) and the *madrasa* al-Firdaws in a southern suburb called the *Maqamat* quarter south of the city wall (fig. 2.1). Both were privileged locations, and thus especially desirable for pious foundations: the former was the residential quarter of the city's notables; the latter already contained several other Ayyubid *madrasas* and mausoleums. Indeed, the location of these two monuments closely corresponds to the two monuments built by Ḍayfa's husband Ghāzī two decades earlier, suggesting a degree of parallelism between hers and her

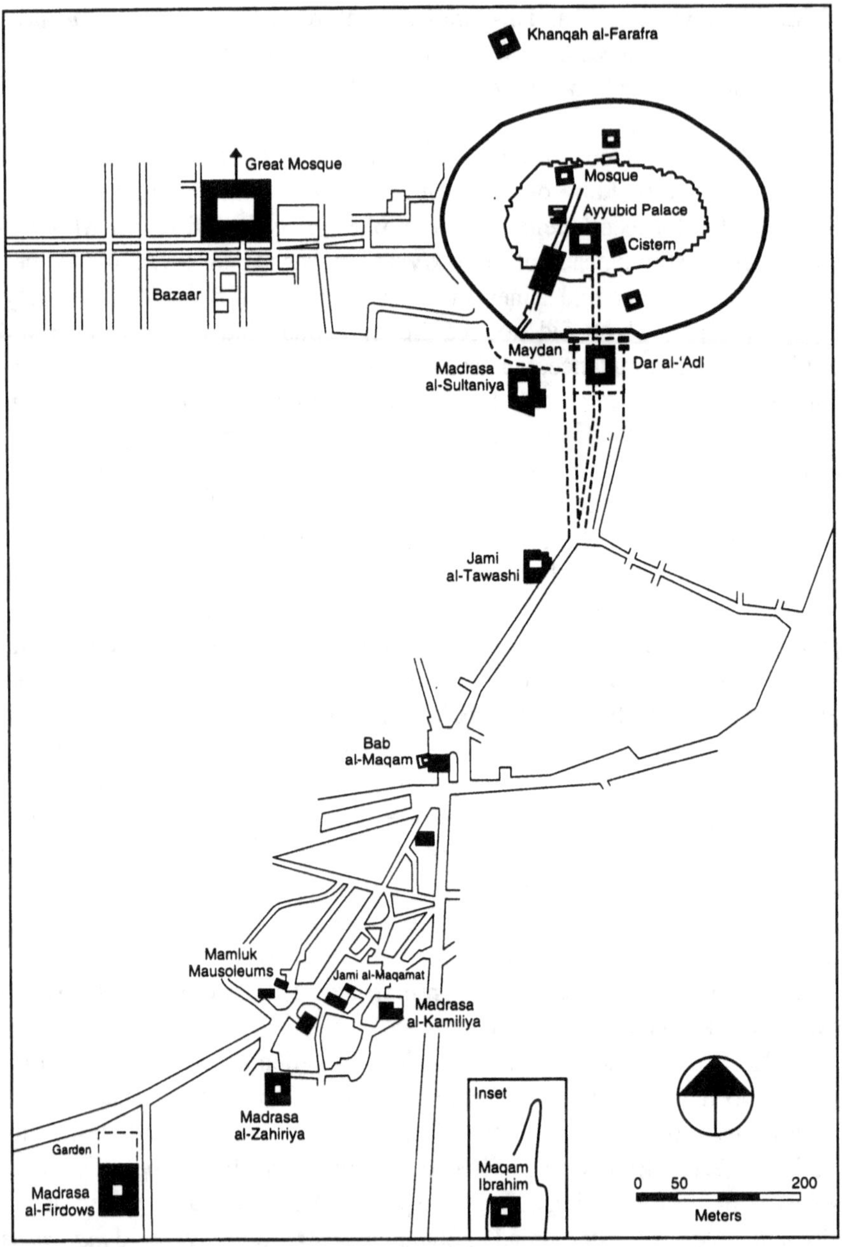


**Fig. 2.1.** Aleppo, Reconstructed plan of central and southern city (*Maqām* Ibrahim is about 300 meters south of *madrasa* al-Firdaws)

husband's patronage. The main difference is that Ghāzī's monuments were *madrasas* whereas those built by Ḍayfa were *khānqāhs*. While this identification is clear in the case of al-Farafra, it goes counter to the accepted function of al-Firdaws as *madrasa.* Elsewhere I have shown that this building was not intended for jurists but for Sufis, making it a *khānqāh,* and this identification sits more comfortably with the pattern of women's patronage in Aleppo.[27] Al-Firdaws, the larger of the two, was founded just before Ḍayfa's ascendance to regency in 1236; and al-Farafra was founded just a year after. This is a clear indication of her already powerful and privileged standing in the dynasty as the daughter, widow, mother and grandmother of Ayyubid sovereigns. Indeed, these attributes seem to have outweighed Ḍayfa's regent status, as an examination of her remaining inscriptions will demonstrate.

Three historical inscriptions for Ḍayfa Khātūn have survived, one in the *khānqāh* al-Farafra and two in the *madrasa* al-Firdaws. The first (fig. 2.2), dated to the first year of her regency in 635/1237, does not name her as the founder but simply states that the *khānqāh* was built during the reign of Ṣalāḥ al-Dīn II, her young grandson, mentioning also his father and grandfather.[28] In fact, her own name does not appear at all. Instead, her identity as a patron was subsumed within the identity of the grandson in whose name and for whose dynasty she governed.

At the *madrasa* al-Firdaws one inscriptional band is located on the exterior along the portal facade and the other on the interior, along the eastern wall of the courtyard. Although dated to 1235, two years earlier

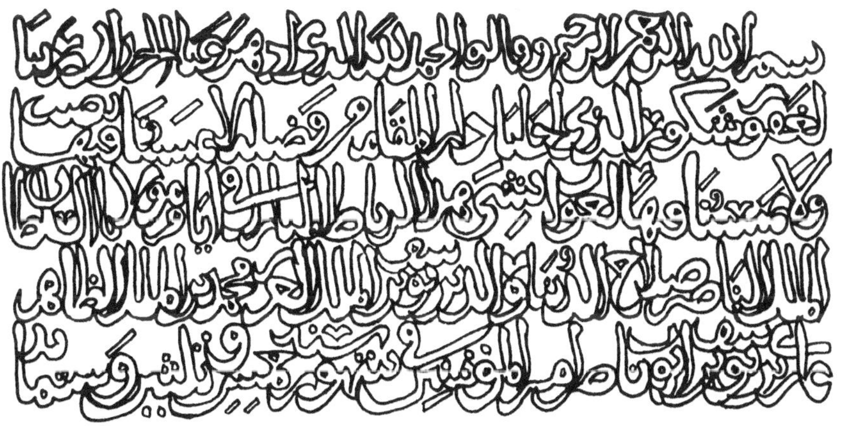

**Fig. 2.2.** Aleppo, *Khānqāh* al-Farāfra: foundation inscription

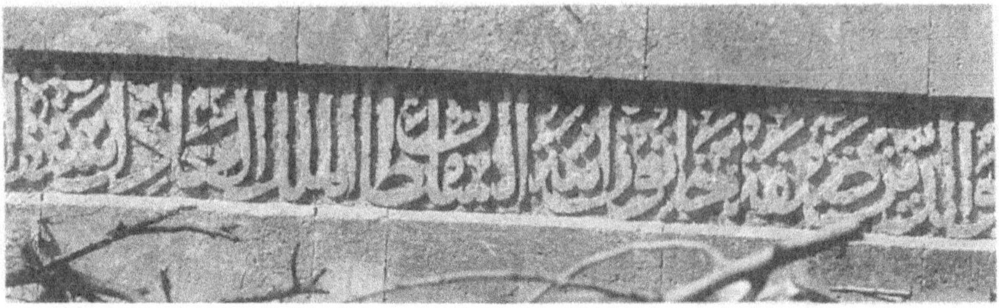

**Fig. 2.3.** Aleppo, *Madrasa* al-Firdaws: exterior inscription: titles of Ḍayfa Khātūn

than the previous inscription, they are somewhat more assertive in their titulature, possibly owing to the extramural location of the *madrasa.* Both mention Ḍayfa Khātūn by name and give her titles, epithets, and royal lineage. The outer one (fig. 2.3) reads as follows:

> This is what has ordered its construction the elevated curtain and impregnable veil, the Merciful Queen . . . Ḍayfa Khātūn, daughter of the sultan al-Malik al-ʿĀdil . . . during the reign of our lord the sultan al-Malik al-Nāṣir, the learned, the just, the warrior for the faith, the defender of the outposts, the assisted by God, the victorious, the vanquisher, Ṣalāḥ al-Dīn son of al-Malik al-ʿAzīz son of al-Malik al-Ẓāhir Ghāzī . . . in the year 633/1235–36.[29]

These are some of the earliest feminine honorific and royal epithets known. The titles "*al-sitr al-rafīʿ w'al-ḥijāb al-manīʿ,*" literally meaning "the elevated curtain and impregnable veil," were sometimes used to describe fortifications. But figuratively they refer to virtue and chastity and should perhaps be translated as "the virtuous veil and chaste lady." These are followed by "the Merciful Queen" and "the refuge of world and religion," titles that were later adopted by Queen Shajar al-Durr of Cairo.[30] The courtyard's historical inscription abbreviates the exterior inscription, omitting the date and title "the Merciful Queen" but adding the unusual though pertinent detail that Ḍayfa Khātūn was the mother (*wālidat*) of the sultan al-Malik al-ʿAzīz.[31] This information augments the exterior inscription and leaves no doubt that the building was built by a royal figure, the mother of the ruling sultan.

The two monuments founded by Ḍayfa share several features of plan and design (figs. 2.4 and 2.5). Both are entered through bent entrances, which were quite uncommon in contemporary *madrasas*, a straight axial or cross-axial entrance being far more common.[32] The bent entrance is more

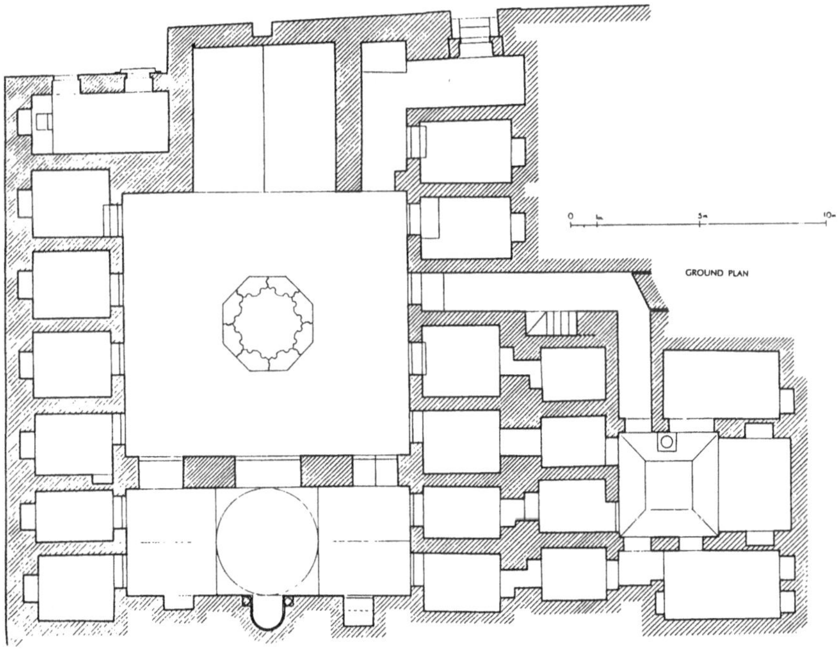


**Fig. 2.4.** Aleppo, *Khānqāh* al-Farāfra: plan (adapted from a plan of Syrian Dir. Gen. of Antiquities and Museums)

commonly associated with residential architecture, where it ensures privacy and protection. This might explain its use in the *khānqāh* al-Farafra, which was intended for women Sufis, whose personal security would have been well guarded, but it does not explain its use in the *madrasa* al-Firdaws, which was most likely for men.

Both buildings employ a fairly typical courtyard plan with an elaborate central pool. The southern quadrant in each is occupied by a mosque that is faced on the north by a large iwan, while the eastern and western flanks are filled with various rooms. The tripartite prayer halls have elaborate marble mihrabs, which is the only concession to ornamentation in these austere buildings. Furthermore, both buildings contain what might be read as residential annexes (for their respective *shaykh*s [scholar-in-residence]) centered around their own little courtyards: one in al-Farafra and two in al-Firdaws. Overall, however, al-Firdaws is larger, better designed, and somewhat less severe in its decoration.[33]

But there are several significant differences between the two buildings. Perhaps the most apparent is that al-Firdaws does not contain individual

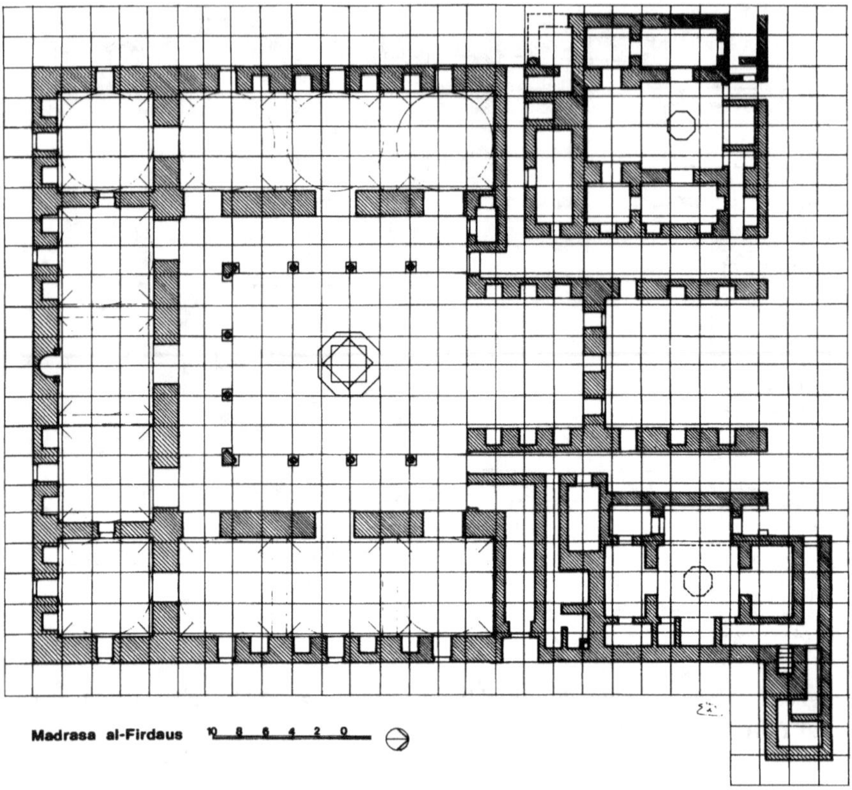


**Fig. 2.5.** Aleppo, *Madrasa* al-Firdaws: plan with applied grid (adapted from a plan of Syrian Dir. Gen. of Antiquities and Museums)

residential cells as was customary in most *madrasas* and *khānqāhs* of any size. Al-Farafra, on the other hand, contains a total of thirty-four such cells, arranged on two levels. Indeed, a second floor is entirely absent at al-Firdaws, whose flanks continue the undulating rhythm of the squat domes that cover the sanctuary for a total of eleven domes. It seems clear, therefore, that these residential units were sacrificed in order to maximize the number of domes, a point to which I will return.

The second most noteworthy difference is the external iwan at al-Firdaws, which adorses the interior one and which originally faced a garden with a pool (fig. 2.6). Such iwans are very uncommon in religious architecture, but have a long history in palatial architecture where they were used as annexed or freestanding pavilions facing a body of water and a

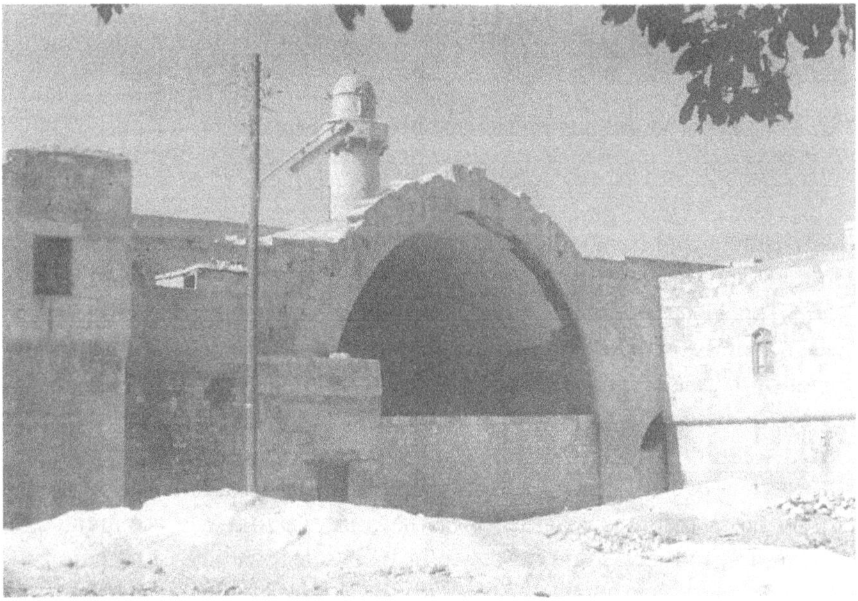

**Fig. 2.6.** Aleppo, *Madrasa* al-Firdaws: exterior iwan

garden. In its present adaptation, the iwan may have served as an audience chamber for the patron where she would have received prominent Sufis. Metaphorically, its use in this building might be the reason behind the name of the *madrasa,* since Firdaws (Paradise) and garden are intimately linked.[34]

This paradisiac imagery is further reinforced by the portal inscription, which begins with Qur'ānic verses (63:68–72) that offer a vision of the faithful entering Paradise where they are offered exquisite food on plates of gold. Indeed, a similarly evocative Qur'ānic passage was also selected for the portal of al-Farafra: "Praise belongs to God who has put away all sorrow from us. Surely our Lord is all-forgiving, all-thankful, who of His bounty has made us to dwell in the abode of everlasting life wherein no weariness assails us neither fatigue" (Qur'ān, 35:34–35). Both excerpts are very rare in public inscriptions and seem to refer to Paradise as the reward for the Sufis who worship in these foundations.[35]

Far more striking are the inscriptions that surround three sides of the courtyard at al-Firdaws for a length of about sixty meters (fig. 2.7). These texts, which are unpublished, are significant because they describe vividly and passionately the actions and aspirations of the Sufis who worshipped at al-Firdaws.[36] Their worship, which took the form of nightly vigils of repeti-

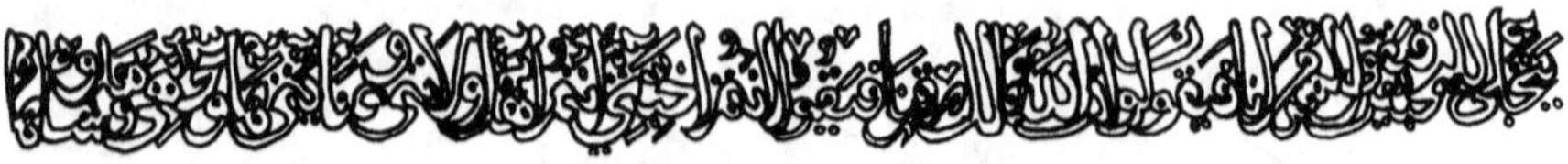

**Fig. 2.7.** Aleppo, *Madrasa* al-Firdaws, courtyard inscription

tive chanting and frenzied dancing, was to culminate in a direct vision of God, whose apparition was seen as the ultimate hope and reward of the Sufis. This vision, which the non-Sufis only experienced in Paradise, was a foretaste of the eternal bliss that awaited the Sufis and a reward that further impelled them in their worship.

It is, of course, impossible for us to determine the extent to which Ḍayfa was involved in the epigraphic program of her *madrasa/khānqāh.* But in view of her known inclination to Sufism and particularly acknowledging the astounding originality of these inscriptions, we are entitled, I believe, to grant her some influence in their selection and formulation. If so, what was their intent and that of the *madrasa* generally? The first motive was to create a Sufi haven in the city where one of the greatest Sufis of all time, Suhrawardī Maqtūl, had been executed forty years earlier. Instigated by conservative theologians and ordered by al-Ẓāhir Ghāzī himself, the execution was widely deplored in the Islamic world.[37] Al-Firdaws may therefore be seen as a long overdue atonement for a grave error and a recognition of the Sufis as an important social force in Islam and particularly in Ayyubid Aleppo. The second motive was to create a Sunni alternative to the highly impassioned Shiʿi ceremonies that were regularly held in some shrines in Aleppo and that exerted a particular attraction in the minds of the populace. Indeed, it is quite likely that the eleven domes of al-Firdaws—unique among all Aleppine *madrasa*s—were intended to compete with the equally large number of domes at the main Shiʿi shrine of al-Husayn just west of the city.[38]

Through her generous patronage of the Sufis, therefore, Ḍayfa Khātūn hoped to ensure the allegiance of this sector of society, who attracted the populace in a manner far more direct than the intellectual appeal of orthodox religious scholars, the *ʿulamāʾ*. It also seem clear that she (as with other Ayyubid dynasts before her) was still engaged in a theological rivalry with Shiʿism, the so-called Sunni Revival, whose origins in Syria date back to the first half of the twelfth century.[39] Indeed, her *madrasa* al-Firdaws might be seen as an attempt to use Sufi ascetic and ecstatic practices as a Sunni paradigm for human salvation.

Ḍayfa Khātūn, Syria's sole female Ayyubid ruler, impresses us today by her influential, though discrete, almost self-effacing form of sovereignty. Before and after her accession to the regency, she worked within the Ayyubid system, avoiding controversial acts and veiling herself from the public eye by using the regency council as an intermediary and by living a life of profound piety. Deeply interested in Sufism, she dedicated considerable energies and funds to promote its well-being and to lead it into new horizons. Compared to the better-known Queen Shajar al-Durr of Egypt, she appears distinctly demure. Although today we might be more attracted to Shajar al-Durr's more assertive personality and disruptive acts, she was in the end far less effective as a queen. The Egyptian queen suffered a horrific death for her alleged transgressions and left the country with a shredded dynasty that was soon taken over by the Mamluks. Ḍayfa Khātūn, on the other hand, left two important monuments and a legacy of piety and tolerance.

## NOTES

1. Fatima Mernissi, *The Forgotten Queens of Islam* (Cambridge: Polity Press, 1992); Leila Ahmed, *Women and Gender in Islam: Historical Roots of a Modern Debate* (New Haven and London: Yale University Press, 1992). By far the weakest chapter in Ahmed's pioneering work is the one entitled "Medieval Islam," pp. 102–24.

2. Caroline Williams, "The Cult of ʿAlid Saints in the Fatimid Monuments of Cairo. Part II: The Mausolea," *Muqarnas* 3 (1985): 39–60; Caroline Williams, "The Mosque of Sitt Hadaq," *Muqarnas* 11 (1994): 55–64; R. Stephen Humphreys, "Women as Patrons of Religious Architecture in Ayyubid Damascus," *Muqarnas* 11 (1994): 35–54; and *Patronage by Women in Islamic Art,* ed. Esin Atıl, in *Asian Art,* 5.2 (Spring 1993).

3. Ibn Jubayr, *The Travels of Ibn Jubayr,* ed. and tr. by R. J. C. Broadhurst (London, 1952): 207–8. The terms *rawḍah* (garden) and *ḥawḍ* (basin) are used figuratively to highlight the paradisiac associations of the shrine of the Prophet. For other accounts of the same women, see ibid., 189–90, 239, and 246. These three women were: Saljūqah, the daughter of ʿIzz al-Dīn Masʿūd, lord of Konya; the wife of Quṭb al-Dīn Mawdūd, the previous ruler of Mosul; and the daughter of Tukush Shah, the prince of Isfahan.

4. Ibn Wāṣil, *Mufarrij al-kurūb fī akhbār dawlat banī Ayyūb,* ed. J. Shayyal (Cairo, 1953), 5:29–30. See also ibid., 3:124.

5. For a discussion of pervasive concubinage in early Abbasid society, see Ahmed, *Women and Gender in Islam,* 81–87. See also Judith Tucker, "Gender and Islamic History," in *Islamic and European Expansion, The Forging of a Global Order,* ed. Michael Adas (Philadelphia: Temple University Press, 1993), 37–74.

6. Leslie Peirce, *The Imperial Harem: Women and Sovereignty in the Ottoman Empire* (New York: Oxford University Press, 1993), 121–22.

7. In Islam, political marriages were given special sanction since they followed in the example of the Prophet himself, most of whose later marriages were political in nature. On Muḥammad's marriages, see Ahmed, *Women and Gender in Islam,* 49–59.

8. The term "Ayyubid confederation" was first coined by R. Stephen Humphreys in his *From Saladin to the Mongols: The Ayyubids of Damascus, 1193–1260* (Albany: State University of New York Press, 1977). See pp. 66–73 for a discussion of the legal and political dimensions of this concept.

9. Shajar al-Durr was in fact referred to in contemporary documents and chronicles as Umm Khalīl, although that prince (her son from Sultan Najm al-Dīn Ayyūb) had died in infancy. See K. A. C. Creswell, *The Muslim Architecture of Egypt* (*MAE*), 2 vols. (New York: Hacker Art Books, 1978), 2:135.

10. *Mufarrij,* 3:213–14.

11. The volume(s) pertaining to women in the famous biographical dictionary of Kamāl al-Dīn Ibn al-ʿAdīm, *Bughyat al-ṭalab fī tārīkh ḥalab,* have been lost. This is especially unfortunate since Ibn al-ʿAdīm (1192–1262) was one of the greatest chroniclers and biographers in medieval Islam and since his *Bughya* contains the most detailed information on the important personalities of his time. See note 14.

12. *Mufarrij,* 3:229–30.

13. A discussion of Shajar al-Durr's monuments and a summary of her rise to power and terrible death are provided by Creswell, *The Muslim Architecture of Egypt,* 2:135–40. Her monuments are also briefly discussed in Doris Behrens-Abouseif, *Islamic Architecture in Cairo: An Introduction* (Leiden: E. J. Brill, 1992), 90–93.

14. On Jamāl al-Dawla Iqbāl al-Ẓāhirī al-Khātūnī, see David Morray, *An Ayyubid Notable and His World, Ibn al-ʿAdīm and Aleppo as Portrayed in His Biographical Dictionary of People Associated with the City* (Leiden: E. J. Brill, 1994), 69–70. Iqbāl is repeatedly criticized by Ibn al-ʿAdīm for his extremely aggressive and arrogant demeanor. It is possible that these very traits would have made him especially suited for his position as chamberlain and mouthpiece of the regent queen.

15. This is entirely different from Shajar al-Durr, who, flaunting tradition, had coinage struck and the *khutba* pronounced in her name. This act of transgression was even criticized by the Abbasid caliph himself, who reputedly wrote to the Egyptian leaders that "if they had no man, he would send them one." Cited by Creswell, *The Muslim Architecture of Egypt,* 2:135, after Maqrīzī, *Sulūk,* 1:358.

16. One indication of Ḍayfa's uncanonical status is that she is not mentioned under the list of the Ayyubid dynasts of Aleppo in C. E. Bosworth, *Islamic Dynasties* (Edinburgh University Press, 1963). This omission most likely has to do

with the absence of her name from the numismatic evidence, which is generally the foundation of Muslim dynastic sequences. Shajar al-Durr, on the other hand, is listed in the same source (p. 63) as the first Mamluk sovereign of Egypt. Since she was at first married to an Ayyubid sultan, she could also be seen as the last of the Ayyubids.

17. Ibn Wāṣil, *Mufarrij,* 5:313.

18. Humphreys, "Women as Patrons," 35–54.

19. For the Mamluks, see Jonathan Berkey, *The Transmission of Knowledge in Medieval Cairo: A Social History of Islamic Education* (Princeton, N.J.: Princeton University Press, 1992), 162–181.

20. Ernst Herzfeld, "Damascus: Studies in Architecture—III," *Ars Islamica* 11–12 (1941): 38–42.

21. Ibid., 19–20 and 64–65; and Humphreys, "Women as Patrons," 43–44.

22. The smallness of some Ayyubid *madrasas* and dearth of students cells within them has been noted by Robert Hillenbrand in "Madrasa," *Encyclopaedia of Islam,* new edition (Leiden, 1960–), 6:1139, and nearly verbatim in *Islamic Architecture: Form, Function and Meaning* (New York: Columbia University Press, 1994), 186–90. Although one might, as Hillenbrand did, question the educational possibilities of a *madrasa* without residential cells, it is equally possible that students would have resided elsewhere and simply used the *madrasa* as a day school.

23. ʿIzz al-Dīn Ibn Shaddād, *Al-Aʿlāq al-khaṭīra fī dhikr umarāʾ al-shām wa'l-Jazīra. Taʾrīkh Ḥalab,* ed. D. Sourdel (Beirut: Institut Français de Damas, 1953), 95–96.

24. Annemarie Schimmel, *Mystical Dimensions of Islam* (Chapel Hill: The University of North Carolina Press, 1975), 432.

25. Berkey, *The Transmission of Knowledge in Medieval Cairo,* 175.

26. Ibid., 174.

27. Yasser Tabbaa, *Constructions of Power and Piety in Medieval Aleppo* (University Park: Pennsylvania State Press, 1997), 163–82. Humphreys in "Women as Patrons of Religious Architecture," p. 35, states that "this was in fact the single madrasa in Aleppo during the Zangid-Ayyubid era to be founded by a woman (out of more than fifty madrasas in the city dating from those 133 years)." This anomaly no longer needs to be sustained since it is clear that al-Firdaws functioned primarily as a *khānqāh.*

28. Ernst Herzfeld, *Matériaux pour un Corpus Inscriptionum Arabicarum: Syrie du Nord.* Deuxième partie, *Monuments et inscriptions d'Alep,* 3 vols. (Cairo: Institut français d'archéologie orientale, 1954–56), 2:305.

29. *Répertoire chronologique d'épigraphie arabe,* 16 vols. in progress (Cairo, 1931–), no. 4084.

30. Herzfeld, *Monuments et inscriptions d'Alep,* 2:298.

31. *Répertoire,* no. 4081.

32. This distinction applies mainly to the *madrasas* of Aleppo, where the two built by al-Ẓāhir Ghāzī, al-Sulṭāniyya and al-Ẓāhiriyya, have straight axial entrances while two others built by notables, al-Sharafiyya and al-ʿAdīmiyya, have straight cross-axial entrances. See Herzfeld, *Monuments et inscriptions d'Alep,* passim and my *Constructions of Power and Piety* for plans and discussion of these buildings. Elsewhere in the Islamic world, matters are different, and *madrasas* with bent entrances are by no means uncommon.

33. For a study of the geometry and design features of the *madrasa* al-Firdaws, see my "Geometry and Memory in the Design of the Madrasat al-Firdaws in Aleppo," in *Theories and Principles of Design in the Architecture of Islamic Societies,* ed. Margaret Ševčenko, (Cambridge, Mass.: The Aga Khan Program for Islamic Architecture, 1988), 23–34.

34. Ibid., pp. 29–34.

35. Erica Dodd and Shereen Khairallah, *The Image of the Word,* 2 vols. (Beirut: American University of Beirut Press, 1981): 2:101–2, list only six other monuments that use this Qur'ānic verse.

36. Tabbaa, *Constructions of Power and Piety,* 173–81, contains a full transcription, translation, and a detailed discussion of the inscriptions of this monument.

37. Schimmel, *Mystical Dimensions of Islam,* 260.

38. Tabbaa, *Constructions of Power and Piety,* ch. 6.

39. For a discussion of the roots of this movement, see George Makdisi, "The Sunnī Revival," in D. S. Richards, *Islamic Civilization, 950–1150* (Oxford: B. Cassirer, 1973), 155–68. For a discussion of its efflorescence during the reign of Nūr al-Dīn (1146–74) and the early Ayyubids, see Nikita Elisséeff, *Nūr al-Dīn un grand prince musulman de Syrie au temps des Croisades (511–569/1118–1174),* 3 vols. (Damascus: Institut français de Damas, 1967), esp. 750–80; and my "The Architectural Patronage of Nūr al-Dīn Maḥmūd ibn Zangī, 1146–1174," Ph.D. diss. (New York University, 1982), 169–85.

# 3

# Princess Safwat al-Dunyā wa al-Dīn and the Production of Sufi Buildings and Hagiographies in Pre-Ottoman Anatolia

*Ethel Sara Wolper*

Sufism, Islam's main mystical tradition, became a collective religious movement by the end of the tenth century. It combined a philosophical outlook with ritual practices meant to provide immediate and personal experience of God's reality.[1] Sufism had its ascetic roots in the practice and spiritual life of the prophet Muhammad, his companions, and a number of important saints (*walīy* /pl. *auliyā'*). One of the most famous of these saints was Rābi'a al-'Adawiyya (d. 185/801) a female ascetic celebrated as an exemplar of spiritual virtue.[2] The example of Rābi'a, whose spiritual achievements freed her from the bonds of slavery, has led recent scholars to ask if Sufism provided other opportunities for women to escape limitations of their class and gender.[3] Before accepting the idea that Sufism gave women more freedom, we must first examine the sources through which our knowledge of Sufi women has been transmitted. Was there, for instance, any relationship between the visibility of women in hagiographies and their role in the organization of Sufi orders formed around a charismatic figure and a set of practices? The present paper looks at this question by investigating the complex issues of representation raised by the case of Princess Safwat al-Dunyā wa al-Dīn and her role in the Maulawī order, a Sufi order named for the Anatolian saint Maulānā Jalāl al-Dīn Rūmī (d. 672/1273).[4]

One assumption that has hindered an understanding of the relationship between the visibility of women in Sufi sources and their role in society is the uncritical assumption that every reference to a woman in historical sources serves as a measure of that woman's agency. Understanding references to women in Sufi literature is problematic because of the source material in which these references are found. The representation of characters and events in sources like hagiographies that are meant to celebrate saintly figures is particularly complex. There is always some kind of balance in these sources between the accurate portrayal of historical events and the promotion of a value system based on the founder of a Sufi order.[5] Moreover, these texts were used to construct Sufi orders, and as such they paid particular attention to the patrons of these orders. Often, elite women are mentioned in these sources because of their connections to the ruling house and their role as guarantors of familial lines.[6] In other words, one way that these women figure in hagiographic sources are as producers of sons or through marriage as symbols of accord between two political lines. Although emphasized in the historical sources, their agency is usually restricted to their biological role as mothers and wives and does not include control over the dispersion of property and resources.[7]

The *Manāqib al-ʿārifīn,* a hagiography commissioned by Ulu ʿĀrif Çelebi, Jalāl al-Dīn Rūmī's grandson, includes many references to the wives of Rūmī and his descendants as well as the wives and daughters of the political figures who supported Rūmī. A Maulawī disciple wrote this text (hereafter referred to as Rūmī's biography) about Jalāl al-Dīn Rūmī and the other personalities who played a role in the development of the Maulawī order.[8] Although the central theme concerned the miraculous acts and pious deeds of this founding figure, the primary function was to establish a spiritual lineage for Rūmī and his chosen disciples. The text was written between the years 718/1318–19 and 754/1343–44, a period when Rūmī's ancestry began to be traced through the maternal line to the Caliph Abū Bakr. With the choice of Rūmī's grandson, ʿĀrif, as leader, a tradition was established whereby the leadership of the order was inherited through Rūmī's descendants.[9] Written at the moment when past and future were so clearly mapped out, Rūmī's biography worked as a history linking a recent past and a historical present represented by the founding and continuation of a spiritual genealogy (*silsila*). Women served as important links in this newly established chain, connecting Rūmī to Abū Bakr and continuing the connection into the future.

Understanding why there were so many references to elite women who were not part of Rūmī's family requires a more complex explanation. Wives of sultans and other political figures are mentioned in a number of places in Rūmī's biography. They, like the men they married, provided examples of Rūmī's enormous popularity and political clout. At the same time, Rūmī's biographer incorporated royal and political figures into the history and future of the order to guarantee continued financial support from these figures and their descendants. The mothers, daughters, and wives of these men were, thus, important links to future and past generations. Some of these women are described as friends of the order and patrons. Yet only one of the female building patrons mentioned in Rūmī's biography can be securely connected to a building act.[10] The biographer's other references to women patrons of architecture are more enigmatic.[11] For example, his biographer states that Princess Safwat al-Dunyā wa al-Dīn supported a Sufi lodge in Tokat. While her name appears in the inscription of the Sünbül Bābā lodge in Tokat, the endowment deed (*waqfiya*) of the same building makes no mention of this supposed patron.[12] Why women who were not patrons were credited with building acts and singled out for mention in Rūmī's biography is an important question. We can assume that these women were significant links in dynastic chains. In some cases, they also may have stood a good chance of inheriting funds from the Seljuk purse. In other words, in times of great political turmoil with newly emerging dynasties, these women functioned as guarantors of familial lines. Rūmī's biographer included references to the generosity of these women to associate the order and its buildings with a range of newly emerging dynasties and wealthy families.

Inscriptions on Sufi buildings include similarly puzzling references to elite women. Women's names appear in building inscriptions from Sufi lodges, institutions meant to house mystics and to offer a place for their communal life.[13] While these references to women would suggest that the women paid for the lodges and that there was a special association between women and mystics, women listed in building inscriptions from the Sufi lodges of thirteenth-century Anatolia did not always pay for the foundation or upkeep of the building.[14] For example, three lodges built in Tokat between the years 689–691/1289–91 have women's names in the building inscription (fig. 3.1). Tokat, a city in central Anatolia that became an important Seljuk center in the latter half of the thirteenth century, was a center of Sufi building activity. Women's names appear on the three Tokat lodges with extant inscriptions: the Shams al-Dīn, Sünbül Bābā (fig. 3.2), and Khalif Ghāzī (fig. 3.3).[15] By itself, these references to women were not unusual. Such famous women as Māhperī Khātūn and Tūrān Malik supported a number of important buildings with building inscriptions that

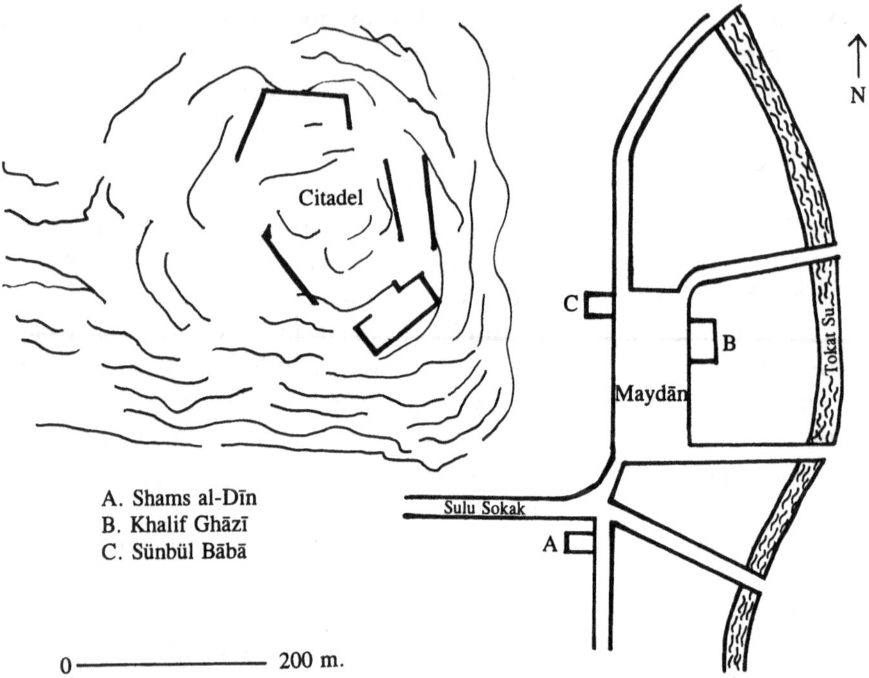


**Fig. 3.1.** Map of Tokat showing the location of Dervish lodges (Wolper and Ruggles)

name them as patrons. By contrast, two of the women mentioned on the three inscriptions in Tokat are introduced with the phrase, "in the reign of" (*fī ayyām daula*). According to Michael Rogers, such a phrase usually excludes the person it introduces from being a building founder.[16]

Although they were neither founders nor financial supporters, there are other reasons why the women may have been listed. Either they were regional leaders with some political power of their own, or they were the wives or mothers of political leaders. In each inscription, their names were given after the name and titles of the reigning Seljuk sultan. Generally, in Anatolian Seljuk building inscriptions, women are referred to by royal titles that are somewhat ambiguous. As a result of this practice, many of these women remain unnamed as individuals.[17] While the royal association is manifest, it is not always clear whether they were wives of the sultan or representatives in their own right.[18]

These Tokat lodges were built after the Seljuk defeat in 1243 when the Seljuks were forced to pay heavy dues to their Mongol overlords and

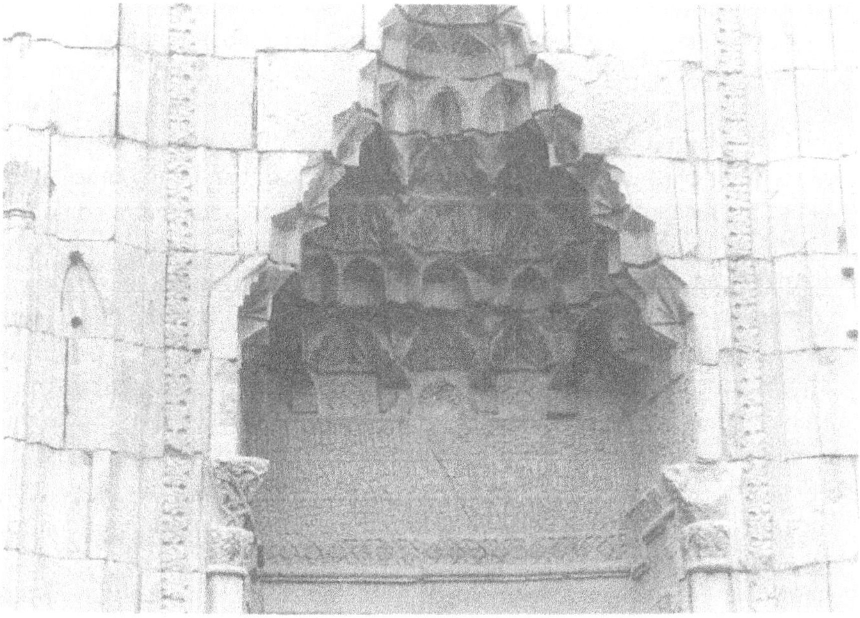

**Fig. 3.2.** Portal inscription of the Sünbül Bābā Lodge, Tokat

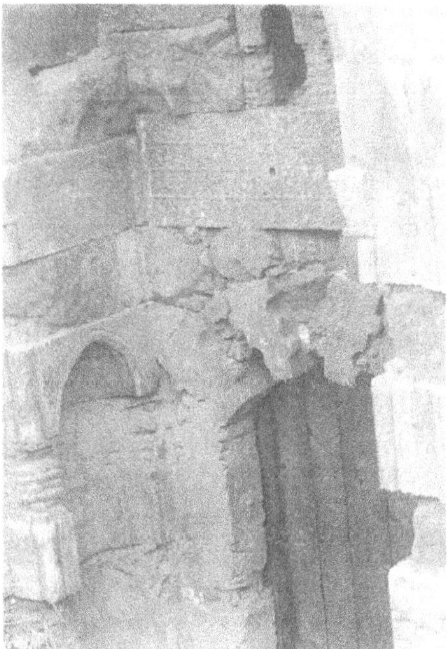

**Fig. 3.3.** Portal inscription of the Khalif Ghāzī Dervish Lodge

could no longer support architecture. As the Seljuk state steadily lost resources, a newly powerful military-bureaucratic elite in alliance with the Mongols, took over the support of building activity. Military bureaucratic elites were increasingly aligned with popular Sufi figures and were responsible for a significant acceleration of Sufi building activity. More Sufi lodges were built in Tokat between 1243 and 1300 than in any other time. One of the reasons for this is that the new patrons of architecture could not muster up enough money to support more expensive foundations like mosques and *madrasas*.[19] Moreover, the support given to these lodges reflected the rising importance of mystic leaders, who became the centers of growing communities in urban centers.

Because Tokat's three lodges were built by anonymous patrons from the rising military bureaucratic elite, the inclusion of the names of royal women gave a stamp of royal legitimation to both the foundation and its patron. The stamp of legitimation was especially important during periods when the Seljuk sultanate was dramatically weakened by Mongol control and local infighting. While the husbands, fathers, and sons of Seljuk women were in danger of losing their lives, the women themselves carried enormous clout as marriage partners because they could always produce a Seljuk heir and, in some cases, may have been able to pass on control of small amounts of the state treasury.

The case of Safwat al-Dunyā wa al-Dīn, the daughter of Muʿīn al-Dīn Sulaymān, a high-ranking Seljuk official who in 1256 was given the title Pervāne (personal assistant of the sultan), raises important questions about why women's names were used in Sufi epigraphy and biography. Her name appears both on the Sünbül Bābā lodge in Tokat and in Rūmī's biography.[20] In a recent article on the Sünbül Bābā lodge, Saim Savaṣ provides a brief introduction to the difficulties encountered in trying to gather information about the identity of Pervāne's daughter.[21] She is referred to by different honorific titles (*laqab,* pl. *alqāb*) in different sources, and although it was characteristic during this period for a person to be referred to by various names and titles, the way in which references to Pervāne's daughter are handled is particularly oblique. Because she is generally referred to by title rather than a personal name, it is her role as princess and daughter that is articulated and not her identity as an individual outside of these roles. By contrast, her brothers, who wielded considerable political power, are referred to by more distinctive names in addition to their titles.[22] For example, the Pervāne's oldest son was named ʿAlī ibn Sulaymān ibn ʿAlī and had the title Muhazzab al-Dīn. Often, the sources refer to him as

Muhazzab ʿAlī (follower of ʿAlī).[23] In the building inscription of the Sünbül Bābā lodge, the princess's honorific titles, such as Safwat al-Dunyā wa al-Dīn (pure of world and faith) and Malika al-Muazzam (august princess), occur in combination with her patronymic title, "daughter of Muʿīn al-Dīn Pervāne." Likewise, in Rūmī's biography, where there are at least two references to her, she is mentioned once by her patronymic title in combination with the title *khāwand-zāde* (princess) and elsewhere simply as the daughter of Pervāne.[24]

There are issues of political and spiritual succession relevant to Pervāne's daughter that can only be understood within the context of her father's dynastic ambitions in Central Anatolia. He came to power at the end of the reign of the Seljuks of Rūm (1077–1302) after their defeat at the hands of the Mongols at the battle of Köse Dağ in 1243. Although he is first mentioned as commander of Tokat, through his association with Mongol generals he was assigned various other positions and awarded territories in Sinope and Tokat. One of these positions was as vizier to the Seljuk Sultan Qılıch-Arslān, who controlled the eastern half of the empire. However, it was not until 1265 when Pervāne arranged to have the sultan murdered and installed the sultan's infant son Kai-Khusraw III that Pervāne became the dominant figure in the Seljuk state. His ability to gain favor with both the Seljuk court and the Mongols allowed him a large measure of power in Anatolia that went far beyond that of the sultan's personal assistant. His meteoric rise to power came to an end in 1277 when he was put to death by the Mongols who suspected him of conspiring against them.[25] Although the standard Seljuk sources give contradictory accounts of Pervāne's death, it would appear from the amount of attention given to this event that his death was unusually gruesome. Some accounts state that Pervāne's body was cut in half and eaten.[26] Although the years immediately following his death marked the end of Pervāne's control over his territories, his sons were able to regain some lands and establish a short-lived dynasty around Qastamonu, where, according to some sources, they ruled from 1295–99.[27]

## Building Inscriptions

During this tumultuous period of rising and falling power, the name of Pervāne's daughter appears in the building inscription of the Sünbül Bābā Sufi lodge in Tokat. The three-line inscription over the main portal of the lodge (fig. 3.2) begins with a Qurʾānic quotation and reads:

> . . . Sünbül, son of ʿAbd Allāh, freed slave of Safwat al-Dunyā wa al-Dīn, daughter of the Amir worthy of His pardon, Muʿīn al-Dīn Pervāne—may God have pity on him and prolong his life!—the magnificent and pure Malika revered by her double ancestry, of noble lineage from her father and mother—may God accept from him the foundation of this blessed place!—called the House of the Pious—to God the highest—in the reign of the August Sultan, Ghiyāth al-Dunyā wa Dīn, son of Kai-Kāʾūs—may God protect his empire!—in the year 691.

In the inscription, Pervāne's daughter is given the honorific title Safwat al-Dunyā wa al-Dīn, the title Malika and is further identified as the daughter of Muʿīn al-Dīn Pervāne. The inscription also states that she came from two noble lines. Because of the royal title, Malika, scholars have assumed that this daughter of Pervāne was connected to the ruling house of the Seljuks. It is unlikely that such a title would have been attached to Pervāne's daughter if her only claim to nobility was through her father, who, though serving as de facto leader of Anatolia, was not of the Seljuk lineage. Various scholars have therefore argued that Pervāne's daughter must have been either the wife of the Seljuk Sultan Ghiyāth al-Dīn Masʿūd II, or the child of a marriage between Pervāne and the daughter of the Seljuk Sultan, Kai-Khusraw II.[28] Even if the inscription does not tell us whether the princess was born into the Seljuk line or married to a Seljuk, it does convey the very important information that there was a merger between two noble households and uses the title Malika to indicate that one of these was royal. The inscription was a prominent way of broadcasting the political rank of her father and his connection to the Seljuks. Thus, while there is disagreement regarding to which Seljuk sultan this princess was married or related, the inscription brooks no dispute as to her social status: she is a royal lady who continues the Pervāne line. In other words, the appearance of a royal female title gave the urban viewer two important pieces of information: one, that the building was associated with a woman connected to the reigning Seljuk sultan, and two that this royal woman was the daughter of Pervāne Muʿīn al-Dīn, detailing his association with the Seljuk house.

The second title, Safwat al-Dunyā wa al-Dīn, has a vast number of royal associations. It is applied in an inscription to Māhperī Khātūn, the mother of the Seljuk Sultan Ghiyāth al-Dīn Kai-Khusraw II. She was an active architectural patron in Kayseri.[29] The same title also appears on an earlier building in Tokat, the Abū al-Shams lodge, dating to 687/1288–89, four years earlier than the Sünbül Bābā lodge. Because the Abū al-Shams lodge is a short distance away from the Sünbül Bābā lodge and belongs to the same social context, it is particularly relevant to this discussion. Its inscription over the entrance into the building is largely intact. It begins with a Qur'ānic citation and states that:

> For drawing near God and in the desire of His consent, the foundation of the construction of this blessed *khānqāh,* in the time of the August Sultan, the King of magnificent Kings, Ghiyāth al-Dunyā wa al-Dīn Abū al-Fath Mas'ūd, son of Kai-Kā'ūs—may God eternalize his empire!—in the days of the magnificent Malika Safwat al-Dunyā wa al-Dīn—may God sustain her empire!—by the weak slave in need of His pardon, Abū al-Hasan, son of al-Shams—May God accept this from him and grant him a favorable outcome—in the month of Rabī' II of the year 687.

As can be seen from the above inscription, the Safwat al-Dunyā wa al-Dīn from the Abū al-Shams lodge is also introduced as a princess. As we have seen, this name is a descriptive title, and it is possible that more than one woman in Tokat at this time may have been so described; thus, the princess of the Abū al-Shams lodge may or may not be the same Safwat al-Dunyā wa al-Dīn who appears in the inscription of the Sünbül Bābā lodge.[30] Unlike the inscription on the Sünbül Bābā lodge, no information is given about this woman's father. As a result, for a modern student removed from the historical and geographical context, the only key to the identity of this Safwat al-Dunyā wa al-Dīn is her association with royalty signaled by the term "Malika" and the mention of "her" empire. One must assume that this woman was so prominent in Tokat that no additional information was necessary and indeed historians have speculated that she was the wife of the Seljuk Sultan Ghiyāth al-Dīn Kai-Khusraw II.[31] It is tempting to conclude that, unlike the Safwat al-Dunyā wa al-Dīn of the Abū al-Shams lodge, the one on the Sünbül Bābā lodge was not so well known and that her father's name was added to specify her social and genealogical position. A more politically construed explanation is that both inscriptions referred to the same woman and that Pervāne's name was added to the second inscription, put up four years later, to draw attention to the family of Pervāne in his former territory of Tokat.

The word "Malika," without the added phrase "Safwat al-Dunyā wa al-Dīn," appears in a third inscription on the Khalif Ghāzī lodge in Tokat (fig. 3.3). The building was built in 691/1291, the same year as the Sünbül

Bābā lodge, and faces it from across the main square (maidān). The four-line inscription begins with a line of Hadith (sayings of the Prophet) and states that:

> The construction of this *buqʿa,* called the house of faith and work, has been ordered in the days of the empire of the August Sultan, Ghiyāth al-Dunyā wa al-Dīn Abū al-Fath Masʿūd, son of Kai-Kāʾūs—may God eternalize his empire!—and in the days of the empire of the magnificent Malika Azmat al-Dunyā wa al-Dīn Seljukī Khwand, daughter of Qılıch Arslān—may God support her kingdom!—by the weak slave who is in need of the mercy of God, Khalif, son of Sulaymān—may God accept this from him—in the year 691.

The inscription from the Khalif Ghāzī Lodge, with its careful elaboration of the patronymic of the female princess, stands out for two reasons. First, it proclaims that this woman, who was the daughter of the Seljuk Sultan Qılıch Arslān, and had the title Malika, was linked through her father to the house of the Seljuks. This building marks the first time in Tokat that the exact details of the woman's linkage to the house of the Seljuks were provided in an inscription. Second, it is a lengthy inscription in which the initial statement of foundation is preceded by a line of Hadith that turns this building plaque into a four-line inscription. Such a long, multinamed inscription typically signaled news about changes in rule to residents of the city of Tokat. For example, one of the most important monuments of Tokat was a bridge at the entrance, built in 648/1250 to mark the end of a fierce dispute between three Seljuk sultans. The bridge gives the full name and titles of each of the sultans as well as the amir who put an end to their fighting. This suggests that among the ways this last building inscription was used to outdo the other two inscriptions was through its claims for social prestige based on bloodlines. The length set it apart from the other two Sufi lodge inscriptions, while Seljukī Khātūn's undeniable royal connections made a final and definitive statement about who had regional rights over Tokat. The inscriptions show that Seljukī Khātūn was decidedly more closely affiliated with the Seljuk house than Pervāne's daughter. Ironically, Seljukī Khātūn's real claim to the region came from what was left unnamed in the inscription, her marriage to a Mongol, linking her with the most powerful group ruling over Tokat in that period.

The changes in the format of the building inscriptions are one of the best indications of the sharing of rule in the city of Tokat. In the last decades of the thirteenth century, the inclusion of more than one ruler considerably lengthened these semi-official public texts.[32] The appearance of women's names after the reigning sultan in building inscriptions also suggests changes in the role of women in dynastic and regional politics. The women in Tokat's inscriptions were meant to be perceived very differently from such earlier Seljuk women as Māhperī Khātūn and Tūrān Malik who were building patrons that supported architecture during a period when the house of Seljuk was strong. In the last quarter of the thirteenth century, Anatolians had no central dynasty ruling over them. At least in Tokat, public allegiances were constantly shifting between the ambitious Pervāne and the Seljuks. Although there were no public references to Mongol rule, this period marked a heightened level of Mongol control over Tokat. All of the women named in Tokat's inscriptions were associated with two power groups, usually one dynastic and one local. During these decades, power was in the hands of various representatives from these three groups. While local officials like Pervāne had regional control, they could not provide the legitimizing stamp of a dynasty. In this scenario, their names were less important than their actions. The value of royal women's names, however, was at a premium and the inscriptions from Tokat show how women (or their names) could serve as public symbols of political unity.[33]

To understand the particular visual significance of writing women's names and their titles on Sufi buildings, we need to think about these names as visible objects meant to be seen by an urban public. Building inscriptions were a public text with a number of properties that separated it from other texts and affected the manner in which it was read. According to Michael Rogers, building inscriptions were a semi-official document requiring permission of the *qādī* (judge). With the authority of religious leaders behind them, inscriptions conveyed important information to the urban public.[34] Collectively, the three lodge inscriptions formed an important urban text whose functions went beyond the semantic context of explaining who supported what structure in what year.[35] On one level, the inclusion of women's names could be read as an indication of newly formed dynastic and political alliances. Their uncharacteristic length and the allusion to several figures of local and dynastic stature would have alerted the public reader to the existence of a new settlement between rival factions and the establishment of joint rule over the area. At the same time, inscriptions such as the ones found on the Khalif Ghāzī and Sünbül Bābā lodge included information about how these alignments were formed. Thus, they became genealogical proofs or reminders of family trees.

Returning to Pervāne's daughter and the Sünbül Bābā lodge, the lodge's inscription clearly heralded important changes in political controls that reflect the dynastic ambitions of Pervāne's family in Tokat. Pervāne's name had been associated with the city of Tokat since the Seljuks gave him control over it in the mid-thirteenth century. When the Mongols took direct control of the city, Pervāne tried to double-cross the Mongols and formed an alliance with the Mamluks that eventually cost him his life. After his death in 1277, Pervāne's sons financed building projects closer to the Black Sea while narrative accounts report that his daughter remained in the city where he had sought rule. Although the Mongols temporarily displaced Pervāne's family's economic and political interests in Tokat, his daughter's presence served as a reminder of Pervāne's family ties to the region.

## Sufi Hagiographies

A comparison of the use of these women's names on public texts at the end of the thirteenth century with Sufi texts from the following century requires a summary of how Sufi biographies were meant to function in Anatolian society. During the first part of the thirteenth century, religious elites and Türkmen *bābās* (military/spiritual leaders) fled to Anatolia, where they began to form a following among the residents and newly settled immigrants. However, it was not until the fourteenth and fifteenth centuries that these informal followings were transformed into hierarchical orders. Sufi biographers were written at least one, and often, several generations after the death of the charismatic leader of the order. Hence, they were not contemporary records but devoted recollections that functioned as parables and precedents of behavior. In this way, Sufi biographies, like building inscriptions, were complex representational practices with their own rules and methods.

Hagiographic descriptions of the daughter of Pervāne are either accompanied by a series of royal titles or like the inscriptions contextualized in a way to stress her royal and elite status while her exact name remains ambiguous.[36] In one anecdote about the arrival of Rūmī's spiritual successor Ulu ʿĀrif Chelebi in Tokat, the biographer states that the nobles of the city, the wives of the sultan, and the daughter of Pervāne received him with great honors and appointed him head of a convent that Pervāne's daughter supported. At the investiture ceremony, Pervāne's daughter made a speech to the effect that Ulu ʿĀrif Chelebi deserved a special place in the lodge.[37] Although at first glance this anecdote would suggest that Pervāne's daughter was an important agent in the development and maintenance of the lodge, a supporting *waqf* endowment drawn up in 725/1325 omits any mention of Pervāne's daughter as either a founder or administrator of the building.[38] According to the *waqf* endowment, the building patron was her freed slave, Hājjī Sünbül, which explains the building's popular title, the Sünbül Bābā lodge.

Pervāne's daughter, to the extent that she appears in Rūmī's biography, is mentioned not as an architectural patron but in relation to her association with royal or pious women. These anecdotes about her are directly related to issues of political and spiritual succession. The inclusion of her name in Rūmī's biography was, by itself, sufficient to mark her as a pious woman. A later reader of Rūmī's biography would find it almost impossible to learn more about Pervāne's daughter than that she was considered fit company for local royal women, supported a dervish lodge in Tokat, and was pious. That reader would most likely not have known whether Pervāne had one daughter or two. More significantly, however, the reader would return to Tokat with a chain of associations that proceeded from Rūmī to his grandson and his grandson's relation to Pervāne's daughter, to Pervāne's daughter and the Sufi lodge in Tokat, and finally back to Rūmī. In this way, the biographer used these names and personages to claim contemporary buildings as Maulawī buildings. He would have done this by order of a grandson, who had supported more Maulawī lodges than any other leader.[39] At the same time, the biographer may have remembered the awful fate of Pervāne. Although Pervāne's mark on Tokat had been hidden behind our Safwat al-Dunyā wa al-Dīn, it was recovered in the mid-fourteenth century when the Mongols were gone and the descendants of Pervāne could remember his accomplishments with pride. This may explain why Rūmī's biographer was able to attribute so many more buildings to Pervāne than any epigraphic or documentary evidence could suggest.

I conclude this essay with some general observations about understanding gender and agency in medieval Anatolia. I have argued that titulature and epigraphy identify women as critical parts within a more extensive, complex network of political and dynastic affiliations. Thus, naming is not necessarily a sign of power. Indeed, many of the women who are mentioned are deprived of personal names. While this can be true of men as well, the particular anonymity of women, brought out so clearly in the case of Princess Safwat al-Dunyā wa al-Dīn in both the city spaces of Tokat and the literary spaces of Rūmī's biography, became the means to enhance the royal associations of a father's dynastic claims.

Because of the way that references to these women were constructed, their names became special objects with important legitimizing functions. In the case of Safwat al-Dunyā wa al-Dīn, the use of her name in the foundation inscription on the building bridged many decades and united the Sünbül Bābā lodge with Rūmī. Although Safwat al-Dunyā wa al-Dīn was not the patron of the Sünbül Bābā lodge, most modern historians have believed her to be; more likely, she played a minimal role in the building's construction and endowment. But her name was of critical importance in the lodge's inscription, for it provided a genealogical bridge between past and present and thus united the Sünbül Bābā lodge with the venerable Rūmī.

## NOTES

I would like to acknowledge the following individuals for their generous help with this essay: Dr. Irene Bierman, Dr. Jamal Elias, Dr. Rudi Lindner, and Dr. Leslie Peirce.

1. For a general introduction to Sufism, see A. J. Arberry, *Sufism: An Account of the Mystics of Islam* (New York: Allen & Unwin, 1950), 11–14 and 74.

2. For more on Rābiʿa, see Margaret Smith, *Rābiʿa the Mystic A.D. 717–801 and Her Fellow Saints in Islam* (Cambridge: Cambridge University Press, 1928).

3. For an important recent discussion of the role of women in the development of the Maulawī order, see Speros Vryonis Jr., "The Muslim Family in 13th–14th Century Anatolia as Reflected in the Writings of the Mawlawi Dervish Eflaki," *The Ottoman Emirate (1300–1389): Halycon Days in Crete I,* ed. Elizabeth Zachariadou (Rethymnon: Crete University Press, 1993), 213–23, especially 220–21.

4. Leila Ahmed suggests that women became Sufis because it provided them with another option than being a wife or slave. Her discussion of the opportunities provided for women within Sufism centers around the rather phenomenal case of Rābiʿa al-ʿAdawiyya. As Ahmed points out, a number of Sufi writers did address gender divisions in their work. More comprehensive analysis of Sufism and gender divisions appear in the work of Jamal Elias, who also brings up the important opportunities that Sufi celebrations and shrine cults offered for women to participate in the public arena. To some extent, these celebrations were as much a part of non-Sufi shrine cults as Sufi ones. See Leila Ahmed, *Women and Gender in Islam* (New Haven and London: Yale University Press, 1992), 95, and her essay, "Early Islam and the Position of Women: The Problem of Interpretation," in *Women in Middle Eastern History: Shifting Boundaries in Sex and Gender,* ed. Nikki R. Keddie and Beth Baron (New Haven and London: Yale University Press, 1991), 58–73; Jamal Elias, "Female and Feminine in Islamic Mysticism," in *Muslim World* 78.3–4 (1988): 209–24; R. W. J. Austin, "The Sophianic Feminine

in the Work of Ibn ʿArabi and Rūmī," in *The Legacy of Mediaeval Persian Sufism,* ed. Leonard Lewisohn (London and New York: Khaniqahi-Nimatullah Publications, 1992), 233–45.

5. Victoria Rowe Holbrook, "Diverse Tastes in the Spiritual Life: Textual Play in the Diffusion of Rūmī's Order," in *The Legacy of Medieval Persian Sufism,* ed. L. Lewisohn, 99–120.

6. For a discussion of Mamluk women as guarantors of familial lines, see Carl F. Petry, "Class Solidarity versus Gender Gain: Women as Custodians of Property in Later Medieval Egypt," in *Women in Middle Eastern History,* ed. Keddie and Baron, 122–42.

7. A survey of pious foundations (*waqfīyas*) that could reveal the control of the most prominent source of power, the control of property, makes relatively few references to women. Likewise, women are rarely mentioned as custodians of property or managers of pious foundations. Given the lack of references in *waqfīyas*, the large number of times that women's names appear in building inscriptions requires a more elaborate explanation than that they were patrons.

Although it is beyond the scope of this essay to discuss the representation of women in all Seljuk sources, there is some need to address some of the issues involved with the representation of Seljuk women in historical sources. The paucity of source material available on the Seljuks of Anatolia has, for example, led some scholars to look to the rich material available for the Seljuks of Iran, or Great Seljuks, in search of material on Seljuk women. The problem with this approach is that Anatolian court life developed under a number of local influences and did not duplicate that of either the Seljuks of Iran or the Mongol Ilkhanids. For information on some of the more notable women from these dynasties, see Ann K. S. Lambton, *Continuity and Change in Medieval Persia: Aspects of Administrative, Economic and Social History, 11th–14th Century* (Albany: Bibliotheca Persica, 1988), 258–96.

8. Shams al-Dīn Aflākī, *Manāqib al-ʿārifin,* trans. Clement Huart as *Les saints des derviches Tourneurs,* 2 vols. (Paris: E. Leroux, 1918–22). From this point on, Huart's translation will be referred to as Aflākī-Huart to distinguish it from Tahsin Yazıcı's edition of the Persian text also used in this study and distinguished as Aflākī-Yazıcı. See Shams al-Dīn Ahmed al-Aflākī al-ʿĀrifī, *Manākib al- ʿārifin,* 2 vols., ed. Tahsin Yazıcı (Ankara: Türk Tarih Kurumu Basimevi, 1976). Yazıcı's Turkish translation will be referred to by its title, *Âriflerin Menkibleri,* 2 vols. (Istanbul: Hürriyet Yayınları, 1973).

9. Holbrook, "Diverse Tastes," 104–5. Conversely, Arberry claims that Rūmī was related to Abū Bakr through paternal descent. A. J. Arberry, *Discourses of Rumi* (London: J. Murray, 1961), 1.

10. Gürcü Khātūn, a widow of the Seljuk Sultan Kai-Khusraw, gave financial support to the tomb of Jalāl al-Dīn Rūmī in Konya. There is some speculation that she still had access to money from the Seljuk treasury, which allowed

her to provide significant financial backing for this project. Michael Rogers, "Waqf and Patronage in Seljuk Anatolia", *Anatolian Studies* 26 (1976): 89, and Aflākī-Huart, 2:26.

11. For more on how buildings were used in Sufi biographies, see Wolper, "Patronage and Practice in Late Seljuk and Early Beylik Society: Dervish Lodges in Sivas, Tokat, and Amasya," Ph.D. dissertation, University of California, Los Angeles, 1994.

12. A photocopy of the *waqfīya* is included in Saim Savaş, "Tokat'ta Hoca Sünbül Bābā Zaviyesi," in *Vakıflar Dergisi* 24 (1993): 206–7. I was able to consult the original text, D. 484 n. 309 (725) Beyler Çelebi bini Tacuddin Muhammed Çelebi at the Vakıflar Genel Müdürlüğü (Directorate of Waqf Archives), Ankara.

13. Sufi lodges were known under a variety of terms in Arabic, Persian, and Turkish. Inscriptions identify them variously as *ribāt, khānqāh, zāwiya, dār al-siyada, buqʿa,* and *dār al-sulahā'.* Later Seljuk and Beylik chroniclers, not to mention modern scholars, use these terms as well as others for the same buildings, further complicating the issue. To avoid a pointless jumble of overlapping labels, I have subsumed all these terms under "Sufi lodge." By the second half of the thirteenth century, these terms designated a group of urban buildings sharing important characteristics that identify them as a common type.

14. See Rogers, "Waqf and Patronage in Seljuk Anatolia," 73. The epigraphic evidence from Anatolia does indicates that royal women descendants of such Türkmen dynasties as the Danişmendids and Mangujaks appear in inscriptions from buildings in Anatolia, suggesting they may have offered some support to the architecture. Among these were Atsuz Elti Khātūn, who was a descendant of Yaghi Basan, and Tūrān Malik, who was a daughter of Bahram Shāh, the last Mangujak ruler of Erzincan. See Howard Crane, "Notes on Saldjuq Architectural Patronage in Thirteenth Century Anatolia," *Journal of the Economic and Social History of the Orient* 36 (1993): 12.

15. The standard source on these inscriptions is Combe et al., *Répertoire chronologique d'épigraphie arabe* (Cairo, 1938), nos. 4959 (Sünbül Bābā), 4903 (Shams al-Dīn), 4960 (Khalif Ghāzī). I was able to study these inscriptions in situ in 1990. Because of the poor quality of the recent renovations to the Shams al-Dīn Lodge, I have not included a photograph of the building. Recent photographs of these inscriptions with Turkish transliterations can be found in Sedat Emir, *Erken Osmanlı Mimarliĝinda Çok-İşlevli Yapılar: Kentsel Kolonizasyon Yapıları Olarak Zaviyeler* (İzmir: Akademi Kitabevi, 1994).

16. Rogers, "Waqf and Patronage in Seljuk Anatolia," 71.

17. Michael Rogers, "The Date of the Çifte Minare Medrese at Erzerum," *Kunst des Orients* 8 (1972): 82–83.

18. In the inscription on the Abū al-Shams lodge, Malika Safwat al-Dunyā wa al-Dīn is introduced by the phrase "in the days of" (*fī ayyām*). By contrast, the Seljuk Sultan is introduced with the phrase "in the time reign of" (*fī zaman*).

Rogers assumes that the handling of the inscription meant that she was the wife of the sultan, yet he does not go into details about why he makes that judgment. For more on the distinction between *ayyām* and *zaman,* see F. Rosenthal, "The 'Time' of Muslim Historians and Muslim Mystics," in *Jerusalem Studies in Arabic and Islam* 19 (1995): 5–35. I thank David Powers for bringing this reference to my attention.

19. E. Sara Wolper, "The Politics of Patronage: Political Change and the Construction of Dervish Lodges in Sivas," *Muqarnas* 12 (1995): 39–47.

20. References to Pervāne's daughter and her connection to the Sünbül Bābā lodge appear in H. Crane, "Notes on Saldjuq Architectural Patronage in Thirteenth Century Anatolia," 53; Halil Edhem, "Anadolu'da İslâmî Kitâbeler (Tokat)," *Tarih-i Osmâni Encümeni Mecmuası* part 35 (Istanbul: Institute of Ottoman Historical Studies, 1931) 650–53; Albert Gabriel, *Monuments turcs d'anatolie,* 2 vols. (Paris: E. de Boccard, 1931–34), 2:103: Hüseyin Husameddin, *Amasya Tarihi,* 4 vols. in 3 (Istanbul: Hikmet Matbaasi, 1327–32 [1909–35]), 3:23; Michael Rogers, "The Date of the Çifte Minare Medrese in Erzurum," 79; Saim Savaş, "Tokat'ta Hoca Sünbül Bābā Zaviyesi," 200–201; E. Yurdakul, "Tokat Vilayetinde Bilinmeyen bir Selcuklu Hankahı," *Önasya* 1970 (Istanbul), 69–70.

21. Savaş, "Tokat'ta Hoca Sünbül Bābā Zaviyesi," 200. A review of the primary Seljuk sources gives almost no concrete information about this daughter.

22. For more information on the building activity of Pervāne's sons, see I. H. Uzunçarşılı, "Kastamonu ve Sinop'ta Pervanezadeler," *Doğu Mecmuası* 7 (1957): 27–31; and M. Z. Oral, "Durağan ve Bafra'da İki Türbe," *Belleten* 20 (1956): 387–88.

23. For full titles, see Crane, "Notes on Saldjuq Architectural Patronage in Thirteenth Century Anatolia," 29. Other sources on Pervāne's sons are Nejat Kaymaz, *Pervane Mu'inu'd-din Suleyman* (Ankara: Ankara Universitesi Basimevi, 1970); I. H. Uzunçarşılı, *Anadolu Beylikleri ve Akkyoyunlu, Karakoyunlu Devletleri* (Ankara: Turk Tarih Kurumu Basimevi, 1988), 148–49; and Claude Cahen, *Pre-Ottoman Turkey* (New York: Taplinger Publishing, 1968), chapter 12.

24. The confusion over her names and titles coupled with the scanty source material available on the Seljuks adds to the difficulty in investigating this woman. See Michael Rogers, "The Dating of the Çifte Minare," 82n14.

25. Cahen, *Pre-Ottoman Turkey,* 280–92.

26. For a discussion of the references to Pervāne's demise, see Anthony Bryer, "Greeks and Turkmens," *Dumbarton Oaks Papers* 29 (1975): 125n33.

27. Cahen, Pre-Ottoman Turkey, 280–92.

28. Pervāne was married to Gürcü Khātūn, the widow of the Seljuk Sultan Kai-Khusraw. It is not clear if the daughter mentioned in the building inscription was Gürcü Khātūn's daughter. In any case, Gürcü Khātūn also had a daughter called ʿAyn al-Dīn who was married to an Atabeg (Kaymaz, *Pervane Mu'inu'd-din Suleyman,* 366–67).

29. Māhperī Khātūn was also the wife of ʿAla al-Dīn Kai Qubad. An inscription on the sarcophagi in her tomb states, "This is the tomb of the lady . . . Safwat al-Dunyā wa al-Dīn Māhperī Khātūn, mother of Sultan" (Ülkü Bates, "The Anatolian Mausoleums of the 12, 13, and 14th Centuries," Ph.D. diss., University of Michigan, 1970, 144–45).

30. Howard Crane suggests that she might have been the wife of Sultan ʿAla al-Dīn Kai Qubad. Crane, "Notes on Saldjuq Architectural Patronage," 53.

31. E. Yurdakal tries to link this Safwat al-Dunyā wa al-Dīn to a Mongol woman (1293–95) who was given control over Kirman and sections of Anatolia. Yurdukal, "Tokat Vilayetinde Bilinmeyen bir Selcuklu Hankahı," 69.

32. Rogers suggests that permission from the *qādī* (judge) gave inscriptions their force as semi-official documents ("Waqf and Patronage in Seljuk Anatolia," 71).

33. For more on Sufi lodges in Tokat, see Wolper, "Patronage and Practice in Late Seljuk and Early Beylik Society: Dervish Lodges in Sivas, Tokat, and Amasya."

34. In one of the earliest works on women as patrons in Turkey, Ülkü Bates studied buildings bearing women's names for information on their role in society. See "Women as Patrons of Architecture in Turkey," in *Women in the Muslim World,* ed. Lois Beck and Nikki Keddie (Cambridge, Mass.: Harvard University Press, 1978), 245–60.

35. Building inscriptions were a type of "public text." I use Bierman's definition here to imply that these texts by nature of their highly visible location and the force of authority behind them provided a suitable forum for reinforcing or altering messages about sovereign power. See Irene Bierman, "The Art of the Public Text: Medieval Islamic Rule," in *World Art: Themes of Unity in Diversity*, ed. Irving Lavin, 3 vols (University Park: The Pennsylvania State University Press, 1989): 2:283–90; and Bierman, *Writing Signs: The Fatimid Public Text* (Berkeley and Los Angeles: The University of California Press, 1998), 1–27.

36. There is even some confusion whether or not Pervāne had two daughters that were associated with the order.

37. Aflākī-Yazıçı, 2:951–53.

38. A copy of this *waqfīya* is published in Savaş, "Tokat'ta Hoca Sünbül Zaviyesi," 206–9.

39. Holbrook, "Diverse Tastes," 108. Holbrook bases her conclusion about the large number of lodges built by Ulu Arif on information found in A. Gölpinarlı, *Mevlânâ'dan Sonra Mevlevîlik* (Istanbul: Inkilap ve Aka Kitabevleri, 1983), 330–440.

4

# Gender and Sexual Propriety in Ottoman Royal Women's Patronage

*Leslie Peirce*

It is a commonplace that patronage is a political tool of monarchies. Royal patronage is not accessible to all members of a dynasty indiscriminately or equally, however. In the Islamic world, the patronage of women is almost everywhere apparent, and, like that of men, it can carry substantial political meaning. But how is a woman's gender a significant factor in determining what forms of patronage are accessible to her? If patronage is an index of one's status *within* hierarchies of power, what distinguishes one female patron from another? Ottoman royal patronage in the fifteenth, sixteenth, and seventeenth centuries was governed by a set of protocols in which gender and sexual identity figured centrally.

Royal patronage was linked to Ottoman dynastic politics generally, and in its gendered aspects to the politics of reproducing the dynasty, that is, to choices about the sexual alliances of male dynasts and the roles of their female partners in the reproduction of sovereignty. Access to power and its prerogatives was determined in large part by the life-cycle stage of the individual and his or her sexual and reproductive status. Monumental architecture—the most conspicuous and enduring form of patronage—offers a visual text from which to read these rules of royal patronage. But in a state that was governed by a single dynastic family for more than six centuries, rules were bound to change: what was effective at one point in time might not be so even fifty years later. This essay explores issues of gender, sexuality, and status by examining the endowments of two women: Hurrem, the favorite concubine and then wife of Süleyman the Magnificent, who died in 1558, and Kösem, royal concubine and then queen mother to three seventeenth-century sultans, who died in 1651. The philanthropic activities of these two women permit us to observe the complex and shifting relationships among patronage, legitimate authority, and the climate of popular opinion.[1]

Why invoke popular opinion? Because the Ottomans governed within a broad consensus on legitimacy and the rights and duties of the ruler. Royal power was restrained by institutional checks (such as the Janissaries, the famed royal infantry) but also by the force of popular opinion. As the dynasty made rules, so the public—elite and masses alike—monitored those rules. Architectural patronage figured in this process as a public index of power. While visual access to the sovereign *person* was for the most part denied, acts of patronage acquainted subjects with their sovereign family. The visible product of the act of patronage—a public monument or a charitable donation—allowed subjects of the empire to gauge the level of influence of the royal patron. Conversely, imperial family politics and personalities were intimately connected to popular reception of the dynasty's philanthropic projects.

Public opinion formed the limits of the possible in all aspects of governance, not least its acts of patronage. While discussed here as an element in political dynamics, these projects were publicly presented, and no doubt sincerely conceived, as pious acts (*hayrât*). Such acts earned God's heavenly reward for their royal patrons while simultaneously enabling subjects to lead religiously and socially enhanced lives. But when the balance between the pious and political objectives of such projects seemed threatened in favor of the latter, the public did not hesitate to express its objection.

A brief look at the checkered building career of Safiye, the third of five influential royal women of this period, demonstrates both the impact of public opinion and the centrality of patronage in an individual's personal political agenda.[2] As queen mother to her son Mehmed III, the unpopular Safiye so exceeded what were perceived as the bounds of her authority that in 1600 the royal troops threatened to drive her from the capital of Istanbul. Commenting on her precarious position, the Venetian ambassador to the Ottoman court reported: "They attribute many disorders to her, in particular the consumption of money for a most superb mosque she is having built; but she has halted its construction."[3] This was only a temporary setback in the queen mother's plans, however; several months later, a member of the English embassy noted that "the Great sultanaes church goeth up apace, and she rayneth as before."[4] Reigning and building, it seems, went hand in hand. Ultimately, Safiye's project was to remain uncompleted, as royal protocol forced her into retirement three years later at the premature death of her son.

What were the rules governing the practice of royal patronage? Gender, age, sexual status, and life-cycle expectations determined access to political power and thus to public patronage. Among the dynasty's males, only the sultan, as head of state, enjoyed the right to full public expression of royal authority, including monumental building. In the very first Ottoman generations, early histories of the Ottomans tell us, the sultan's sons governed alongside their father and, like him, undertook architectural endowments. However, the princely right to imperial patronage was soon revoked as a sign of the growing centralization of power in the person of the reigning sovereign and the political subordination of his sons. But if the sultan was the sole *male* dynastic patron, the privilege of patronage was shared by numerous females of the dynasty, slave concubines of the sultan as well as princesses of the blood. Here again, protocol operated to create a hierarchy of female patronage that was linked to the dynasty's politics of reproduction—that is, to its policies regarding marriage, concubinage, production of offspring, and the roles of royal mothers and fathers in the education and training of their children.

One group of women is conspicuous through the absence of public building in their careers: the foreign princesses who, until the mid-fifteenth century, were joined to the Ottoman dynasty through formal marriage. It may seem odd that slave concubines were privileged in this regard over women of royal blood, but the key here was motherhood. Except in the very first generations, the Ottoman dynasty did not reproduce through formal diplomatic marriages but rather by means of slave concubinage. The absence of public building by royal *wives* is a compelling statement about their second-class status, and a compelling statement about the prerogatives of political motherhood. Royal motherhood was simply assumed to embody the political knowledge necessary to training future rulers and their sisters. Through a kind of reverse lineage linking these slave consorts to the dynasty as royal mothers, their status was publicly symbolized by the privilege of building. The monuments of the dynasty's concubines were modest at first, but by the late fifteenth century royal mothers were undertaking the endowment of significant urban complexes.

It was a requirement that the imperial patron of public projects be an elder. No matter what his age, the sultan was by definition the male elder of the dynasty. Female seniority was established less by advanced age (one could be an "elder" as early as one's mid-thirties) than by postsexual status. Women who built were women no longer perceived to be sexually active, whether through abstinence, widowhood, or postmenopausal incapacity. In other words, the female patron's identity was independent of a marital or sexual linkage with a male. This is one manifestation of the broad social pressure to seclude women in the child-bearing cycle of their life. Norms of sexual propriety, subscribed to by the dynasty and its subjects alike, granted public stature and influence only to the female elder.

Among royal women, political motherhood, as we have seen, was an essential criterion for status. That concubine mothers were often "elders" by their mid-thirties was a result of the dynasty's management of reproduction, which arbitrarily ended the sexual phase of a concubine's career once she had borne a son.[5] With the birth of a son, which might occur when a concubine was around the age of seventeen, she ceased to be the sexual partner of the sultan. Henceforth her identity was that of mother to the prince, and her duty was his political training. When the prince reached the age of sixteen or seventeen, he was considered to have attained the threshold of legal and political maturity, a crucial passage in his life, which was acknowledged by his appointment to the governorship of a provincial capital. As the prince thus began the public phase of his career, so did his mother. According to Ottoman tradition of the fifteenth and early sixteenth centuries, a royal mother accompanied her son to his post and acted as head of his domestic household. As the elder member of this satellite royal establishment, she, not her son, enjoyed the privilege—indeed, the duty—of adorning the provincial capital.

This leads us to the final principle governing royal patronage until the reign of Süleyman (1520–66): the clear separation of the architectural theater of the sultan from that of his concubines. The endowments of royal concubine mothers were confined to provincial cities, while the sultan alone was responsible for the most splendid projects in the capital of Istanbul. Confinement to a provincial theater did not however mean that a royal mother's endowments were unimposing. In the city of Manisa, one of the main provincial capitals to which princes were sent, the principle religious monuments were the mosques of two royal mothers. Only at the end of the sixteenth century did the city acquire a sultanic endowment, when Süleyman's grandson, Murad III, chose to build his imperial complex in the city of his princely governorate rather than in the seat of his sultanate. In a late sixteenth-century view of Manisa (fig. 4.1), the mosque of Hüsnüshah

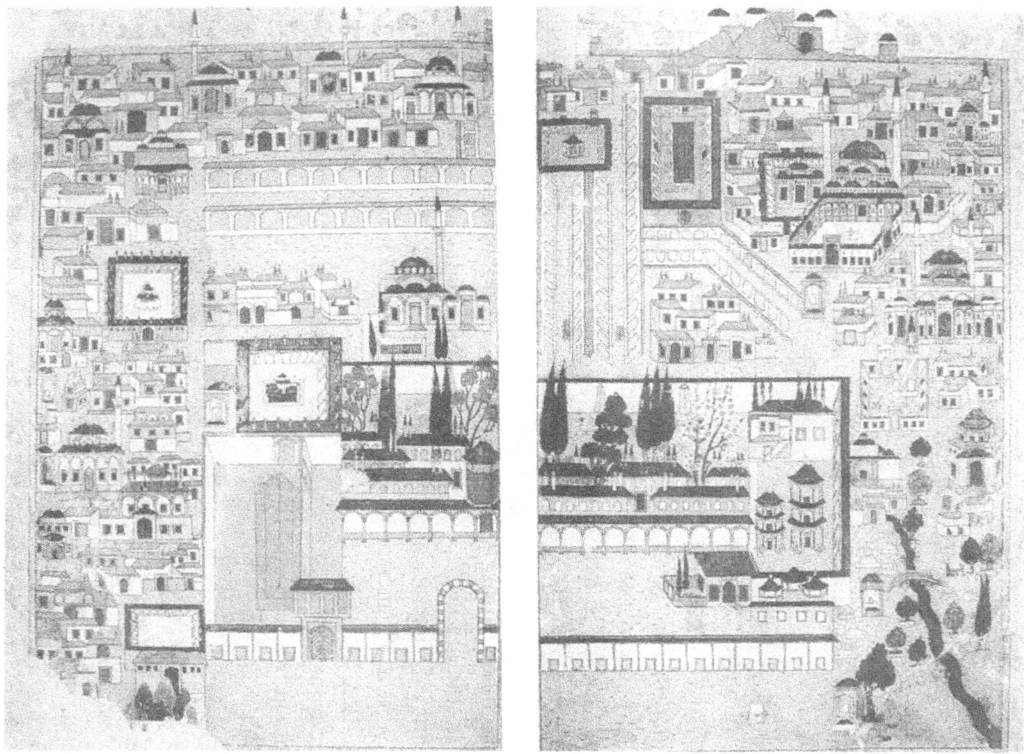

**Fig. 4.1.** A view of Manisa in the sixteenth century, showing the palace in the foreground and the Mosque of Murad III and Hafsa's Sultaniye complex in the upper right (Talikzade, *Şahname-i Al-i Osman*, f. 10b–11a. Courtesy of the Topkapı Palace Museum Library, Istanbul)

lies just above the princely palace, situated in the lower center, while the mosque of Süleyman's mother Hafsa, with its two minarets and outdoor prayer courtyard, lies slightly below the larger mosque of Murad III in the upper right. Known as "Sultaniye" ("the Imperial"), Hafsa's mosque complex included a religious college, a dervish hostel, a primary school, and a soup kitchen (Süleyman later added a hospital and a public bath to his mother's endowment). A successful example of the Ottoman deployment of mosque complexes as a strategy in urban development, the Sultaniye became the nucleus of a thriving new neighborhood, setting the stage for the subsequent endowment of its patroness's great-grandson.[6]

The reign of Süleyman introduced major innovations in dynastic politics, which not surprisingly were reflected in the practice of royal patronage. Outstanding was the sultan's devotion to a single concubine, Hurrem.[7] A major tradition was broken by Hurrem when she became Süleyman's only sexual and reproductive partner; their union produced five sons and one daughter. Other innovations included the sultan's formal marriage to her, and her continuing residence in the royal palace: she did not accompany any of her sons to their provincial governorates. But while these innovations gave Hurrem a unique monopoly within the imperial harem, at the same time they made it difficult for her to establish her political maturity. Unlike her predecessors, female elders whose careers were played out in the provinces, separate from and relatively independent of the sultan, Hurrem was unable to make the transition from a zone marked by sexuality and reproduction to the public zone of political leadership. Significantly, she continued to be known popularly as *Haseki,* the sultan's favorite. Her inability to escape this sexualized status is suggested by a comment made around 1540 by Luigi Bassano, a Venetian page in the palace: "All Süleyman's subjects say that she has bewitched him; therefore they call her '*ziadi*', which means witch. For this reason the Janissaries and the entire court hate her and her children likewise, but because the sultan loves her, no one dares to speak. I have always heard every one speak ill of her and of her children."[8]

Not unexpectedly, the radical architectural profile of this extraordinary woman broke with earlier tradition. What was unusual was the location and the number of works undertaken by Hurrem herself and by Süleyman in her name. Unlike her concubine predecessors, whose works were confined mainly to Anatolian provincial capitals, architectural endowments in Hurrem's name existed in all the principal cities of the empire: Istanbul, the secondary capital of Edirne, the holy cities of Mecca, Medina, and

Jerusalem, and other major cities as well. For the first time in the history of the Ottoman dynasty, the building career of a royal concubine encompassed the whole empire.

Hurrem's special status was first announced in the capital of Istanbul, where the first royal mosque complex associated with Süleyman's reign was built in Hurrem's name. Later came the magnificent bath, with separate sections for women and men, constructed to serve the staff and congregation of the great church-turned-mosque of Hagia Sophia (Aya Sofya) and located in the symbolically charged ceremonial center of the city. In the Arab lands recently conquered by Süleyman's father, where the sacred cities of Mecca, Medina, and Jerusalem were located, Hurrem's patronage carried the new overlord's message of beneficence and piety. In Jerusalem, for example, was located the large public foundation that was the special object of Hurrem's endeavors in her later years.

Two of Hurrem's major projects, the early Istanbul complex and the later Jerusalem complex, demonstrate the range of images she projected through her patronage. The Istanbul complex, begun in 1537, was the first of Hurrem's public philanthropic acts, and may have figured in the problematic reputation she suffered. There is some disagreement over whether Hurrem or Süleyman endowed the mosque itself, but in any event the complex's religious college and primary school were commissioned by Hurrem the year following the mosque's completion.[9] The soup kitchen and the hospital (the latter still functioning today) came later, the former built by Süleyman and the latter by Hurrem. The mosque itself was modest (with only a single minaret, it did not claim the imperial status signified by the presence of two or more minarets); it was the complex's location in the capital as well as its eventual size that was noteworthy.

The date when the mosque was begun is surely significant. In 1537, Hurrem's eldest son was sixteen, the threshold of a prince's political adulthood. So, in a sense, the rule that a public profile might be enjoyed only by a female *elder*—that is, the mother of a politically mature son—was not broken, and it is likely that Hurrem intended to convey a change in her status with this public charitable act. The years around 1537 marked a life-cycle turning point not only in Hurrem's career but also in that of Süleyman. With the birth of their last child in 1531, the royal couple—for so had Süleyman fashioned their image by marrying his concubine—had moved beyond the reproductive phase of their reign. The sultan turned forty, the traditional beginning of male elderhood, during the celebrated two-year military campaign of 1534–36 which captured the city of Baghdad, historic seat of the Sunni caliphate, from the Ottomans' greatest Muslim opponent. Upon his return, Süleyman initiated an important series of policy changes that gave increased emphasis to the legal and religious aspects of Islamic monarchy and less to the glories of military conquest.[10] This period has been described as a time of widespread discontent among the empire's subjects, and the shifts in policy may have been both symptom and cause of tensions.[11]

Hurrem's unpopularity may therefore have stemmed from general dissatisfaction as well as from more focused public resistance to changes in the dynasty's politics of reproduction made manifest in the building of her complex. Despite the image of female maturity that Hurrem may have wished to project with her Istanbul endowment, she continued in people's minds to be thought of as the sultan's favorite (it is about this time that Bassano reported people calling her a witch). It is not surprising that the mosque became known as "Haseki," as did the district that grew up surrounding it. In fact, it is possible that the planning for the Haseki mosque was undertaken in an effort to mitigate Hurrem's problematic status. The mosque was located in a relatively undeveloped part of the city, near an area known as the "Women's Bazaar" (at the end of the century, the secretary to the English embassy described it as "the markett place of women, for thither they come to sell their wourks and wares"[12]). The historian Peçevi commented that this association of the complex with women was a manifestation of the sultan's "utmost sensitivity."[13] In his *Book of Travels,* the seventeenth-century writer Evliya Çelebi emphasized the association of women with structures in the area: in a humorous passage where he matched different classes of the city's population with appropriate public baths, women were assigned to a bath near the Haseki complex.[14] What I am suggesting here is that Hurrem's endowment may have been deliberately presented as an act of concern for women in order to disarm public rumblings over this unprecedented act by a royal consort. In this regard, it is noteworthy that the simple mosque built by Gülfem, another prominent member of Süleyman's harem (probably its senior administrative officer) was, according to local legend, intended for the use of women and opened to men only in recent times.[15]

Hurrem's Jerusalem complex, in contrast, appears to have been an untroubled act of patronage. The fact that it was located away from the capital and undertaken later in Hurrem's life, when her sons were governing in the provinces and her maturity beyond doubt, probably affected its reception. This well-endowed establishment, completed in the early 1550s, contained a mosque, a fifty-five-room dwelling for religious pilgrims, an inn and stable for travelers, and an area devoted to numerous charitable services for the poor including a soup kitchen and public toilets. The ceremonial importance attached to Hurrem's public works is highlighted by the magnificence of the property deeds granting her income sources to provide for the complex's upkeep. Witnessed by the highest officers of the empire, the deeds are superb specimens of the chancery art of the Ottomans, with their exquisite calligraphy and illumination. A deed from the year 1552 provided revenues from villages in the province of Trablus.

The complex's site was already associated with pious acts by women: it was reputed to be the location of a pilgrim's hospice built by Helena, the mother of the Byzantine emperor Constantine and legendary discoveror of Christian holy sites in the city, followed in Mamluk times by the residence of a wealthy religious pilgrim to the city.[16] The implicit reference to pious female predecessors confirmed the legitimacy of Hurrem's enterprise. This historical appeal was no doubt linked to Süleyman's program to establish himself, the first Ottoman overlord of the holy cities of Islam, as worthy successor to earlier caliphs, sultans, and even Byzantine emperors (to whose "Roman" sovereignty the Ottoman sultans of "Rum" claimed successorship through their conquest of Constantinople). In the Ottoman appropriation of previously sanctified or imperialized space, the women of Süleyman's family figured centrally, foremost among them Hurrem. Inscription into a tradition of pious benefactresses in an ancient sacred environment was for Hurrem certainly a safer means of self-representation than the novel act of patronage by a sultan's favorite.

The subsequent history of royal female patronage owed much to Hurrem, to both the positive and negative aspects of her ambivalent legacy. On the one hand, her career offered a powerful precedent for conspicuous imperial patronage by women. On the other, it taught the lesson that political motherhood—a public role—should not be confused with conjugal status—a private role. Henceforth, a concubine, even the favorite, might wield a good deal of influence, but it was not demonstrated beyond the borders of the household. To do so, as Hurrem's experience showed, was understood by the public as a violation of social and sexual propriety.

Royal concubines continued to undertake charitable works, but like their persons, their efforts were not publicly manifest. Instead of building, they established endowments for such "invisible" pious works as recitation of the Qur'an in a major mosque or the provision of relief for the poor. Moreover, such charities were usually dissociated from their patron through their enactment in distant places, in particular the sacred cities. At issue here is a paradoxical clash of female piety and pollution, that is, the problematic relationship of the patron herself to the space whose function and status are constituted by her act of patronage. What happens, in other words, when the person of the patron can defile the space—the sanctuary of a mosque, the male society of the religious college or the dervish lodge—that she has brought into existence through her pious act?[17] A contemporary reading of religious law by the official Ottoman authority, the *mufti* Ebu Suʿud, ruled that a group of women desiring to attend the Friday congregational prayer might be prevented from doing so if there were young women among them (implying that the *mufti* sanctioned the participation of older women in the communal mosque prayer).[18] The rules of seclusion were most stringently enforced for the married child-bearing woman for two related reasons: unlike the virgin, the married woman was considered to have an awakened sexual apppetite, and as a result, her reproductive capacity was a potential threat to the integrity of her husband's bloodline. In the matter of female patronage of religious structures, Süleyman's family appears to have tried different solutions to this dilemma: his mother and his only daughter Mihrimah safely endowed mosques as female elders, while the mosques of women associated with his harem (Hurrem and Gülfem) were justified, legend suggests, as endowments for the use of women.

The difficulties experienced by Hurrem, and thus by Süleyman as well, led to the abandonment of the second option. The female patron of public endowments was henceforth always a postsexual elder. Beginning with Nurbanu, the concubine favorite of Hurrem's son and Süleyman's successor, Selim II, the privilege of public building was reserved for the royal female as mother of the sovereign, in which capacity she now acquired an official title, *valide sultan* ("queen mother"). The endowment of imperial complexes in the capital in fact now became the prerogative of queen mothers rather than sultans. With one major exception (Ahmed I), sultans—if they built at all—established their endowments in lesser cities of the empire. This privilege of adorning the capital paralleled the gradual institutionalization of the queen mother's political influence into what by the seventeenth century had become the formal *office* of *valide sultan*.

This essay might have concluded with an account of Nurbanu, whose career was instrumental in transforming the paradigm of royal female patronage from favorite to queen mother. As the first of the powerful queen mothers, Nurbanu's considerable authority was noted in ambassadorial circles. Her large and splendid mosque complex, which Evliya Çelebi described as "a mountain of light," was constructed in the Üsküdar district of Istanbul between 1570 and 1582 (Nurbanu's son, Murad III, built his own mosque in the provincial capital of Manisa, as we have seen). However, paradigms are rarely stationary or absolute. The career of our second patron, Kösem, demonstrates that protocols of patronage, like any rules for managing power, contain inherent tensions and are subject to the vagaries of politics.

Kösem's long career passed through the two stages of favorite and queen mother.[19] Her influence was first manifest as favorite to the sultan Ahmed I (who ruled from 1603 to his death in 1617), and then as *valide sultan* to two sultan sons and a grandson who ascended the throne at the age of seven. A dominant political figure during the first half of the seventeenth century, Kösem's increasing control of power was terminated by her murder in 1651 by the rival faction of her daughter-in-law Turhan, mother of the child-sultan.

Kösem's influence as favorite was noted by the Venetian ambassador, who reported that "she can do what she wishes with the King and possesses his heart absolutely, nor is anything ever denied to her."[20] Like Hurrem, Kösem was the only other royal concubine for whom the rule of a single son was broken: she and the sultan were the parents of three, perhaps four sons, and three or four daughters. But unlike Hurrem, Kösem did not suffer ill repute for her "possession of the sultan's heart," for the rules of propriety were observed. As concubine, Kösem undertook "invisible" charities: the annual distribution of shirts, woolen cloaks, shoes, and turban materials to poor pilgrims and to the poor of the sacred cities of Mecca, Medina, and Jerusalem; recitation of the Qur'an in the sanctuaries of these cities; and the supply of water to pilgrims making their way to Mecca and Medina (for this purpose Kösem's endowment funded thirty camels, six drovers, and six water carriers).[21] Moreover, Kösem appears to have learned from her predecessors the valuable lesson of managing her power without flaunting it: another Venetian ambassador noted that "she restrains herself with great wisdom from speaking too frequently of serious matters and affairs of state."[22]

One might have expected that as queen mother, Kösem would undertake an architectural project commensurate with her power and reputation. She did not, however, although she spent enormous sums of money on philanthropic endeavors. And here we encounter the political vagaries and tensions suggested above. The most obvious tension was the delicate balance of power between sultan and queen mother. By Kösem's time, the experience of several influential royal women had rendered their public influence a continual focus of popular scrutiny. Indeed, as the *valide sultan*'s authority became routinized into an *office,* criticism of individual queen mothers became less personal and therefore culturally and politically more feasible. During the reign of Ahmed I, whose consort Kösem was, royal women had almost no public profile as a result of Ahmed's determination to avoid the appearance of being dominated by a woman as his father had been dominated by his own mother, the notorious Safiye. Reviving the practice of his forebears, neglected for four generations, Ahmed chose to build his own mosque (the "Blue Mosque") not in a distant province but in the capital. Located in the imperial center of the city, on the ancient Byzantine hippodrome, the sultan's monument asserted itself as peer to the venerable Hagia Sophia.

During the reign of her first sultan son, Murad IV, Kösem may have held back from an architectural project of imperial scope because of Murad's dynamism: he was a military hero and aggressive ruler. Furthermore, Murad himself was rumored to be planning a large project in the "new traditionalism" of his father Ahmed.[23] But Murad's early death in 1640 at the age of twenty-nine put an end to any such plans. It was at this point that Kösem did build: her own mosque was undertaken in 1640, shortly after Murad's brother, her emotionally unstable son Ibrahim, inherited the throne. It might have been expected that this weak son would provide his mother with the opportunity for a large project, but once again this did not happen. Kösem's complex, which consisted of a mosque, a primary school, a school for the study of Prophetic tradition, two fountains, and a public bath, was of modest scale and materials and located in an out-of-the-way neighborhood in Üsküdar. I would suggest that the reason for its modesty was the precarious state of the dynasty at this moment in its history: in 1640, Kösem shared with others the fear that the collapse of the Ottoman dynasty was imminent, and this may well have led her to the hasty endowment of a mosque complex before the demise of her career, indeed of the empire. Because of Ibrahim's disabilities, he had not been expected to become sultan, but as a result of the vagaries of dynastic reproduction, he was the sole surviving male of the Ottoman royal house at his brother Murad's early death. This grave danger was compounded by Ibrahim's sexual aversion to women at the beginning of his reign. Ambassadorial reports from 1640 and 1641 discuss the probable collapse of the dynasty and speculate as to the ensuing political dénouement.[24] Kösem's effort at architectural patronage may reveal genuine pious intent as well as, perhaps, a wish to memorialize the sultanic generation of her own sons, during whose reigns no other royal mosques were endowed.

Kösem's failure to endow a substantial religious project *later* in her career had to do, in part at least, with the challenge to her status from others. The increasingly eccentric Ibrahim tried to exile his mother, and while he was unsuccessful in this, he was able to limit her public prerogatives. When Ibrahim was eventually overthrown in 1648 and replaced by his seven-year-old son (a political manuever in which Kösem played a central role), she did not count on the ambition and authority of the child's young mother, Turhan, whom she herself had groomed for the responsibility of political motherhood. After three years of waiting in the shadow of the venerable *valide sultan,* Turhan appears to have sanctioned Kösem's murder, a move that provoked divided response in both governing circles and the urban populace. Once her own career as queen mother was consolidated, Turhan would restore the *valide sultan*'s prerogative of endowing an imperial complex in the capital (see chapter 5 in this volume by Thys-Şenocak).

If Kösem did not follow the paradigm of endowing a major religious monument, she nonetheless amply fulfilled the role of patron expected of royal female elders. Kösem's most prominent building project was a large khan, or business complex, in the commercial center of Istanbul, close to the Grand Bazaar. Appropriately, this endowment, the grandest of such structures in the capital and still functioning today, became known as the Valide Khan, or Khan of the Queen Mother. At Kösem's death, her own treasury, consisting of twenty chests of gold, was found secured in her khan.[25] Significantly, it was at the city's nexus of money and politics, not at the ceremonial nexus of religion and politics, that this veteran political strategist's major act of architectural patronage was located.

While Kösem may not be remembered for the number of charitable structures she endowed, her philanthropic career is notable for the number of charitable acts she undertook. For example, she regularly made provision for dowries to poor girls, and during the three holy months of the calendar she would furnish stipends to two hundred descendents of the Prophet. Once a year Kösem would leave the palace incognito and personally arrange for the release of imprisoned debtors and other criminals (except murderers) through payment of their debts or recompense for their crimes. She was famous for her largesse toward her own slaves, whom she freed after half the usual term of service.[26]

As actions rather than architecture, these charities may have been "invisible," but they were hardly private. Kösem's stature and influence—

or notoriety in the eyes of some—made these donations controversial, since acts of largesse could be an effective means of cultivating partisan support. One contemporary historian lamented the fate of peasants who worked Kösem's landed holdings and suffered extortionate taxes that provided the revenue for her charities. Another countered that had her substantial revenues gone straight into the general treasury, they might have been squandered rather than spent for the benefit of the populace, as they were through her philanthropic efforts.

Kösem's legacy as a patron, like Hurrem's, was ambivalent. While she avoided Hurrem's dilemma by undertaking the endowment of public establishments only as an elder, she encountered an obstacle that Hurrem did not: resistance among members of the dynasty itself to her high profile. But Kösem's failure to endow a religious complex may not have been due solely to inability, for it is possible that she consciously decided to avoid such a project. She may have recognized that to survive as a political actor in the circumstances of her times and to achieve the goals she desired for the empire and for herself, she would be forced to engage in a good deal of factional maneuvering. In other words, her political profile might have been so public that any major act of patronage would have seemed an abuse of her access to extraordinary resources. There was the example of Safiye to warn her that undertaking a mosque complex on an imperial scale might move the debate about the uses of her wealth from the pages of historians into the streets of the capital.

I have argued here that Ottoman royal women's choices regarding patronage were embedded in protocols of sovereignty, in which gender was deployed as one of a number of strategies to project royal legitimacy. Yet such protocols were successful only insofar as they met with popular approval, hence the need to conform to broadly shared notions of gendered space and sexual propriety. But within these protocols, gender was not a sole determinant, nor was it static over time. We have observed a significant overlap in the rules for female and male patronage, and in addition significant differences among forms of female patronage. We have also seen that rules can be overwhelmed by contingent factors, which, through their construction in the public's understanding, in turn cast a particular meaning on the act of patronage, a meaning not necessarily intended by the patron herself. In sum, the Ottoman case suggests that gender should be understood *not* as an essentializing category of analysis ("*female* patronage"), but rather as a dynamic and nuanced element in the religiously, socially, and politically complex act of patronage in Islamic societies.

## NOTES

I am grateful to Rebecca Foote for help in clarifying some of the ideas expressed in this paper.

1. The patronage of Ottoman royal women of this period is discussed by Ülkü Bates, "Women as Patrons of Architecture in Turkey," in *Women in the Muslim World,* ed. L. Beck and N. Keddie, (Cambridge Mass.: Harvard University Press, 1978), 245–60, and "The Architectural Patronage of Ottoman Women," *Asian Art* (Spring 1993): 50–65. See Leslie Peirce, *The Imperial Harem: Women and Sovereignty in the Ottoman Empire* (New York and Oxford: Oxford University Press, 1993) for a study of these women and their peers, their political and diplomatic roles, and their patronage.

2. For a biographical sketch of Safiye, see Susan Skilliter, "Three Letters from the Ottoman 'Sultana' Safiye to Queen Elizabeth," in *Documents from Islamic Chanceries,* ed. S. M. Stern (Cambridge, Mass.: Harvard University Press, 1965), 144.

3. Nicoló Barozzi and Giglielmo Berchet, eds., *Le Relazioni degli stati Europei* (Series 5: Turkey) (Venice, 1871–72), 1:39.

4. John Sanderson, *The Travels of John Sanderson in the Levant 1584–1602,* ed. Sir W. Foster, Hakluyt Series no. 67, second series (London, 1931), 204.

5. A concubine might however give birth to one or more daughters before bearing a son. This policy results statistically in an equal ratio of male to female births overall.

6. On this complex and its endowment deed, see Ibrahim Hakkı Konyalı, "Kanunî Sultan Süleyman'ın Annesi Hafsa Sultanın Vakfiyesi ve Manisa'daki Hayır Eserleri [The Endowment Deed of Hafsa Sultan, Mother of Sultan Süleyman, and Her Pious Works in Manisa]," *Vakıflar Dergisi* 8 (1969): 47–56; see also M. Çağatay Uluçay, *Manisa'daki Saray-ı Amire ve Şehzadeler Türbesi* [*The Royal Palace in Manisa and the Princes' Tomb*] (Istanbul, 1941), 9.

7. For a brief biographical treatment of Hurrem, see Susan Skilliter, "Khurrem," in the *Encyclopaedia of Islam,* new ed. (Leiden and London, 1954– ), 5:66–67.

8. Luigi Bassano, *Costumi et i modi particolari della vita de' Turchi,* 18 vols. (Munich, 1963). "Ziadi" is Bassano's Venetian rendering of Turkish *cadi,* "witch."

9. Aptullah Kuran, *Sinan: The Grand Old Master of Ottoman Architecture* (Washington, D.C. and London: Institute of Turkish Studies, 1987).

10. On this issue see Gülru Necipoğlu, "A *Kânûn* for the State, a Canon for the Arts: Conceptualizing the Classical Synthesis of Ottoman Arts and Architecture," in *Soliman le Magnifique et son temps,* ed. G. Veinstein (Paris: Documentation Française, 1992), 195–98; Cornell Fleischer, "The Lawgiver as Messiah," in ibid., 167–68.

11. Ahmet Yaşar Ocak, "Idéologie officielle et réaction populaire: un aperçu général sur les mouvements et les courants socio-religieux à l'époque de Soliman le Magnifique," in *Soliman le Magnifique,* 185–90.

12. Sanderson, *The Travels,* 77.

13. Ibrahim Peçevi, *Tarih-i Peçevi* (Istanbul, 1281–84/1864–67), 1:425.

14. Evliya Çelebi, *Narrative of Travels in Europe, Asia, and Africa,* trans. J. von Hammer (London, 1834), 1:179–80.

15. On the identity of Gülfem, sometimes thought to be an early concubine of Süleyman, see Peirce, *The Imperial Harem,* 302n12.

16. For the foundation deed of this complex, see St. H. Stephan, "An Endowment Deed of Khâsseki Sultân, Dated the 24th May 1552," *Quarterly of the Department of Antiquities in Palestine* 10 (1944): 170–99. For the Mamluk residence of the Lady Tunsuq Al-Muzaffariya, see Michael Burgoyne, *Mamluk Jerusalem* (London: World of Islam Festival Trust, 1987), 485–87. Hurrem's foundation is the subject of a study by Amy Singer, "The *Mülknāmes* of Hürrem Sultan's Waqf in Jerusalem," *Muqarnas* 14 (1997): 96–102; she is preparing a monograph on the subject as well.

17. On pollution and piety in Muslim societies, see Kevin Reinhart, "Impurity/No Danger," *History of Religions* 30.1 (1990): 1–23; Shahla Haeri, *Law of Desire: Temporary Marriage in Shi'i Iran* (Syracuse: Syracuse University Press, 1989); Carol Delaney, *The Seed and the Soil: Gender and Cosmology in Turkish Village Society* (Berkeley and Los Angeles: University of California Press, 1991); Julie Marcus, *A World of Difference: Islam and Gender Hierarchy in Turkey* (London: Zed, 1992).

18. M. E. Düzdağ, ed., *Ebussuûd Efendi Fetvaları Işığında 16. Asır Türk Hayatı* [*Sixteenth-Century Turkish Life in the Light of Ebussuûd Efendi's Fetvas*] (Istanbul: Enderun Kitabevi, 1983), 60.

19. For an account of Kösem's career, see the fine article "Kösem Sulṭān" in the *Encyclopaedia of Islam,* new ed., 5:272–73, an abridged translation of M. Cavid Baysun's article of the same title in the Turkish *Islam Ansiklopedisi* (Istanbul, 1940–86).

20. Barozzi and Berchet, *Le Relazioni,* 1:302.

21. Mücteba Ilgürel, "Kösem Sultan'ın Bir Vakfiyesi [A Foundation Deed of Kösem Sultan]," *Tarih Dergisi* 16.21 (1966): 86–92.

22. Barozzi and Berchet, *Le Relazioni,* 1:134.

23. Ibid., 2:95.

24. Ibid., 1:372–73, 2:110.

25. Mustafa Naima, *Tarih,* 6 vols. (Istanbul, 1280/1863–64), 5:113.

26. Naima, *Tarih,* 5:113.

5

# The Yeni Valide Mosque Complex of Eminönü, Istanbul (1597–1665)

## Gender and Vision in Ottoman Architecture

*Lucienne Thys-Şenocak*

The Yeni Valide mosque complex is a large pious foundation located on the shores of the Golden Horn in the Eminönü district of Istanbul (fig. 5.1). Construction on the mosque began in 1597 under the auspices of Safiye Sultan, the mother of Sultan Mehmed III, but was abandoned shortly after Mehmed's death in 1603. The succession of her grandson, Ahmed I, to the Ottoman sultanate marked the end of Safiye's tenure as *valide,* the title given to the mother of the reigning sultan. She was moved from the harem to the Old Palace and replaced by the new *valide,* the mother of Sultan Ahmed I.[1] With the death of Safiye in 1605, the momentum of the Yeni Valide project was lost.

What had been built of the Yeni Cami's foundations was left untouched for fifty-seven years. The building site that had been expropriated at great cost from the largely Jewish population in the Eminönü quarter was re-inhabited by these minorities and others involved in the bustling trade surrounding the customs depots located there. It was not until 1660, after a fire had devastated a large section of the city from Unkapanı to Eminönü that interest in the Yeni Cami project was reawakened. At the suggestion of the head imperial architect, Mustafa Ağa, the Valide Hatice Turhan Sultan, mother of Mehmed IV, decided to resume construction in 1663 and inaugurated in 1665, along with several other dependencies: a *hünkâr kasrı* (imperial pavilion), *türbe* (tomb), *sebilhane* (large fountain), *sibyan mektebi*

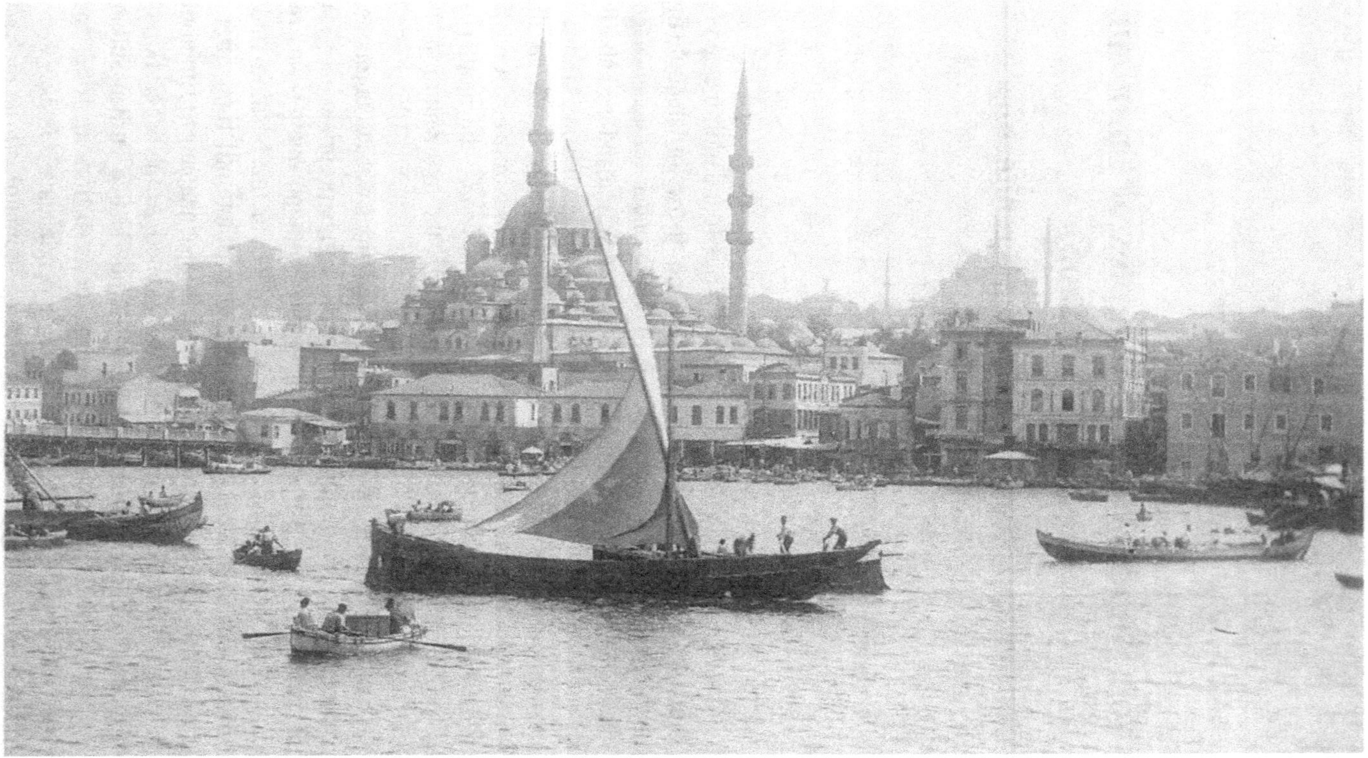

**Fig. 5.1.** The Yeni Valide Mosque complex of Eminönü as seen from the Golden Horn (photograph by Sebah and Joaillier; courtesy of the German Archaeological Institute of Istanbul)

(primary school), a *darülhadith* (school for the instruction of hadith), and a formidable commercial venture, the *Mısır Çarşısı,* known today as the Egyptian or Spice Market (fig. 5.2).[2]

From inception to completion, the building of the Yeni Valide complex spans a major part of the seventeenth century, and thus the story of its creation reflects the historical circumstances of that century. The central and often competitive role that dynastic women played in the Ottoman power structure, the policies and attitudes toward the expropriation of property, and the economic, political, and military crises of that era were all factors that shaped the Yeni Valide mosque complex. The study of its patronage adds an important dimension to our understanding of the roles that imperial women played in the late-sixteenth-century and seventeenth-century Ottoman world and the complex dynamics of the Ottoman architectural enterprises in the postclassical age.

In the Eminönü complex we can see the planning mechanisms that shaped the large pious foundations, or *külliye*s, built in the capital of the Ottoman empire. In particular, the nonsymmetrical layout of the buildings in the Yeni Valide complex calls into question certain traditional analyses of mosque-complex planning in Istanbul that see the development of these socioreligious centers in evolutionary terms. That approach assumes that the optimal spatial relationship between the mosque and its dependencies was a rational, symmetrical one.[3] Accordingly, the royal Ottoman complexes of Istanbul have been described as emerging from "organically-shaped" early imperial complexes of fourteenth- and fifteenth-century Bursa and Edirne, reaching the apogee of architectural expression in Mimar Sinan's symmetrically arranged Süleymaniye complex of the sixteenth century (fig. 5.3). Mosque complexes built in Istanbul after the so-called classical era that have nonsymmetrical layouts have been interpreted as manifestations of an increasingly deteriorating political order in the empire.[4] Thus the Yeni Cami complex, commonly referred to by Ottoman architectural historians as the benchmark between the classical age of Sinan and a postclassical era of decline, has been described as lacking an organizing agenda, an example of a "freely arranged ensemble."[5]

The history of the project's construction reveals that an immense quarter of Eminönü had burned just prior to the building of the Yeni Valide complex and large tracts of land were expropriated for the complex on two occasions. Thus the most frequently invoked explanations for the absence of symmetrical planning in Ottoman mosque complexes—uneven terrain, extant street patterns, and an inexperienced architect—do not answer the

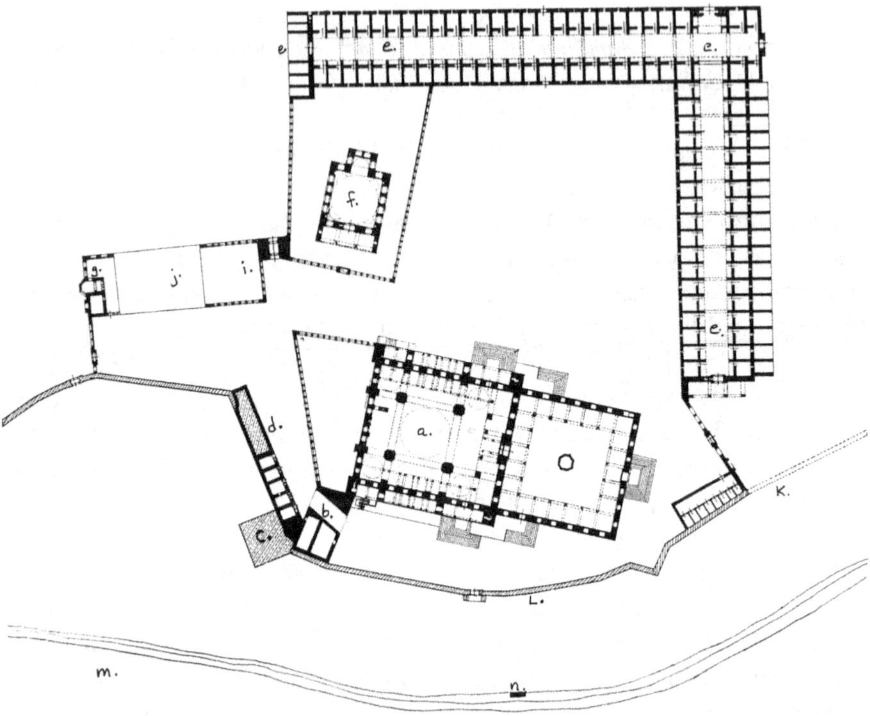


**Fig. 5.2.** Plan of the Yeni Valide Mosque Complex (Ateş and Alcı, *Istanbul Yeni Cami ve Hünkâr Kasrı*). Key: a) mosque, b) *hünkâr kasrı,* c) garden of the *hünkâr kasrı* on the Vasileus tower, d) *taht-ı revan yolu,* e) Egyptian market, f) tomb, g) fountain, h) fountain converted to time-keeping center, i) primary school (no longer extant), j) customs house (no longer extant), l) sea wall (no longer extant), m) Golden Horn, n) *valide* entrance to complex from Golden Horn

first question posed in this paper: what are the factors contributing to the unique layout of the Yeni Cami and its dependencies? I suggest that while the Eminönü complex does not emphasize symmetrical relationships to the same degree as the Süleymaniye, there was a logical agenda for the layout of the Yeni Valide complex that can be better understood in terms of the gender of its patrons.

The Yeni Valide complex reflected the efforts of two powerful dynastic women. Patronage by women, as the papers in this volume demonstrate, was not unusual, but due to either a lack of interest or the assumption that female patronage was of secondary importance, our understanding of royal women's architectural patronage in the Ottoman past, and the larger issues

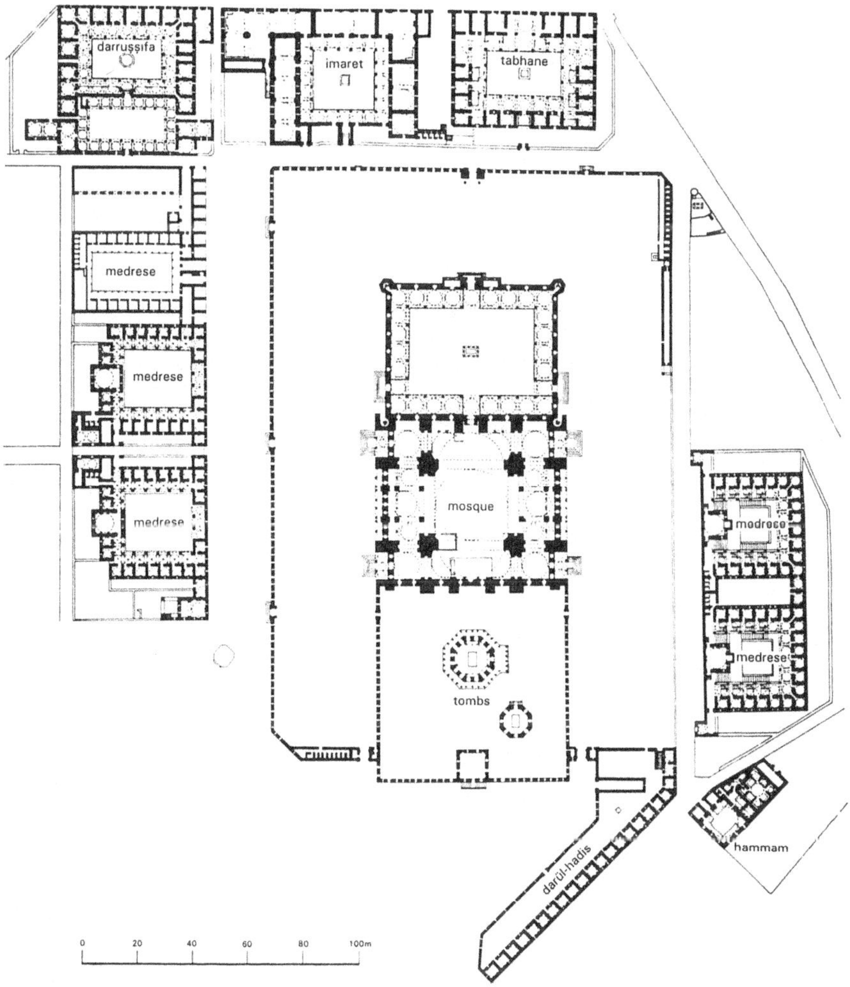


**Fig. 5.3.** The Süleymaniye complex (after G. Goodwin)

of gender and its impact upon architectural expression in the Islamic world is limited. Typically, the role of royal women in the politics of the Ottoman Empire has been perceived as a negative and destabilizing influence. Their actions in this critical period of Ottoman history have not been seen as legitimate but as manipulations that, among other factors, contributed to the decline of the empire.[6] But the present study of the two women patrons of the Yeni Valide *külliye* reveals a different and more complex picture that calls into question the traditional decline paradigm for the post-classical

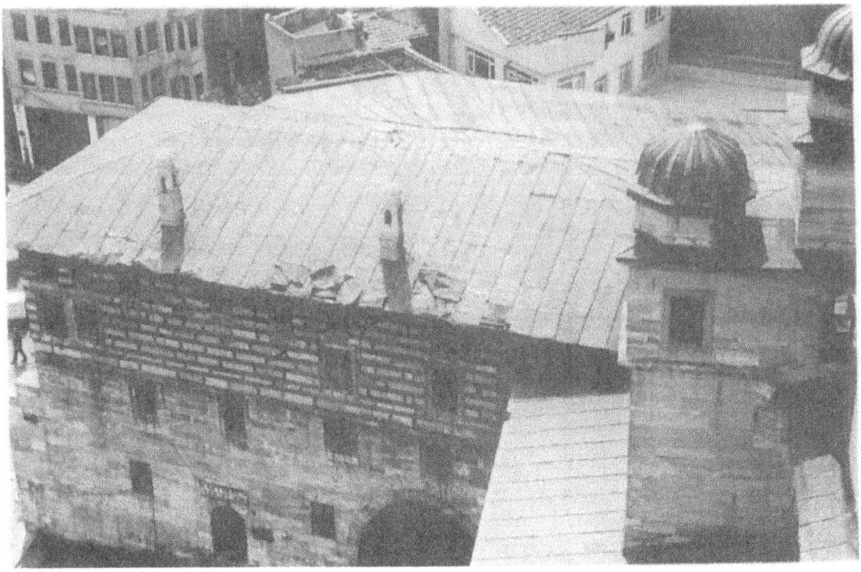

**Fig. 5.4.** The Yeni Valide Hünkâr Kasrı

Ottoman period. Therefore, the second question raised here is: did the gender of the patrons, the mothers of two sultans, influence the location of the complex, the type of buildings in it and, specifically, the physical organization of the Eminönü *külliye*?

To further our understanding of the mechanisms involved in the planning of imperial mosque complexes in the Ottoman capital, and determine the impact that the gender of the patron may have had upon various aspects of the Eminönü building campaign, we must turn to the most unusual building in the complex, the *hünkâr kasrı,* or royal pavilion (fig. 5.4). When considered in light of its typological origins, its organizing role in the complex and, finally, its stage for royal ceremonial, the pavilion holds the key to the location and orientation of the subsidiary buildings in the complex. The supposedly "freely arranged ensemble" is, in fact, a collection of structures whose locations are not arbitrary but quite deliberately organized around the position of the *hünkâr kasrı.*

A three-story, richly tiled structure, reached by a long covered ramp, the pavilion was erected on the remains of the Byzantine Vasileus tower and may have served initially as a vantage point from which to observe the construction of the complex.[7] Once completed, it served as residence

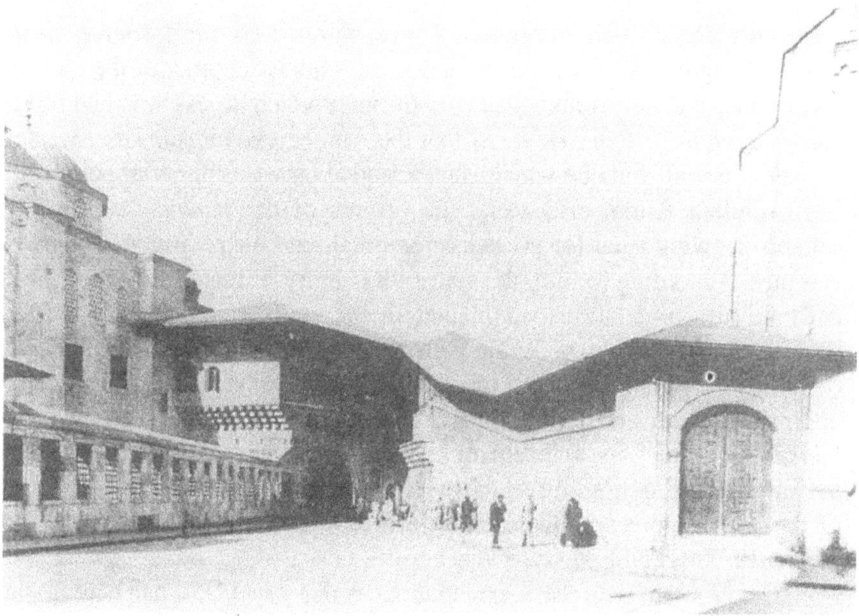

**Fig. 5.5.** The Yeni Valide Hünkâr Kasrı and Taht-ı Revan Yolu (Ateş and Alcı, *Istanbul Yeni Cami ve Hünkâr Kasrı*)

outside of the palace for the *valide,* sultan, and other members of the royal entourage and played an important role in the ceremonial surrounding the Eminönü complex.

As a building type, the Ottoman *hünkâr kasrı* is a curiosity. It makes an abrupt debut in the early seventeenth century at the Sultan Ahmed complex in Istanbul's Atmeydanı, the site of the ancient hippodrome.[8] One historian has remarked that the ramp leading to Sultan Ahmed's *hünkâr kasrı* is "the first appearance in Ottoman architecture of a ramp to the royal kiosk and has been considered a baroque development."[9] The ramp, or *taht-ı revan yolu,* at the Sultan Ahmed Mosque leads to a platform and loggia and, finally, a two-room suite that served as retiring rooms for the sultan after prayer.[10] The Yeni Valide *hünkâr kasrı,* completed fifty years later, is even more impressive in size and the presence of the great ramp, here completely enclosed (fig. 5.5).

The origins of the *hünkâr kasrı* building type is said to have evolved from the *hünkâr mahfili,* the sultan's private prayer area.[11] Howard Crane, for example, states that "beginning with the Ahmediyye this imperial portal (*hünkâr mahfili*) undergoes a further transformation in both conception and scale. In place of a simple portal, a great ramped corridor, a *taht-ı revan yolu* (palanquin way) was constructed at the southeast corner of the mosque giving onto a series of antechambers through which access was had to the *hünkâr mahfili.*"[12] Later he states that the Ahmediyye *hünkâr kasrı* was an "imperial portal" but one which "far exceeded previous imperial portals."[13]

Aptullah Kuran also seeks the origins of the *hünkâr kasrı* in the sultan's growing need for greater ceremonial, and hence a more extensive entrance. According to him, the sixteenth-century Sultan Süleyman had no need for the ostentatious portal that in the seventeenth century was to become the *hünkâr kasrı.* While there was a great deal of ceremonial surrounding the sultan's visit to the mosque, "the pomp was not dependent upon special architectural features."[14] Like Crane, Kuran believes that the *hünkâr kasrı* had its antecedent in the sultan's private entrance to the *hünkâr mahfili.* According to these explanations, as the ceremonial needs of the sultan increased, the architecture developed to accommodate, and the *hünkâr kasrı* building type was born.

The problem with these explanations is that royal Ottoman ceremonial and ostentation described by Kuran and Crane existed as early as Fatih Mehmed's reign in the late fifteenth century, indeed was codified in the *kanunname,* or sultanic regulations established by this earlier sultan.[15] Yet the *hünkâr kasrı* building type does not appear until almost two centuries later and then, without prior experimentation, in a well-developed and extensively decorated form, first at the Sultan Ahmed mosque, and next in the second building phase of the Eminönü complex. It is clear from the problems in the traditional analyses of the *hünkâr kasrı*'s origins that the hitherto accepted emphasis on evolutionary architectural forms explains neither the variance in Ottoman mosque complex organization nor the appearance in the seventeenth century of the *hünkâr kasrı* as a building type.

Furthermore, I suggest that the origins of this type are not to be found exclusively in the imperial portal of the mosque or the *hünkâr mahfili* but lie closer to the shores of the Bosphorous in the various kiosks that were built to accommodate the sultan and his retinue on outings from the palace. It is important to note that the *hünkâr kasrı* type emerges in the seventeenth century, at a time when royal Ottoman women were establishing themselves as prominent patrons of architecture in the capital and exercising a greater amount of political power in the palace. While any discussion of the plan and appearance of the Sultan Ahmed *kasr* is problematic due to its successive restorations, we can posit that the existence of the *hünkâr kasrı* building type at Sultan Ahmed's complex was related to the increasingly powerful and central role that royal Ottoman women exercised at court in this period of history.

Among Ahmed I's harem favorites, or *haseki*s, was Mahpeyker Kadın who, upon the accession of her son Murad IV to the throne in 1623, became the Valide Kösem Sultan, one of the most powerful regent mothers in Ottoman history.[16] Ahmed I's grandmother was Safiye Sultan and it was her architectural project in Eminönü that had been terminated by Ahmed when he ended Safiye's powerful tenure as *valide* and moved her to the Old Palace. While extant architectural evidence does not provide absolute proof, it is likely that the first *hünkâr kasrı* was actually conceived during the initial phase of his grandmother's Eminönü mosque and may have served Ahmed I as the model for his own *kasr*.[17]

In the sixteenth and seventeenth centuries, seashore kiosks were not just places for relaxation for the sultan and his harem, but also reception areas for ambassadors, viziers, and other distinguished visitors to the Ottoman court.[18] Many of these kiosks were perched high on Byzantine walls above the water's edge and decorated lavishly with inlaid mother-of-pearl doors and calligraphic tile panels. Like the seashore kiosks below the Topkapı Palace, the Eminönü *hünkâr kasrı* was a place where the *valide,* sultan, and other members of the imperial family could gather after prayer for rest and to seek a tranquility not possible in the busy quarters of the palace harem. The *kasr* building type found at Eminönü, thus, had similar functions to the many waterfront kiosks located below the Topkapı Palace.

Female members of the harem frequented these shoreline kiosks, and thus the architectural environment with which the royal women would have been most familiar were the quarters of the Topkapı harem, the Old Palace near Beyazid Square for older retired women of the court, and the interiors of many of the sultans' kiosks. Throughout the sixteenth and seventeenth centuries there are numerous reports of visits by royal women to the İnci Kiosk. Safiye Sultan's husband, Murad III, is reported to have visited the İnci Kiosk with his harem twice a week.[19] The late-sixteenth-century chronicler Selaniki recorded the festivities surrounding the opening of the İnci Kiosk in 1591 and mentioned that the harem women were invited to attend the fourth day of the celebrations and given a banquet and tour of the kiosk.[20] And it was from the İnci Kiosk that Mehmed III and his mother Safiye Sultan watched Queen Elizabeth's organ and an elaborate carriage, the former a gift to the sultan and the latter intended for the Ottoman queen mother, arrive in Istanbul on Her Majesty's ship.[21]

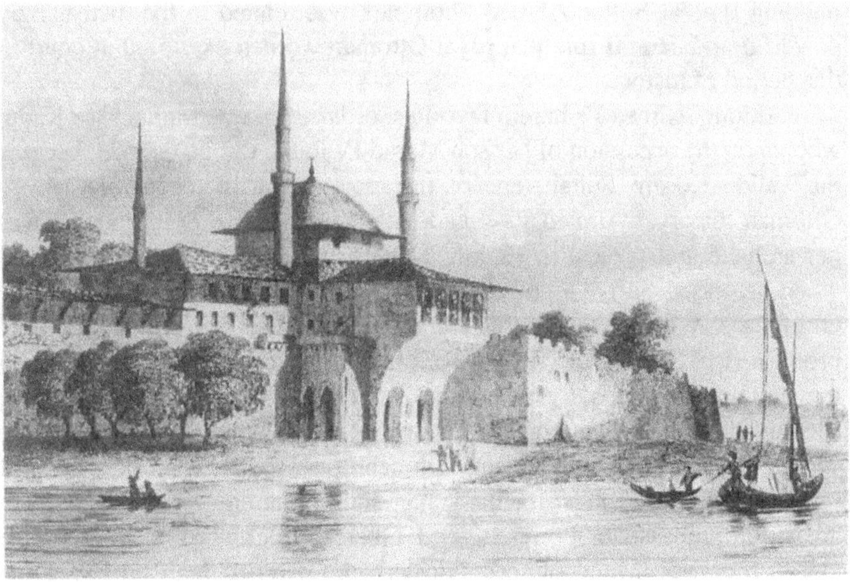

**Fig. 5.6.** Nineteenth-century engraving of the İnci Kiosk (J. Arnoul)

Of all the royal kiosks, the İnci Kiosk was the most frequently visited by the harem and had the reputation of being the most splendidly decorated. Ottoman chroniclers described the kiosk in great detail and remarked upon its advantageous, all-seeing position. Selaniki reported that, "His majesty the world-protecting Sovereign had described the construction of a pavilion with no peer, near the wharf of the gates of the Stables in the imperial palace, on top of the city walls of Istanbul, along the seashore, so that it would overlook both the horsemen's Maidan of the Gourd, inside the imperial palace, and the sea."[22] The interior of the İnci Kiosk was decorated with Iznik tiles, gilded muqarnas decoration and painting. There were exquisite textiles and inlaid jeweled decorations as well.[23] The early-seventeenth-century chronicler Hasanbeyzade, in one of the most elaborate descriptions of the İnci Kiosk, wrote, "Its dome resembling the vault of heaven was decorated with infinite stars, colorful paintings and shining jewels."[24] Necipoğlu has concluded that Hasanbeyzade was not describing the exterior dome of the İnci Kiosk because a repair document from 1681 indicates that the original pyramidal roof of the kiosk was replaced by the domical vault shown in the later engraving (fig. 5.6). Rather, the "vault of heaven" was an interior dome.[25] Thus, the phase of the İnci Kiosk that the *valide* Hatice Turhan would have seen in the later seventeenth century had a pyramidal roof and a central hall that afforded visual access to the sea on one side and to the square on the other, and was flanked by two side wings. The interior reception area had a painted wooden-domed ceiling, and the entire structure was elevated on a bastion of the sea wall.

When the site and building type for Valide Hatice Turhan's *hünkâr kasrı* was chosen, it is not surprising that the Eminönü *kasr* would emulate the reknowned İnci Kiosk, in terms of its location, and architectural and decorative features. While only the vaulted basement and wall fountain of the İnci Kiosk remain today, contemporary descriptions by chroniclers, repair documents, later engravings of it, and the fact that the İnci Kiosk and at least the foundations of the Eminönü *kasr* were built by the same court architect, Davud Ağa, strengthen the link between Murad's famed building and the one in Eminönü. The *kasr* constructed for Hatice Turhan Sultan, like the İnci Kiosk, was elevated on a section of the Byzantine sea wall, it is clear that the *valide*'s pavilion was also built to serve as a platform upon which one could watch the world. Indeed the theme of watching—or vision—is key.[26]

The Yeni Valide's *hünkâr kasrı* is clearly a very complex structure that draws its meaning from a variety of architectural sources in the Ottoman past. The positioning of the *kasr* on the Vasileus Tower, in addition to being a practical way to elevate the building, recalled the many belvedere pavilions that Mehmed the Conqueror used to link the Topkapı Palace visually to the outside world.[27] The incorporation of the Byzantine tower into the design of the structure indicates an interest in the appropriation of the architectural past of the conquered Byzantine empire, a practical reuse of serviceable architectural fabric but, on the ideological level, an empowering and meaningful choice.

The models that directly shaped the design of the *hünkâr kasrı* were the İnci Kiosk from the late sixteenth century and the *hünkâr kasrı* of the Sultan Ahmed complex from the early seventeenth century. The *kasr* at the Sultan Ahmed mosque (which could have looked to the first phase of construction at the Eminönü mosque for inspiration) established a firm precedent for this building type, its connection to the Friday mosque, and the long access ramp.

The appropriation of this particular building type into the Eminönü complex reflects the dominant role that imperial women were playing in the center of the empire, for this building reflects the female patron's more limited experience with architectural space: primarily harem quarters and sultanic kiosks. The gendering of the Eminönü complex is evident in the unique physical relationships among the *hünkâr kasrı,* the mosque, and the subsidiary structures of the complex, but the connections of these are discernible only in the view obtained from the *kasr.* The *kasr* was a site for visual surveillance, a privilege offered only to those who could enter the exclusive imperial quarters. The view afforded by the Eminönü *hünkâr kasrı* was not expansive or encompassing like that of the Süleymaniye or Sultan Ahmed complexes, nor was it for public consumption. It was an active controlling gaze that had its antecedents in the gaze of the Ottoman sultan who watched his subjects, hidden from view, behind screens such as the grated window of the tower above the Divan-i Humayun, the public council hall of the Topkapı Palace.[28]

As the drawing of the complex illustrates (fig. 5.7), the lines of vision from the *kasr* (b) intersect with several strategic points and activities in the complex: The southern congregational side entrance to the mosque (q), and the imam's private entrance (o) where a cool sweet refreshment, *sherbet,* was served to worshippers after prayer time, one of the many benefits bestowed upon the Eminönü congregation by the *valide.* These key points in the complex were all visible from the side of the *kasr* that faces the water. Additionally, as at the İnci Kiosk, naval exercises at the entrance to the Golden Horn (m) could be observed on this side of the *kasr* as could the activities of commercial vessels bringing goods into the customs houses of Eminönü (k).

From the interior land side of the *kasr* several key locations were clearly visible, particularly because the present wall which adjoins the *sebil*-turned-*muvakkithane,* or time-keeping center (r), was not extant at the time of the original construction, leaving a more uncluttered space and more open lines of vision. The interior side of the *hünkâr kasrı* afforded privileged visual access to all the dependencies in the complex: the entrances, the incoming and outgoing traffic of Hatice Turhan's immense tomb (f), the eastern gate of the Egyptian marketplace (e), the entrances to the primary school (i), and the school for instructing hadith (j). The large fountain at the easternmost end of the complex (g) is the only feature that was not visible from inside the *kasr,* but it was easily seen from the private garden behind the crenellations of the Vasileus tower (c).

For the *valide,* physical access to the Eminönü complex and particularly the *hünkâr kasrı* would have constituted an increasingly important part of the royal ceremonial. Hatice Turhan's visits to the Eminönü *hünkâr kasrı* were regular enough to have necessitated her own quay, the Porte de

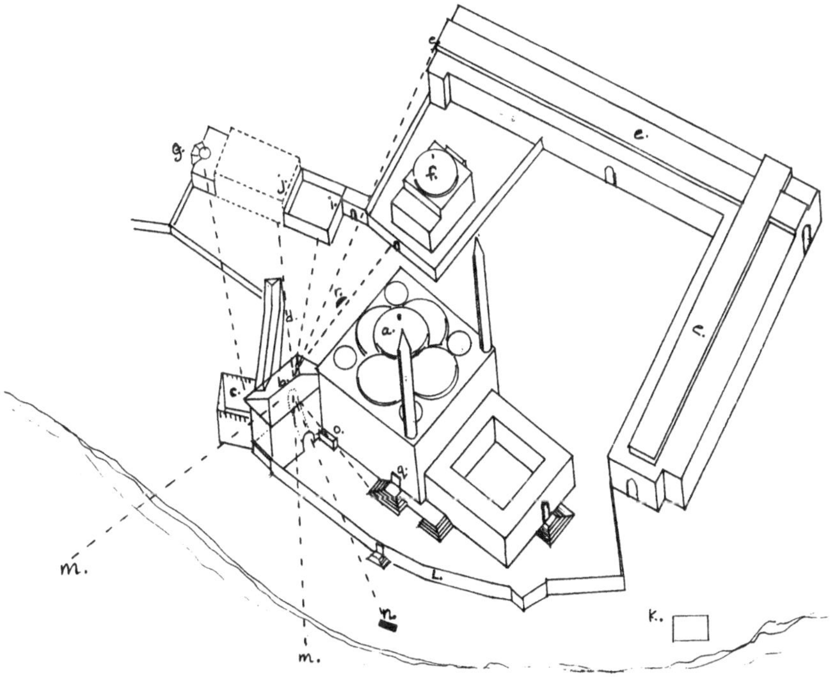

**Fig. 5.7.** The sight lines from the Hünkâr Kasrı extend to the Golden Horn (m), the *valide*'s sea entrance (n), and the entrance for the imam on the northern side of the mosque (o). The sight lines on the opposite side of the *kasr* provide visual access to the other buildings in the interior of the complex (refer to fig. 5.2 for key) (M. Şenocak)

la Validée. In her late thirties, and as the mother of the reigning sultan, the *valide,* by the accepted norms of the time, had more mobility than she would have had in her younger years. However, it would not have been within the rules of protocol for her to frequent all the buildings in the complex, especially the Egyptian market, primary school, tomb, Koran school, and various fountains of which her foundation was comprised.

The layout of the Yeni Valide complex was organized to allow a visual access to the various components of the complex for a royal female patron whose actual physical access was restricted. The manipulation of the royal gaze, the ability to control who and what was seen from a specific vantage point, was a power that had been traditionally an imperial prerogative of the sultan.[29] The fact that it is appropriated here by the *valide* indicates that the *hünkâr kasrı* and mosque complex, rather then representing a deterioration in planning principles, was an innovative response to the changing status of Ottoman royal women, and particularly the queen mother.

Beginning in the early sixteenth century with Süleyman's renowned wife, Haseki Hürrem, we have seen that royal Ottoman women had developed a "right" to build in the center of the empire, rather than in the provinces, thereby signaling their growing political power. By engaging in public displays of royal power, dynastic women began to exploit the architectural and ceremonial iconography that had been, since the conquest of Istanbul by the Ottomans in 1453, the domain of the Ottoman sultan. In contrast to the institutionalized isolation of the sultan, the political role and physical presence, albeit a veiled or palanquined one, of the royal Ottoman women, increased.

The impressive spectacle and size of the *valide*'s processions in the seventeenth century served to deflect attention from the political instability and economic problems facing the empire at this time. Within Istanbul, the move from the Old Palace to the Topkapı, called the *Valide Alayı,* as well as weddings, funerals, and visits to the Friday mosque formed part of the *valide*'s expected ceremonial repertoire. These highly public events were more than displays of self-glorification, for the pageantry ultimately served the state. Hatice Turhan's magnificent procession to and from Edirne to visit Mehmed IV (her wayward son who found the hunting ground of Thrace more appealing than those surrounding Istanbul), is well documented by Ottoman chroniclers and Europeans alike. From the number of participants and the expense of the processions, it is evident that these sojourns were intended to be brilliant exhibitions. And as her son Mehmed IV shifted his allegiances from Istanbul to the old Ottoman warrior capital of Edirne, the enactment of royal ceremonial in Istanbul became increasingly the responsibility of the *valide.* When age-old tension between Edirne and Istanbul, as competing centers for the location of the Ottoman court, resurfaced in Hatice Turhan's tenure as regent mother, it was she who reaffirmed Istanbul as the chosen administrative center of the empire by creating opportunities for the staging of royal ceremonial and ultimately by building a large mosque complex there.

Whether the *valide* arrived in Eminönü and entered the *hünkâr kasrı* by the sea gate or through the Bahçekapı entrance closer to the Topkapı grounds, it is clear that the *taht-ı revan*—the long, diagonally oriented and elevated ramp leading to the *hünkâr kasrı*—as well as the *kasr* itself were an integral part of the ceremonial surrounding royal visits to the site. Carried

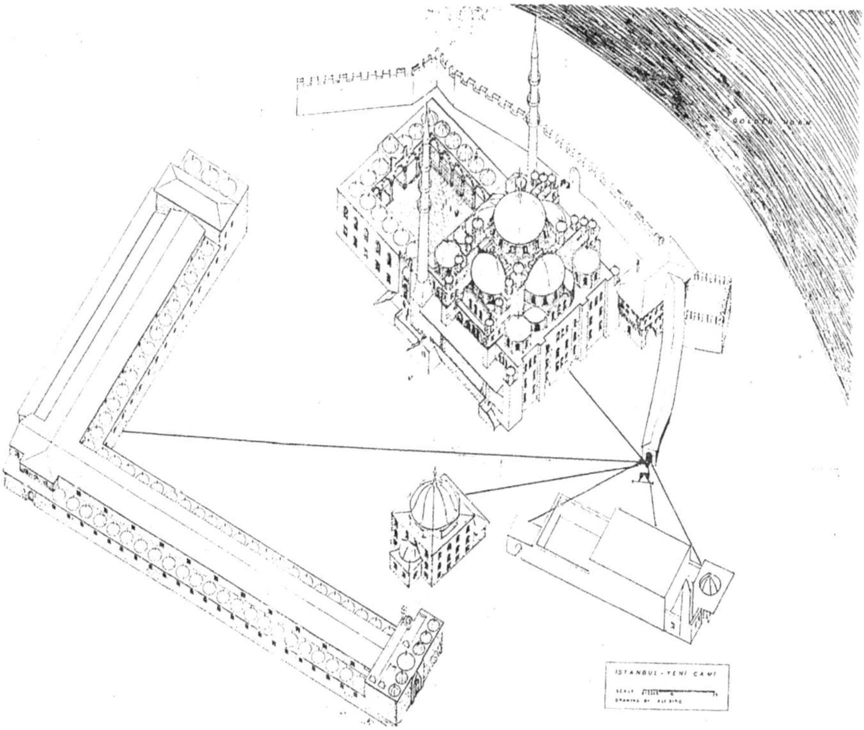


**Fig. 5.8.** The sight lines of the ceremonial converge at the point where the *taht-ı revan yolu* begins and extend to the exterior of the mihrab wall, the tomb, the Egyptian Market, the fountain, the primary school, and the school for instruction in hadith (the latter two structures are no longer extant) (Ali Biro)

by caique or palanquin, the *valide*'s entrance to the covered ramp occurred at a symbolically charged point in both temporal and physical terms (fig. 5.8). Directly aligned with the *mihrab*'s location on the exterior *qibla* wall of the mosque and surrounded by other components of the complex that provided tangible evidence of royal largesse and good works, the street entrance to the ramp was a matrix where the *valide,* as a visible symbol of Ottoman royal power, was transformed into an "aniconic" symbol of piety and political control. It is at this point that the imperial entourage, its centerpiece the *valide*'s palanquin, disappeared from sight, moving into and up the ramp, reaffirming the elevated status, inaccessibility, and inviolable space that separated the members of the imperial procession from their Ottoman subjects. Once in the *kasr,* the ceremonial was completed when the royal entourage which moments before had been the object of the

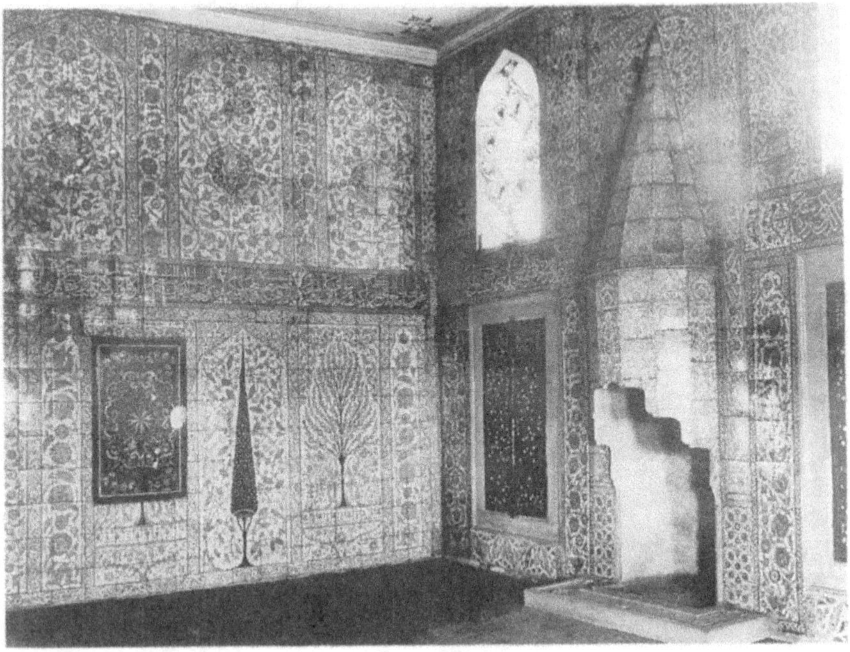

**Fig. 5.9.** The richly tiled interior of the Yeni Valide Hünkâr Kasrı includes an extensive epigraphic program. Here above the cypress tree is the line from Asimi's poem (courtesy of the German Archaeological Institute of Istanbul)

public gaze, now, from the privileged vantage of the *kasr,* became the controller of that gaze and hence of the subjects below.

The importance of both these views is revealed in the line of Asimi's poem in the *kasr* that appears on the wall of the domed room in the imperial suite (fig. 5.9). It reads: "*Yanında kasr-ı hünkârı ʿaceb özge temaşâdır,*" which translates loosely as "The *kasr* next to the mosque is a special place to behold." Here, the *kasr* as object and generator of vision is recognized.[30] One interpretation of the line is that the *kasr* is, from the exterior, an extraordinary sight, a spectacle to behold.[31] An alternative explanation is that the verse acknowledges the *kasr* and its dramatic ramp as a stage upon which the royal theater of arrivals and departures was staged. The *kasr*'s theatrical exhibition was manipulated in such a way as to emphasize the power and exclusivity of a view that was only obtainable from within the *kasr* itself. However, these two interpretations do not conflict; it is quite likely that the variant readings of the couplet were recognized and intended to describe the multiple functions of the *kasr.* Ultimately royal spectacle reaffirmed the image of imperial munificence and authority of the sultan, or, as in the case of the Eminönü ceremonial, the *valide.*

Ottoman miniatures and contemporary descriptions of imperial ceremony such as the Circumcision Festival of Murad III in 1582, with its many stagelike props, reveal a fascination with the skillful manipulation of boundaries separating the viewer and the viewed, the producers and consumers of spectacle.[32]

It also appears that there was an interest along members of the Ottoman elite in the science of optics. This is evidenced by the existence in a number of Istanbul libraries of copies of Ibn al-Haytham's eleventh-century manuscript, *Kitāb al-Manāẓir,* or the *Optics,* as well as other important treatises on the nature of light and vision.[33] It is of particular interest that most of the extant books on the *Kitāb al-Manāẓir* are in the library belonging to the Köprülü family, from which Hatice Turhan chose two of her Grand Viziers.[34] In the *Optics,* Ibn al-Haytham describes experiments he conducted using devices such as sighting tubes and dark chambers to explore the ways in which light could be manipulated. Further, he investigated theories in ancient optical treatises which claimed that sight was made possible by "visual rays" that were emitted from the eye to illuminate the object.[35] The impact of Ibn al-Haytham's investigations on the architecture of the Ottomans in the seventeeth century is tempting to speculate upon, particularly because the eleventh-century optical theorist is known to have written a treatise on architecture that has been lost.[36] Could the long ramp leading up to the *hünkâr kasrı* have been an application of experiments with optical sighting tubes? The ancient concept of visual rays issuing from the eye to illuminate an object, while largely refuted by Ibn al-Haytham, was a widely accepted hypothesis on the mechanics of vision. Could the sight lines used in positioning the buildings at the Yeni Valide complex have been influenced by these controversies over the nature of visual perception?[37]

The planning of the entire Yeni Valide Sultan complex, although neither symmetrical nor organized according to a rigid rectilinear ground plan, reveals a sophisticated manipulation of the lines of sight. The location of some of the structures in the Eminönü complex was dictated by pre-existing conditions; the mosque had to be oriented on the *qibla* axis and the *kasr* attached to the *qibla* wall to allow access to the *hünkâr mahfili.* But the placement of the remaining structures in the complex was clearly decided by the visual principle in which the sight lines extending from the royal pavilion was the primary determinant.

The *hünkâr kasrı* is the fulcrum of the complex, and its location and the impact it had upon the orientation of the various dependencies in the Eminönü complex, its dialogue with the Byzantine and early Ottoman architectural past, and finally the role that it played as a stage for the theatrical ceremonial of the *valide* sultan is unique to the Yeni Valide complex. The Eminönü project reveals that the imperial female patron of the Yeni Valide complex, while adhering to the basic protocols of architectural patronage employed by imperial men, chose a type of building which she knew well; hence the kiosk model for the *kasr,* the royal ceremonial surrounding the complex, and even the physical layout of the Eminönü foundation. With the skillful manipulation of the built environment, the *valide* extended the space and stage upon which she could exercise her authority and brought gender as a nuanced and important factor into the "optical politics"[38] of the Yeni Valide complex and the Ottoman architectural enterprise.

## NOTES

1. For information regarding names and dates of harem favorites and the queen mothers of Sultans Murad III, Mehmed III, and Ahmed I, see M. Cagatay Uluçay, *Padişahların Kadınları ve Kızları* (Ankara: Turk tarih Kurumu Basimevi, 1985), 43–50.

2. A comprehensive study of the Yeni Valide mosque complex is presented in my doctoral dissertation, "The Yeni Valide Mosque Complex in Eminönü, Istanbul (1597–1665)," Ph.D., University of Pennsylvania, 1994; see also L. Thys-Şenocak, "The Yeni Valide Mosque Complex of Eminönü," *Muqarnas* 15 (1998), 58–70. For earlier studies of the Yeni Cami, see A. Ülgen, "Yeni Cami," *Vakıflar Dergisi,* 2 (1942): 387–97; S. Tekindağ, "XVII Yüzyil Turk Sanat Eserlerinden bir Abide: Yenicami Külliyesi," *Tarih Derdisi* 28–29 (1974–75): 67–183; E. Yücel, "Yeni Cami Hünkâr Kasrı," *Türkiye Turing ve Otomobil Kurumu Belleteni* (Istanbul, n.d.); Ateş and F. Alcı, *Istanbul Yeni Cami ve Hünkâr Kasrı* (Istanbul, c. 1942–44; reprinted Istanbul: Vakıflar Genel Mudurlugu, c. 1977).

3. G. Necipoğlu has criticized this approach to understanding the Mimar Sinan's buildings. She states that our understanding of the complex relationships among monuments built by Sinan has been obfuscated by traditional analyses involving a "linear evolution of style driven by some mysterious impulse toward creating centralized schemes." G. Necipoğlu-Kafadar, "Challenging the Past: Sinan and the Competitive Discourse of Early Modern Islamic Architecture," *Muqarnas* 10 (1993): 176.

4. H. Crane, "The Ottoman Sultan's Mosques: Icons of Imperial Legitimacy," in *The Ottoman City and Its Parts: Urban Structure and Social Order,* ed. I. Bierman, R. Abou-el-Haj, and D. Preziosi (New Rochelle: A. D. Caratzas,

1991), 173–243. Crane's analysis of the Süleymaniye is typical of the evolutionary approach to understanding Ottoman *külliye* planning. He states, for example, that the Süleymaniye is "widely regarded as the climax of the evolutionary process of Ottoman imperial mosque architecture at Istanbul," pp. 185–86.

5. Crane, "The Ottoman Sultan's Mosques," 185–86.

6. L. Peirce, *The Imperial Harem: Women and Sovereignty in the Ottoman Empire* (New York: Oxford University Press, 1993), viii.

7. Aptullah Kuran, "The Evolution of the Sultan's Pavilion in Ottoman Imperial Mosques," *Islamic Art* 4 (1990–91): 284n4.

8. For various interpretations of the origins of the *hünkâr kasrı* building type, see Kuran, "Evolution of the Sultan's Pavilion," 281–300, and Thys-Şenocak, "The Yeni Valide Mosque (1597–1665)," 114–29.

9. G. Goodwin, *A History of Ottoman Architecture* (London: Thames and Hudson, 1971), 346.

10. The restorations of the Sultan Ahmed *kasr* complicate any comparison between it and the Yeni Valide *kasr.* The Sultan Ahmed *kasr* was partially destroyed in the seventeenth century by a fire, rebuilt in the nineteenth century, and again burned in 1949. The restoration of the present structure was completed in 1963 and was modelled after early engravings of the building before it burned and the Yeni Valide *kasr.* From the original foundations of the Sultan Ahmed *kasr,* it is evident that the original pavilion was elevated, reached by an open ramp, and of much smaller scale than the Eminönü *kasr.* Yücel, "Yeni Cami," 31; and Zeynep Nayır, *Osmanlı Mimarlığında Sultan Ahmet Külliyesi ve Sonrası (1609–1690)* (Istanbul: ITU Mimarlik Fakultesi Baski Atolyesi, 1975).

11. E. Yücel, for example, sees the roots of the *hünkār kasrı* as connected to the early private prayer areas in the Beyşehir Eşrefoğlu Mosque, the sultan's gallery in the Yeşil Mosque of Bursa, and Sultan Beyazıd II's mosque in Edirne ("Yeni Cami," 30).

12. Crane, "The Ottoman Sultan's Mosques," 211.

13. Ibid.

14. Kuran, "Evolution of the Sultan's Pavilion," 281.

15. G. Necipoğlu, *Architecture, Ceremonial, and Power: The Topkapı Palace in the Fifteenth and Sixteenth Centuries* (Cambridge, Mass.: MIT Press, 1991), 21.

16. For information concerning Kösem Valide, see Uluçay, *Padişahların Kadınları ve Kızları,* 47–65; M. İlgürel, "Kösem Sultan in Bir Vakfiyesi," *Tarih Dergisi* 16.21 (1966): 83–94; and Peirce, *Imperial Harem.*

17. Kuran, "Evolution of the Sultan's Pavilion," 284n4.

18. Necipoğlu, *Architecture, Ceremonial, and Power,* 210–41.

19. Ibid., 230.

20. Ibid., 227–28.

21. T. Dallam, "The Diary of Master Thomas Dallam, 1559–1600," in J. T. Bent, *Early Voyages and Travels in the Levant* (London: Hakluyt Society, 1893), 58–60.

22. Mustafa Seliniki, *Tarih-i Selaniki,* 2 vols., ed. Mehmed Ipsirli (Istanbul, 1989), 289–91; trans. Necipoğlu, *Architecture, Ceremonial, and Power,* 227n79.

23. Necipoğlu, *Architecture, Ceremonial, and Power,* 226.

24. Hasanbeyzade, "Hasanbeyzade Tarihi," ed. Nezihi Aykut, Ph.D., Istanbul Üniversitesi Edebiyat Fakultesi, no. 1256, 1980, pp. 136–37; trans. Necipoğlu, *Architecture, Ceremonial, and Power,* 227.

25. Necipoğlu, *Architecture, Ceremonial, and Power,* 228, n. 82, 83.

26. See Thys-Şenocak, "The Yeni Valide Mosque (1597–1665)," 13–23, for information on the Vasileus Byzantine tower.

27. Necipoğlu, *Architecture, Ceremonial, and Power,* 31–40.

28. For information related to the importance of the gaze in Ottoman architecture and particularly in the Topkapı Palace, see G. Necipoğlu-Kafadar, "Framing the Gaze in Ottoman, Safavid, and Mughal Palaces," *Ars Orientalis* 23 (1993): 303–4.

29. Mustafa Naima (*Tarih-i Naima,* 6 vols. [Istanbul, 1281–83/1864–87], 6:359) and Antoine Galland (*Journal d'Antoine Galland pendant son séjour à Constantinople [1672–1673],* ed. C. Shefer, 2 vols. [Paris, 1881], 1:215) record Mehmed IV's processions with the Valide Turhan Sultan in September 1658 and December 1672 respectively. For the French merchant Jean Baptiste Tavernier's eyewitness description of the *valide*'s spectacular entrance into Istanbul in 1668, see *Nouvelle Relation de l'Intérieur du Serrail du Grand Seigneur contenant plusiers singularitez qui jusqu'icy n'ont pas esté mise en lumière* (Paris, 1681), 158–61.

30. For a documentation and analysis of the epigraphic program of the Eminönü *hünkâr kasrı,* see Thys-Şenocak, "The Yeni Valide Mosque Complex (1597–1665)," 164–71; also Thys-Şenocak, "The Yeni Valide Mosque Complex of Eminönü." Regarding architectural pavilions as the subject and object of the view in the Hispano-Islamic context, see D. F. Ruggles, "The Eye of Sovereignty: Poetry and Vision in the Alhambra's Lindaraja Mirador," *Gesta* 36 (1997): 180–89, and *Gardens, Landscape, and Vision in the Palaces of Islamic Spain* (University Park: Pennsylvania University Press, 2000).

31. My thanks to Gülru Necipoğlu for this reading.

32. D. Terzioğlu, "The Imperial Circumcision Festival of 1582: An Interpretation," *Muqarnas* 12 (1995): 84–100.

33. G. Necipoğlu has commented extensively on the importance of Ibn al-Haytham's optical studies in *The Topkapı Scroll: Geometry and Ornament in Islamic Architecture* (Sketchbooks and Albums Series, The Getty Center for the History of Art and the Humanities) (Santa Monica, Calif.: Getty Center, 1995), 201–4. See also *The Optics of Ibn al-Haytham: Books I–III on Direct Vision,* trans. A. I. Sabra, 2 vols. (London: Warburg Institute, 1989), and Sabra, "Ibn al-Haytham," *Dictionary of Scientific Biography* (New York: Scribner, 1972), 6:189–210 (my thanks to D. F. Ruggles for directing me to this reference). For information on Ibn

al-Haytham's manuscripts in Istanbul libraries and works by other Islamic mathematicians, see M. Krause, "Stambuler Handschriften islamischer Mathematiker," *Quellen und Studien Geschichte der Mathematik, Astronomie und Physik,* Abt. B, Studien 3 (1936): 437–532; *Transfer of Modern Science and Technology to the Muslim World,* ed. E. Ihsanoglu (Istanbul: IRCICA, 1992); and *Catalogue of Manuscripts in the Köprülü Library,* 3 vols. (Istanbul, 1986).

34. Sabra, "Ibn al-Haytham," 206.

35. Ibid., 191–92.

36. Ibn al-Haytham's lost work on architecture was *Kitāb al-abniya wa al-'uqūd* (The Book of Buildings and Constructions). Necipoğlu also mentions al-Karaji's *Kitāb 'uqūd al-abniya* (The Book of Architectural Constructions) as an additional eleventh-century manuscript that was known to the Ottomans but which did not survive (*Topkapı Scroll,* 140–1).

37. I am currently researching the potential impact of manuscripts such as Ibn al-Haytham's *Optics* on the architectural planning of the Ottomans because more evidence is needed before any concrete links between visual theory and architectural practice can be assumed. The presence of a manuscript in the Yeni Cami library (MS Yeni Cami T217) that has been attributed to Ibn al-Haytham indicates that this link merits exploration; see Krause, "Stambuler Handschriften," 478.

38. For the usage of this term see Necipoğlu, "Framing the Gaze," 303–42.

# 6

# Women's Wealth and Styles of Giving

## Perspectives from Buddhist, Jain, and Mughal Sites

*Ellison Banks Findly*

The monuments of the Mughal empire established an enduring presence of elegance and stability. In that, they reflected the desires of their patrons for a large empire that both included the wide range of religious traditions within India and celebrated the greatness of their imperial lineage. Most, in fact almost all, of these monuments were patronized by men—by the Mughal emperors themselves, as well as by princes, in-laws, and colleagues of Mughal families. Just a few were patronized by Mughal women, and the most well-known of these matrons was Nūr Jahān, last wife of the fourth Mughal emperor, Jahāngīr (r. 1605–27). Nūr Jahān's matronage extended broadly into a variety of the arts: not only did she fund and design gardens in north India and Kashmir, but there is good evidence that she had a hand in developing new themes and interests (particularly of women) in miniature painting,[1] and that her trade with European sources in embroidered textiles contributed to the flower designs on the surface of the Tāj Maḥal.[2] Nūr Jahān also patronized architectural sites, and one of the most precisely identified as stemming from her hand is the Scrai Nūr Maḥal in Jullundur. This site not only reflects clear patronage by an Indian queen, but a style of donation in which the donor's sense of herself as a ruler is manifested in the syncretism of Hindu and Islamic surface design. More than any other Mughal woman of prominence, Nūr Jahān affirmed and took advantage of the South Asian culture that was her ruling milieu. We will argue, then, that this Muslim queen worked out of a context where patronage by women of many backgrounds had a long and enduring history.

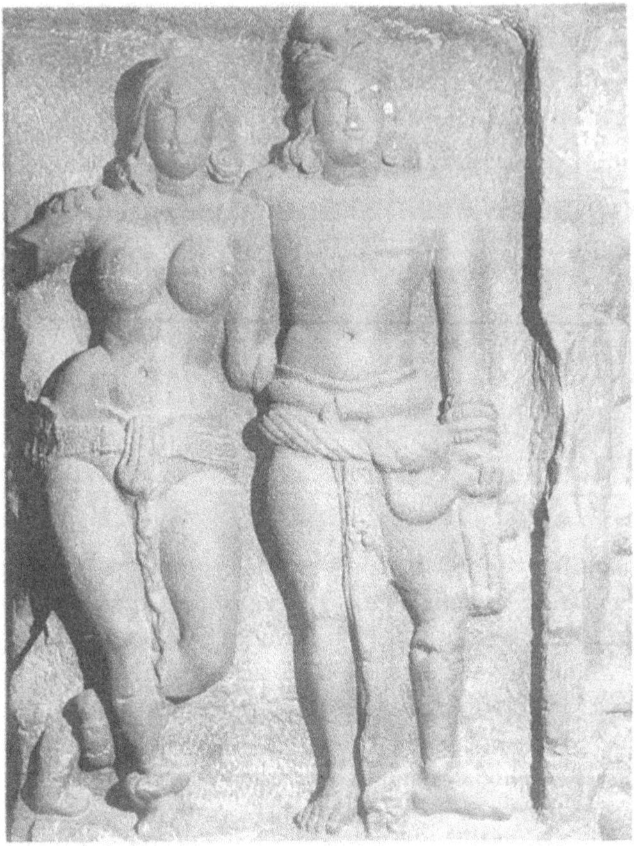

**Fig. 6.1.** Donor couple, *dampatī*, from the facade of the *caitya* at Karle caves, Maharashtra, Śātavāhana period, first century C.E. (Mario Bussagli, *5000 Years of the Art of India* [Harry N. Abrams, Inc., n.d.] pl. 79; courtesy of MPI Books, member of Roto Smeets)

Standards for donation (*dāna*) by women in non-Muslim India are based in traditional Brahmanic (priestly) codes of social duty, or Dharmaśāstras, which define a wife's economic identity as based in her relationship to two areas of property: her own personal property (*strīdhana*) anchored in a cache of jewelry and clothing, which a husband normally cannot touch[3] and which traditionally devolves upon daughters as inheritance,[4] and the property of the household. Although the traditional Brahmanic view of marriage is of a single, whole unit,[5] expressed in a theory of joint ownership by the couple over the household and its property (the *dampatī,* "the two masters of the house," fig. 6.1), the traditional wife is viewed as manager of this household property[6] with certain rights concerning its disposal. One of these rights stems from the wife's principal agency in representing the household at the time of honoring a guest, an act performed by the wife but for the honor of the family as a whole.[7] Donative activity is, then, an extension of the hospitality of guest etiquette, particularly in the offering of cooked food to students and renunciants whose petitioning also falls under Dharmaśāstric jurisdiction. This paradigm, of giving food at the household door, then becomes one of several ways women's gift-giving activity is prescribed in the texts, and special categories of giving, which cover the construction and dedication of properties for public use, such as temples, wells, and parks, come to be particularly noteworthy for women.[8] While the exact source of wealth a wife might use in *dāna* is not altogether clear from the texts—whether from her own property or from general household property—that women can and do give is a defined Dharmaśāstric norm.

Women's donation activity in South Asia can be found in varied religious and social settings. Observing examples of women from three different backgrounds who gave support to religious institutions in north India, we will argue that the matronage of a queen like Nūr Jahān was not a singular activity but one which had as its larger context many sectors: householder women giving to Buddhist monastic complexes, a courtesan giving to a Jain complex, and royal women giving to Buddhist complexes. Although none of these examples is specifically Brahmanic, the traditional statutes about giving and, in particular, about the role of women in giving, may have been known and, in many cases, may have been informative. The exact relevance of Dharmaśāstric norms to the actual lives of women is open to some debate,[9] but it does seem that several of the sites discussed here had Brahmanic culture available to them. Schopen notes, for example, the importance of studying Brahmanic and Buddhist behavioral codes together,[10] as "it appears likely that most early Buddhist communities arose in . . . highly brahmanized areas."[11] Moreover, the evidence we will look at reflects some marking out of the wife, that kin relation which in the Dharmaśāstras "is most significant for a woman's identity and activities."[12] While "wife" is not the only kin designation conspicuous in the material which follows, its presence may denote the Brahmanical model as one of the several identifying structures at work in women's donative self-representation,[13] a structure for which there is ample textual description.

In the following examples of matronage from Buddhist, Jain, and Muslim sites, the traditional Brahmanic ideal may have varying degrees of influence. Orr has noted that there are probably a number of ways to conceptualize the axes "along which women's identities and activities might . . . be located"[14] other than public and the private, and the Dharmaśāstric norm is certainly only one of several shaping the context and self-representation of women as they give. As we examine each of these cases from the South Asian context in which Nūr Jahān herself later worked, then, we will be mindful of the source of a woman's wealth, the pluralistic context in which the matronage takes place, whether a woman's gift is in any way gender-bound as to beneficiary, and whether her gift customarily or self-consciously reflects a particular sense of self vis-à-vis the culture at large. On this last, we will pay special attention to whether there may be clear donor intention to personalize the gift in some way or whether the evident individuation belongs to other peculiarities of the tradition.

## Patronage by Householder Women: Lay Buddhist Inscriptions at Mathurā and Sāñcī

Buddhist texts in the Pāli language from the early centuries B.C.E indicate that views about patronage by the householder and housemistress develop in relationship to the emergence of a Brahmanic ideal. It has been argued that the Buddhist disciplinary texts did not serve monastic communities in proximity to Brahmanical cultures.[15] In fact, however, Brahmanic notions about the defining place of women in the family and the role of property within the marital unit are clearly at hand in canonical discussions. It is in reference to the *strīdhana* model of property, for example, that the representation of a wife and property in these texts is one of greater autonomy in decisions regarding disposal of materials for which she is responsible and of considered independence in the actual disposal of them a marked and self-conscious change from older priestly notions. The stories of several monks,[16] for example, show their mothers' own wealth as separable and freely available stockpiles offered in the negotiations for the sons' return to lay life.

As agents of donation, moreover, Buddhist women like their Brahmanic colleagues are ever present at the household door. There they give food to petitioners but not, following the Brahmanic model, as representatives of a household's hospitality function; rather, they are independent donors deciding for themselves on religious alliances and on the worthiness of each cause.[17] In the Buddhist donation context, further, the exchange element is clearly present whereby donors give the four requisites of food, robes, lodgings, and medicine in exchange for teaching, and for merit usually made evident in the next life.[18] Because the donor is not under a specific hospitality obligation to give, however, the burden of the transaction rests upon the renunciant who must generate the goodwill of the donor (usually the housemistress)[19] by his humble stance at the door.

In Pāli texts, women stand out as donors also in the making of large substantial gifts, and no one so clearly as the lay housemistress Visākhā, who gives not only food and textiles in abundance but a residence, the Migāramātupāsāda, as well.[20] While part of Visākhā's resources may indeed be the property due her as wife,[21] she clearly has other property to draw upon, as seems to be the case for many householder women of the Buddhist Canon.

Recent work attests that there are more textual and inscriptional references to patronage by women in the Buddhist context than in the Brahmanic context, probably because in the latter women are under "considerable social constraints."[22] Matronage is a feature for example, of the Buddhist rock caves of Bedsā, Kanheri, Nānāghāt, and Nāsik, and at the shrines of Nāgārjunakoṇḍa, among several other places.[23] Two such spots, in fact, Sāñcī and Mathurā are, as we will see, especially significant for the great number of women donors noted in their inscriptions.

With the appearance of sites like Sāñcī, it is clear not only that the "lasting medium of stone" will play a rôle in Buddhist monumental art but that patronage at such venues is not primarily "the result of any royal decree" but of a "collective and popular" persuasion.[24] While royal patronage is clearly attested at many sites,[25] the overwhelming material support for Buddhist monuments in India comes from "the cooperative effort of the people,"[26] who give in worship of the Buddha or the *stūpa,* "temple," and who have hope for blessings in return. Sāñcī, whose original *stūpa* was erected by King Aśoka around 250 B.C.E., has over 631 donative inscriptions, the earliest dating from about the first century B.C.E.,[27] with donors ranging from individuals like royal scribes, artisans, teachers, stone masons, bankers, troopers, weavers, cloaksellers, and merchants to whole families, sects, and guilds.[28] One important group of donors, in fact the single largest, is nuns and monks, a donor category much discussed in recent years.[29] The reason for gifts of worldly property by those thought to have renounced it is ascribed to several things: either as surplus from what had been given to them and to the community by patrons,[30] gifts made on their behalf by lay donors,[31] or as real gifts made from wealth privately held by the monks and nuns themselves.[32] Renunciants are known to have been involved in raising funds for the monastic complex, and presumably traveled "to numerous towns and villages collecting subscriptions,"[33] making private wealth a considerable possibility.

Donation inscriptions at Sāñcī are found on pavement slabs, cross-bars, railing pillars, copings, and sculptures and, of the individual patrons listed, about one-third are women.[34] In fact, the large number of women and their prominence in these inscriptions is quite remarkable.[35] The appearance of the term *ghariṇīye,* "housewife," for example, indicates a strong donative basis in the lay community, and many of the nonrenunciant women clearly come from urban settings, an especially significant feature:

> Taking into account the urban base of the majority of women donors as well as the fact that ladies belonging to artisanal and mercantile classes figured more prominently as donors, it would be perhaps safe to assume that it was the emergent commercial spirit of the age which was to an extent responsible for transforming a section of women into an important category of donors.[36]

While this assessment is not peculiar to the Sāñcī site, it does point up the important changes taking place in mercantile and urban life which facilitate the rise in women donors such as those found at Sāñcī.

While there are a number of visual representations of women donors in the sculpture of Sāñcī—for example, Sujātā offering to the meditating Gautama, prostrating women presenting donations before trees[37]—one key to the self-representation of women donors, here particularly lay women donors, is that in the donation inscription, we find kin designation giving central context for the gift. Although kinship is used to identify men as well, it is more often the sole identifier for women.[38] These kin designations often tie the woman donor to a male relative and, of them, "mother" is the most frequently designated.[39] Next in number are designations of "wife" donors,[40] followed by "sister-in-law" donors, "sister" donors,[41] "daughter" donors, "daughter-in-law" donors and "niece" donors. What is significant here is that while kin designations for male donors do occur in inscriptions—e.g., "father," "son," "brother"[42]—they are far fewer than for female donors.

Inscriptional evidence from Buddhist sites at Mathurā in northern India indicates similar use of kin designations by women donors. Located fortuitously, Mathurā was at a crossroad of an important caravan route, with branch routes leading west to Taxila, east to Patna and Tamluk, and south to Ujjain and Brach. As a meeting place for travelers and traders who halted there over the centuries, Mathurā thrived off of the accumulating wealth and the heavy investments in its monuments. As at Sāñcī, donors covered a wide range of vocations from generals to troopers, from merchants and bankers to perfumers and cloakmakers, and Buddhist, Jain, and Hindu followers built complexes which were dominant at the site until the renewal of Brahmanism around the seventh century C.E. Buddhist monasteries at Mathurā were numerous, the Chinese traveler Fa-hien noting twenty such establishments with three thousand monks in the late fourth century C.E., and sites such as Kaṭrā, Saptarṣi, Bhūteśwar, and Govindnagar have all yielded Buddhist materials.[43]

One of the most well-known gifts by a woman at Buddhist Mathurā is the so-called Kaṭrā Bodhisattva or Buddha (fig. 6.2), seated in full lotus position on a lion throne with a *kapardin* (*kaparda,* "snail") styled knot on top of his head. This stele was commissioned by Amoghādāsī, the mother of Buddharakṣita, and her parents for the welfare of all beings and set up in her own monastery. It is not clear what Buddharakṣita's status was, whether a monk or a lay Buddhist,[44] but notable here is that in the donation inscription Amoghādāsī is not only designated as Buddharakṣita's mother but, because of the joint sponsorship of her parents, tied publicly to the preceding generation as well.

Another image at Mathurā, given by the nun Dhanavatī, confirms the centrally defining pattern of family designations for women donors. In her inscription, Dhanavatı notes that she is the sister's daughter of the nun Buddhamitrā, who has been identified with the nun Buddhamitrā, the donor of a large standing image at Kauśāmbī. This Kauśāmbī image is the "earliest dated cult image set up at Kauśāmbī," leading Schopen to conclude that it is the nun Buddhamitrā "who introduced at Kauśāmbī the cult image," and to say even further and more importantly that "nuns, and laywomen as well, seem to have been very actively involved in the development of the 'new cult'" of images.[45] This is a significant conclusion regarding the role of women, both as nuns and as laywomen, in the development of Buddhist iconography, and that Dhanavatī calls herself the "niece" of Buddhamitrā in her inscription not only supports the place of kin designation as an expressive feature of Buddhist women donors in general, but provides a central clue to a monastic woman's role in establishing the Kauśāmbī image cult.

As at Sāñcī, about one third of the donors at Mathurā are women.[46] Among women donors in Jain settings, there is a full range of kin relations

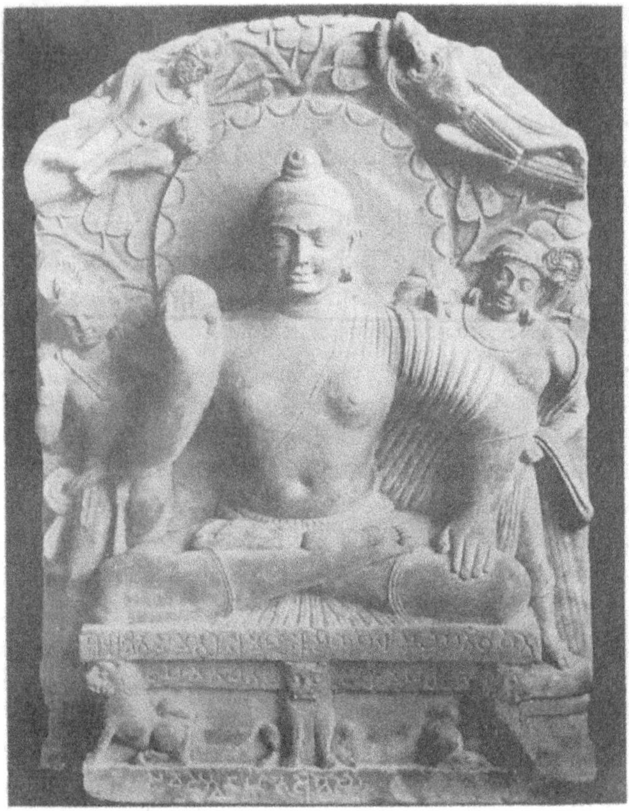

**Fig. 6.2.** Seated *kapardin* Bodhisattva or Buddha, Kaṭrā mound, Mathurā, Uttar Pradesh, first-second century C.E. Government Museum, Mathurā. (J. C. Harle, *The Art and Architecture of the Indian Subcontinent* [Yale University Press, 1994], pl. 43; courtesy of the Government Museum, Mathurā, U.P., India)

used to identify the matron: for example, "mother,"[47] "grandmother,"[48] "wife,"[49] "daughter," "daughter-in-law," and "granddaughter,"[50] and these women portray themselves together with their families, and even their servants, in the bas-reliefs.[51] Women donors in Buddhist settings show a similar range of kin relationships, each building on the place the matron has within the larger family network: for instance, "mother," "wife," "daughter," "daughter-in-law," and "niece."[52] While "mother" and "wife" are most prominent as designations at these two sites, that others are used as well underscores the importance of precisely defined place within kin matrices as a significant identity marker for women donors.

Turning to the larger gender issue in self-referencing at patronage sites we find that men seldom set themselves within kin relations in a donation inscription and when they do, it is primarily with the single, particular designation of "son."[53] In contrast, the dominant pattern for householder women making gifts at both sites is for women to use at least some kin identification in their inscriptions. Moreover, kin identification among women is often much fuller—with two or three relationships named (e.g., "daughter-in-law/granddaughter," "daughter/daughter-in-law," "daughter/wife/mother")[54] rather than just one. The multiple kin networking is made especially clear in the case of a Buddhist nun mentioned earlier, Dhanavatī, who names herself not only the sister's daughter of Buddhamitrā and the female pupil of the monk Bala, but the co-donor with her father and mother as well. This is in contrast with a few monks' inscriptions—those, for example, of Yaśadinna and Budhavāla—who say they give simply for the benefit of their parents.[55]

Mindful, then, of Brahmanic ideals that would have been known to early Buddhist communities arising in highly Brahmanized areas, it is no surprise that householder women at Buddhist sites understand themselves primarily within the protracted network of family relations. In this way, they are like women donors from other South Asian areas, medieval Tamil Nadu, for example, where kin relationships were an essential aspect of their self-definition.[56] While it is not clear from the inscription what material resources women actually use in making donations to Buddhist monuments, the very fact that many do so in Buddhist contexts signifies a considered autonomy in the allocation and disposal of resources—a pattern evident textually in the Pāli Canon.[57] This autonomy is made evident not only as an economic act but within a context that is decidedly public. So, while the Brahmanic ideal of hospitable women as defined by family relational status is present, a different venue for it is affirmed: a public display of economic agency.

## Patronage by a Courtesan: A Jain Tablet at Mathurā

We have seen that in the Hindu context men's primary identity is given by caste or occupation and that women's is given by family and kin ties. In the case of patronage by courtesans, kin ties remain, but occupational ties are seen as defining the female donor as well, perhaps in this case even more explicitly. A striking example of this is a tablet from a Jain site at Mathurā given by the courtesan (*gaṇikā*) Vāsū. This example is different from previous examples of female patronage because of the resources she might have used to make the donation, how she styles herself in the donative inscription, and how the iconography of the image may be related to her profession or to peculiarities of the Mathurā locale.

Unlike householder women, courtesans, even when adhering fully to their duties, are not admired in Indian legal texts. Food offered by them is to be shunned by Brahmins, for example, and they are to be noted by kings as improperly depriving others of property.[58] While early Buddhist texts are aware of prevailing negative views of courtesans, they also portray them as a category of professional women who not only are open to hearing and converting to the Buddhist doctrine but are increasingly available as donors to the monastic community as well. Women like Ambapālī, Sirimā, Sulasā, Sāmā, Kālī, and Sālavatī garner high fees and are thus eminently wealthy and Ambapālī, especially, is known as a generous and pious donor to the tradition. Her gift of a mango grove to the order of renunciants, for example, is one of the most famous in the early Buddhist texts.[59]

Kauṭilya's *Arthaśāstra,* a detailed guide to Indian political administration from around the fourth century B.C.E., identifies several unusual ways of getting revenue and one of them is the organization of courtesans into different grades under the guardianship of a superintendent. Hoping to increase state coffers, the system placed courtesans and prostitutes into ranked categories that identified the annual salaries they would receive based on services rendered. Each courtesan's income went directly to the superintendent who controlled her salary in return; she then retained "full authority" over all her personal assets that included her salary, her jewelry, and the gifts she received from her lovers. Discussing the system as described by Kauṭilya, Chandra notes:

> [H]igh living was a characteristic feature of a courtesan's life, and was not calculated merely to satisfy their personal vanity, but was a trade trick to attract wealthy merchants and officers. In the free institution of *gaṇikā,* the courtesans, or at least the leading ones, earned a great deal of money and could live in luxury. But since prostitution was a state managed institution there is every likelihood that their palatial establishments and gardens were state property with life interests.[60]

A different aspect of courtesan life is given by the *Kāmasūtra,* a text attributed to Vātsyāyana in the early centuries C.E. In addition to detailed discussions of courtesan education and lifestyle, this manual of sensuality explores ways courtesans are encouraged to acquire fees and gifts from wealthy clients. While the advice may seem to encourage cleverness, pretense, and trickery, it is underscored by the clear message that this is courtesan livelihood and that, as a norm, the multigenerational network of women had to give preeminent focus to financial security.[61] One important aspect of the economic material in the *Kāmasūtra* is Vātsyāyana's advice on what the wealthiest of courtesans should do with their profits: use them to build temples, reservoirs, and gardens, to give cows to brahmins, to perform religious ceremonies, and to carry out religious vows.[62]

One such gift by a courtesan is found at Kaṅkālī mound, the site of a Jain *stūpa* at Mathurā dating to Kuṣāṇa times,[63] in the early centuries B.C.E. and C.E. While excavations at the mound have revealed Brahmanic and Buddhist remains, those belonging to the Jain tradition predominate and among the significant Jain finds are about two dozen *āyāgapaṭas,* votive tablets used for worship.[64] Although these may have been used as altar sites for the deposit of offerings,[65] or set in a high place to be seen and worshipped from afar,[66] their full ritual use is not yet clear.[67]

We have already seen that there is substantial patronage of Jain objects by women donors at Mathurā. Items such as images and gateways at the Kaṅkālī mound have all been gifted through matronage: for example, by a merchant's wife, a goldsmith's daughter, a jeweler's daughter, and an ironmonger's daughter-in-law.[68] Moreover, the sculpted slab tablet, the *āyāgapaṭa,* is also an item given by donors and is an item "donated almost exclusively by Jain women."[69] Often these tablets were made at the request of a Jain nun, perhaps a widow who became a Jain nun as a way of easing her dependence upon her family.[70] Patronage by women and for women, then, is a critical aspect of these tablets that are used in worship.

The Kaṅkālī mound tablet given by the courtesan Vāsū is noteworthy in this context. Normally, the inscription is understood to read that the tablet is a gift of the courtesan Vāsū, daughter of the courtesan Lavaṇa Śobhikā, the disciple of the ascetics, in honor of the Arhat Vardhamāna. The use of honorific epithets in the inscription, one each with the mother's name and the daughter's name, is interpreted as a designation of "their ranks among the co-professionals or their status in the society," that is, as a designation of senior and junior.[71] The inscription also notes that Vāsū's co-donors are her mother, her daughter, her son, and her whole household—significant because, first, it reflects the multiple kin networks found in other female donation inscriptions and, second, because it reflects the matrilocal basis of courtesan families. While the tablet is accompanied by a gift of a shrine, a hall of homage and a cistern, it is the tablet itself that is of interest here: it depicts a *stūpa* (temple) accessed by steps and a gateway with three architraves, the lowest one supported by lion brackets, and surrounded by a railing and bordered on either side by two pillars, the left holding a wheel and the right holding a seated lion.[72] The *stūpa,* whose portrayal here is a fairly complete representation of contemporary *stūpa* architecture,[73] has a *yakṣī* (female protector deity)[74] on either side of the drum, a *kiṃnara* (male celestial attendant) on either side above, and, at the top, two flying figures which may be *munis* (silent sages).

This particular act of matronage highlights several issues in the Jain tradition. In particular, while the restrictive Hindu context for women is certainly influential here, the Jain vision is open (along sectarian lines) to the possibility of full salvation for woman.[75] In light of this and of the fact that Jainism disapproves of prostitution without socially punishing it, salvational opportunities are expressed as available for women of even the lowest status. Socially, the Jain tradition deals with prostitution "in a matter-of-fact and candid way," being most concerned that the presence of prostitutes and courtesans not weaken the ascetic vows of renunciants.[76] With regard to spiritual salvation, however, courtesans are seen as imperfect beings just like any others who are caught in the cycle of birth and rebirth.

To improve the chances for a better rebirth, then, Jainism, like Buddhism, emphasizes donation for its laity, a practice that had its most public manifestation in the construction of temple architecture and images.[77] We have seen that Jain women have always been involved in the donative process, either as housemistresses at the door giving out food to renunciant petitioners or as matrons funding monumental works. For a courtesan with her own particular cache of resources, the support of monuments may stem from a number of uniquely configured motivations: not only may the donor be sensitive to improving the material lives of her donees and to acquiring merit for her own future rebirths, but she may be mindful as well of the role giving has in securing "a creditable reputation" for herself, in a culture where donation "serves as a means by which . . . [one's] moral and financial status can be established."[78] Moreover, in addition to the issue of status, courtesans may have donated in order to assuage guilt: like ruling and mercantile groups who give out of "a sense of guilt produced by the exploitative nature of their economic pursuits as well as the increasingly impersonal and unscrupulous manner of their social dealings," courtesans may give because they are "still not looked upon with approval by the traditional moralists of the time," and may be exceptionally sensitive to the manner in which they have procured their wealth.[79]

In turning to the donor-specific marks of the image itself, we focus on the two *yakṣīs* (female protective deities) on either side of the *stūpa* drum.[80] Much has been made of the extensive cult of male *yakṣas* and female *yakṣīs* at Mathurā, including their ties to tree deities and other folk divinities, their mythological wealth and their use as protecting attendant figures in both Buddhism and Jainism, and their possible place in the development of the Buddha image.[81] They may also be linked, we argue, with courtesans like Vāsū. The voluptuous rendering of *yakṣī* figures on Mathurā railing pillars, for example, with their large round breasts, exaggerated heavy hips, thin calves, and seductive, unabashed postures and gestures, may represent the courtesan ideal and even particular courtesans.[82] The merchants and rulers who patronized monuments at places like Mathurā also patronized courtesans and the

> *Yakshī* figures [depicted at Mathurā may reflect] the memory of these licentious beauties. They reveal undreamt of pleasures of the flesh. They depict them inviting and soliciting men or engaged in their toilet or enjoying the pleasures of drinking and dancing, singing and roaming in gardens in the company of their lovers.[83]

Another suggestion develops the Jain designation of *yakṣīs* as the female attendants of Jain saints (Tīrthaṃkaras) by identifying them with "the leaders of the women converts," some of whom would clearly be of courtesan status.[84] The use of actual sculpted figures to represent donors to a monument is common in India (fig. 6.1); the depiction of them as something other than ordinary human beings is unusual. The suggestion that the *yakṣī* figures reflects not only the occupation of the donor (through its voluptuousness), but the social position of the donor within the religious community (through its attendance on the Tīrthaṃkaras) makes these images especially significant.

The *yakṣīs* on the tablet gifted by Vāsū the courtesan, then, can be interpreted in at least two ways. First, they may be the idealized representations of courtesans patronized by wealthy men of Vāsū's extended community, images with which she identifies herself or through which she represents herself publicly to the audience of Jain worshippers; second, they may be associated with women converts to Jainism, which may include Vāsū herself. However the two *yakṣīs* on this *āyāgapaṭa* tablet are interpreted, the categories of self-representation used by Vāsū remain within familiar boundaries set by the contextual traditions: a network of multiple kin designations placing her within an extended family and household; an appellation of *gaṇikā* tying her to a South Asian tradition of courtesan wealth and giving; and a figural image of the *yakṣī* tying her to gender or occupational patterns well-established within the (Jain) setting at Mathurā.

## Patronage by Royal Women: Kambojikā at Mathurā and Nūr Jahān at Jullundur

A third type of matronage is that by women of royal position. Donation by queens is known from many sources in South Asia and in any list of female donors their names are prominent.[85] Royal women have considerable wealth with which to support large acts of donation, and often do so in ways that reflect their particular religious habits and persuasions. The Cōla queen Sembiyan Mahādevī, for example, supported an ambitious temple building program tied to specific sacred sites, in the context of which she promoted the worship of Naṭarāja.[86] And the widow of the emperor Humāyūn, Hājī Begam, built a tomb for her husband in Delhi that borrowed its use of the wide base platform from Hindu architecture; allowing for circumambulation of family cenotaphs, the spacious structure confirmed the Mughal lineage's establishment within the broad Hindu environment.

We focus here on monumental gifts made by two royal women of very different background: patronage of a Buddhist monastery (*vihāra*) by Kambojikā, wife of the Scythian (Śaka) king Rājula (Rajuvula) who was father of Śoḍāṣa, at Mathurā (first century C.E.), and patronage of a traveler's rest house (*serai*) in Jullundur by the Mughal queen Nūr Jahān. What these gifts have in common is not only that they are located at points of substantial convergence for travelers and traders but also that, because of their location and their specific royal matrons, they signify a synthesis of several cultural traditions. In this way, we see Nūr Jahān's patronage of the *serai* not only as a donative act understandable to her subjects familiar with the kinds of patronage undertaken by housewives and courtesans, but as an act of donation commensurate with similar acts done by other high-ranking women.

In the case of the Mathurā site, two works are of interest: a lion capital from the Saptaṛṣi mound with a Kharoṣṭhī inscription recording the building of a Buddhist cave monastery, *Guhā Vihāra,* by Kambojikā the chief queen of the Mahākṣatrapa Rājula,[87] and an almost life-size figure, made of schist stone in the Gandhāra style, of a royal woman, also from the Saptarṣi mound. This figure is usually identified as Kambojikā (fig. 6.3).[88] Our interest here is both the context of the matronage and the details of the female figure, as both suggest a significant convergence of elements from different cultural traditions—a process facilitated, perhaps, by the high status of the donor.

The lion capital inscriptions, which were engraved at a time of significant religious patronage, suggest an origin among a nonindigenous elite, as Mathurā was generally beyond the range of Kharoṣṭhī inscription.[89] Issuing from their original homeland in Central Asia, the Śakas may well have reached Mathurā independent of their progress up the Indus River Valley.[90] As members of a foreign ruling class who, in Indianizing fashion, styled their rulers Mahākṣatrapas ("great governors"), the Śakas retained their distinctive styles of dress at the same time as they followed the local religion of Buddhism.[91] To the artistic heritage of Mathurā, they contributed materials gleaned in the course of their other invasions of Hellenistic and Parthian lands in the first centuries C.E. The Śakas, then, acted as middlemen passing on cultural and artistic elements acquired from their contacts with Iranians, Greeks, Romans, and others.[92]

The female figure commonly identified as Kambojikā exhibits traditional Gandhāra drapery style, notable for the knot just above the left leg, and the clasp at the left shoulder, arm decoration, and multiple neck wear. The wreath on her head (fig. 6.4) is fastened with fillets in the back, and "an ornamental tress showing bead and floral motif suspends on her back."[93] The attention to anatomical detail is noteworthy here, as is the slightly left-bent cast of the head, the lidded eyes, and the clear symmetry of the face. If this figure is indeed Kambojikā, it establishes portraiture, here of women, as an early mode of representing high-ranking donors giving to South Asian monuments. While there are clearly elements generic to the Gandhāra style, the fact that the figure comes from the same find spot as the lion capital with its inscription dedicating the *Guhā Vihāra,* personalizes the features of face and dress. Whether this is an example of *self*-representation is not clear, but it does stand in contrast to the inscriptional and representational milieus we have seen for women in donative art so far.

Many of the objects now extant in Gandhāra style belong in some measure to the Buddhist tradition, and the Saptarṣi mound at Mathurā, significantly, was under the considerable sway of the Sarvāstivādin sect. It is quite possible that the Śakan allegiance to Buddhism at Mathurā was based on the religion's appeal as a liberal, universal, and non-exclusive

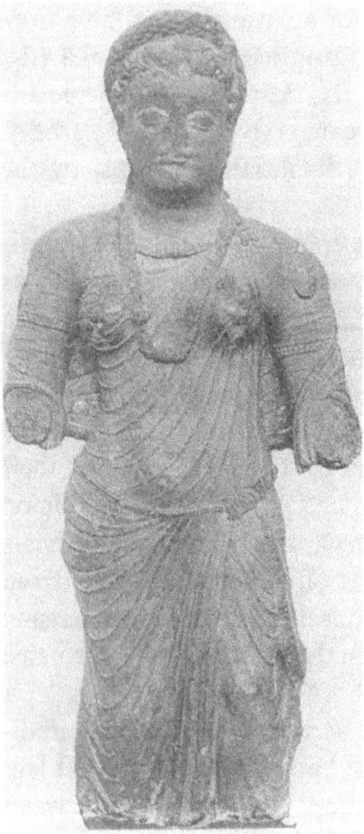

**Fig. 6.3.** Female figure, in Gandhāra style, said to be Kambojikā, wife of Mahākṣatrapa Rājula, Saptarṣi mound, Mathurā, Uttar Pradesh, first century C.E. Government Museum, Mathurā. (R. C. Sharma, *Buddhist Art: Mathura School* [Wiley Eastern Limited, New Age International, 1995], pl. 11; courtesy of Government Museum, Mathurā, U.P., India)

tradition,[94] which allowed members of any group, including their own, to support its institutions. Interpretation of the ties between the Śakan and the Sarvāstivādin Buddhists range from the renunciants enjoying the "royal favor" of the foreign rulers[95] to their active lobbying for royal support—the monastery being given "at the instance of the Sarvāstivādin ācāryas,"[96] for example—but, whatever the vantage point, the commitment to the religion seems to be a strong component of Śakan presence in Mathurā and, in particular, of Queen Kambojikā.

The female figure thought to be this matron reflects a number of features of Mathurā art found across the site: the assimilation of foreign components, the introduction of images styled as portraits, and the treatment of female figures with particular care and delight.[97] While the convergence of each of these three elements in the Kambojikā figure single her out aesthetically among woman donors at Mathurā, her multiple kin designations

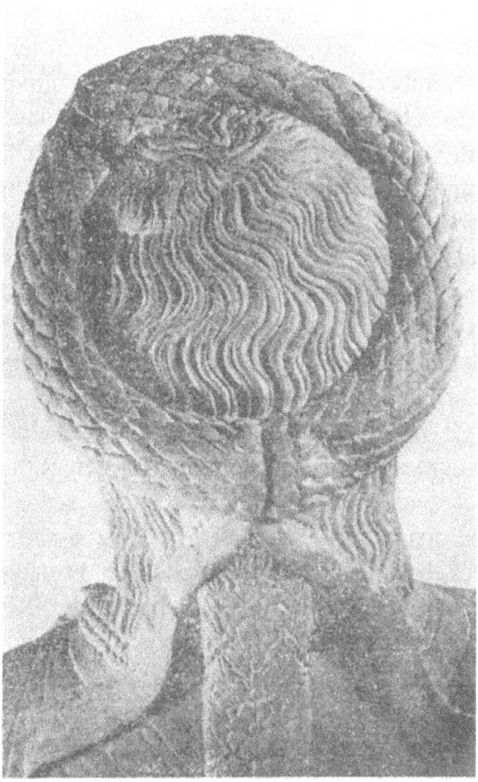

**Fig. 6.4.** Detail of back of head, figure 6.3. (R. C. Sharma, *Mathura Museum: Introduction* [Government Museum, 1971], fig. XXIII-B; courtesy of Government Museum, Mathurā, U.P., India)

tie her directly to the matronage practices of other South Asian women. Not only does the lion-capital inscription name her as the chief queen of Rājula, but related artifacts designate her as a daughter and as a mother.[98] Thus, kin designations continue to be useful identification markers for women donors, though they are not, by any means, exclusive to them.

A final element pertains here as well. It has been noted that patterns of royal Cōla patronage show royal women over long periods of time sponsoring costly and enduring religious monuments while kings focused, contemporaneously, on other types of legitimizing behavior. While kings looked to established ritual patterns to provide mandate in the Cōla context, queens—particularly Sembiyan Mahādevī—turned to conspicuous and often extended patterns of *dāna*.[99] The donation activity of Kambojikā may well fit this pattern, supported as it would be by the positive nature of Buddhist attitudes towards female giving.

Like Kambojikā, Nūr Jahān was married to a ruler sovereign in a land not originally his family's own and over a people of predominantly different cultural persuasion. Unlike Kambojikā, however, who joined other followers of Buddhism, Nūr Jahān retained her family's Islamic heritage all the while developing a receptivity to the Hindu culture around her.[100] The last wife of the Mughal emperor Jahāngīr, Nūr Jahān (1577–1645) came to power in 1611 at the time of her marriage, strengthening the hand of her already entrenched Persian family and shoring up the rule of a husband vulnerable to intoxicants. She had been married before, to a Persian adventurer known as Sher Afghān and, after his death in 1607, came to the women's quarters at the Mughal court in Agra under the sponsorship of Ruqayya Sultān Begam where she and her daughter lived until 1611.[101]

Upon her marriage to Jahāngīr, Nūr Jahān acquired not only considerable power but the substantial resources available to Mughal women at the time. Although there is not direct evidence that she came to this second marriage dowered in the traditional manner by her family,[102] we can assume that her upwardly mobile relatives, headed in India by her father I'timād-ud-daula, supported her materially in whatever ways were appropriate. We do know that members of her own family benefited, primarily through promotions, as a result of her marriage and that she herself was the object of sizable gift-giving at the time.[103] Not only were gifts given on the occasion of her marriage, but women of the *zanāna* (women's apartments) received regular increases in their allowances from the imperial purse. Akbar's *Āʾīn-i Akbarī,* memoirs of his reign, describes a system of entitlements for palace women designed to reflect internal social hierarchies as well as to keep control over the often extravagant expenditures, which were frequently devoted to luxury items of toilet and ornamentation brought in from local and overseas markets.[104] Not only did Nūr Jahān routinely receive such entitlements, but she was the chief beneficiary of the estate of her father who died early in 1622. This estate, which reverted by escheat to Jahāngīr, might ordinarily have benefited Nūr Jahān's brother Āṣaf Khān, but was bestowed upon her as part of Jahāngīr's normally extravagant largesse toward his favorite wife.[105] Finally, Nūr Jahān's substantial wealth was augmented through various channels of trade, both domestic and foreign, which she cultivated from the very beginning of her power. Her domestic revenues derived from collecting duties on textile goods, spices, and other consumer stuffs as they passed through trading centers,[106] and her foreign trade involved the export of textiles and indigo and the import of various luxury items.[107]

Although the disposal of these many resources went in part for enhancing life in the women's apartments, it was also turned toward acts of patronage. Reflecting, perhaps, Islamic tradition in which "the wife has often been the agent through whom monies or goods have been distributed to the poor,"[108] Nūr Jahān is said, by chroniclers such as Muḥammad Hādī and Muʿtamad Khān, to have been exceptionally liberal in her generosity and to have, for example, dowered five hundred orphan girls during her lifetime.[109] Her patronage also extended to buildings and, like a few other Mughal women of rank, though perhaps to a far greater extent, she used her resources to build monuments that were not only useful and necessary, but innovative and trend-setting as well: the tomb of her father in Agra, the Pattar Masjid in Srinagar, the tomb of her second husband in Lahore, her own tomb in Lahore, and many gardens on the plains and in the mountains.[110]

One of the earliest of her projects was a caravanserai located on a Mughal roadway between Agra and Lahore. Jahāngīr had called for wells and rest houses to be made for travelers along the major roads under Mughal sovereignty, and one of Nūr Jahān's contributions was the handsome Serai Nūr Maḥal in Jullundur district of the Punjab, with quarters for travelers and a mosque. Begun in 1618–19 and completed two years later with much fanfare by both Nūr Jahān and Jahāngīr,[111] the Serai Nūr Maḥal could accommodate upwards of two thousand travelers and their mounts, each traveler for a modest fee.[112]

The inscriptions on Serai Nūr Maḥal leave no doubt that the complex is the product of Nūr Jahān's patronage, effected within the context of the ruling Mughal family. The building is small but beautifully detailed,[113] and it is thought to be one of the most magnificent made under Jahāngīr. Francisco Pelsaert, a senior factor for the Dutch East India Company, noted while in India in the 1620s, "she [Nūr Jahān] erects very expensive buildings in all directions—*sarais,* or halting-places for travellers and merchants, and pleasure-gardens and palaces such as no one has ever made before—intending thereby to establish an enduring reputation."[114] This enduring reputation impressed Peter Mundy, an English factor in Agra during the 1630s, about ten years later who happened upon the *serai* "built by the old Queene Noore mohol . . . for the accommodation of Travellers;" it was "a very faire one," he noted, and compared favorably to what he had encountered heretofore.[115]

The facade of the western gateway of Serai Nūr Maḥal (fig. 6.5) is subdivided into several panels, many of them carved with abstract angular

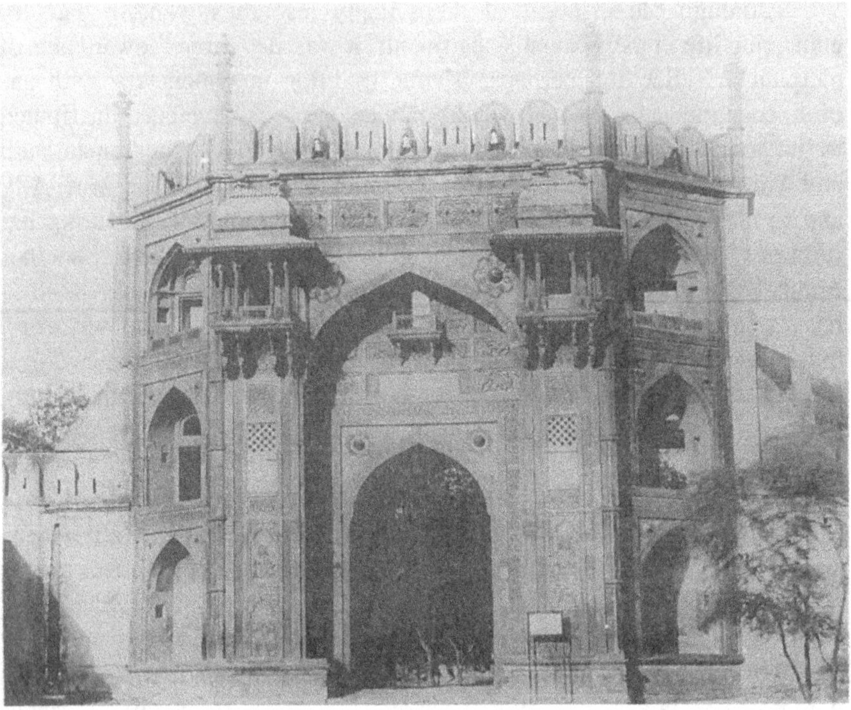

**Fig. 6.5.** Western gateway, Serai Nūr Maḥal, Jullundur, Punjab, ca. 1620. (Courtesy of the Archaeological Survey of India, New Delhi)

and vegetal arabesques alternating with panels of figural representations: women, men on elephants, peacocks, and plants (fig. 6.6). It is important to note here that, like Kambojikā, Nūr Jahān found herself at a point of substantial cultural convergence, among a goodly array of religious and aesthetic traditions and, through monumental patronage, sought ways to syncretize normally divergent, even antithetical, visual heritages. Thus, in her caravanserai, Islamic skill in repeated and interconnectic arabesque pattern (geometric and organic, linear and planar) is neatly blended with the naturalistic representation that is a hallmark of Hindu art.

The appeal of Hindu female forms to Mughal women is first expressly reflected by Gulbadan, sister to Humāyūn (r. 1530–56), who in her *Humāyūn-nāma* marvels over the gift of dancing girls, sent "as curiosities of Hind."[116] The contrast of the open, loose, and revealing clothes of the dancers to the modest covering layers of the Muslim women is stark, especially when

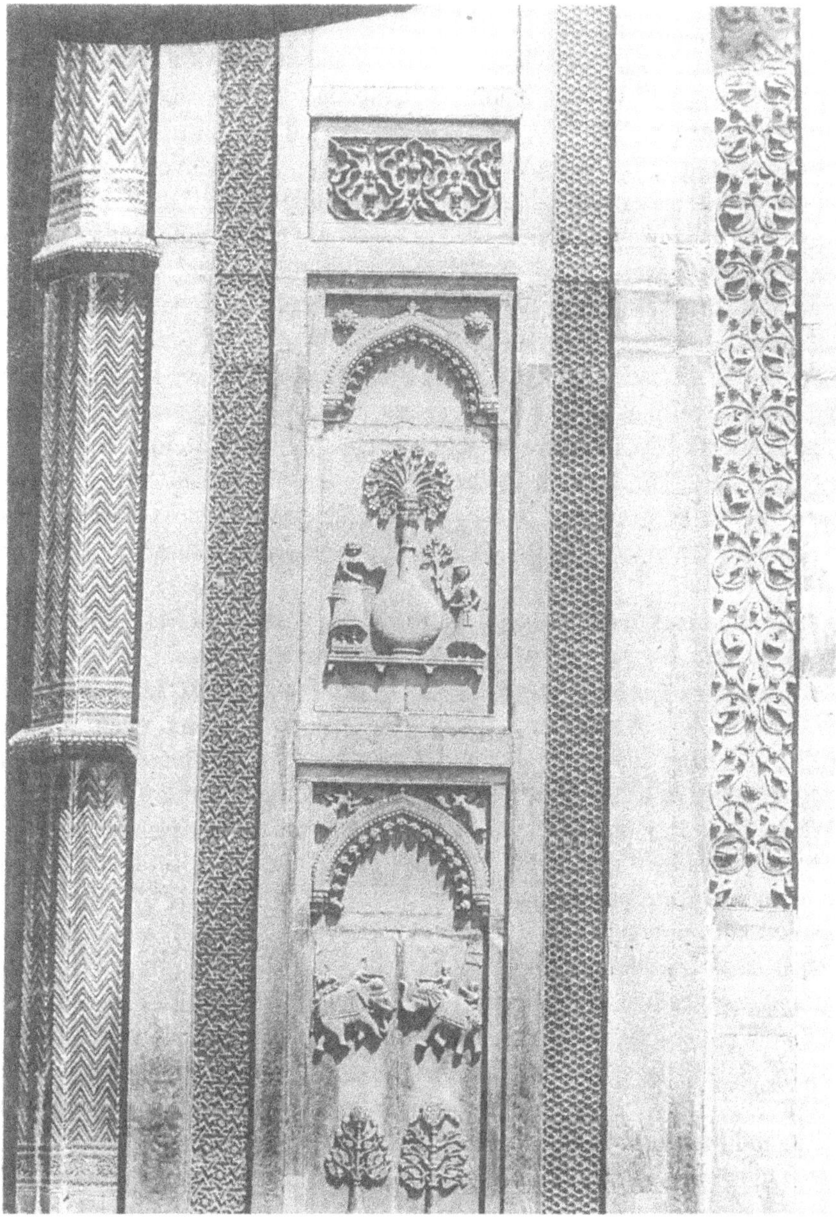

**Fig. 6.6**. Detail of facade, figure 6.5. (Courtesy of the Archaeological Survey of India, New Delhi)

coupled with the women's elaborate jewelry and the intoxicating movements of the dance and, in a biography of Gulbadan, Rumer Godden interprets this experience as "the first sight of a new world . . . [stirring] a great deal of excitement."[117] In the next generation, Akbar would favor Hindu forms of dress and, under Nūr Jahān, Hindu sensibilities toward the female body would find renewed receptivity.[118] The argument here is not whether figural representation was Hindu or Muslim in origin—indeed there are long traditions of figuration in both religiocultural contexts—but rather that in the early seventeenth century in the time of Nūr Jahān, peacocks, lotuses, and elephants had a Hindu connotation. Their inclusion in Nūr Jahān's *serai* along with Islamic curvilinear arabesques and geometric repetitions signal not merely a passive eclecticism but the self-conscious collocation of traditions. The women of the reliefs, then, though in Mughal dress, nevertheless betoken an affirmation of the Hindu willingness to express the feminine form in stone relief and three-dimensional sculpture.[119]

These examples reflect several of the ways women in South Asia have been visible as patrons of monuments—donation patterns that render matronage by the Muslim queen Nūr Jahān, for example, fully consonant with the values of her ruling milieu. Not only have women given, historically, and been named as givers, but they have represented themselves in ways reflective of their peculiar social roles within the prevailing culture. While there may be a variety of axes used to locate the self-identification of women as they give,[120] the influence of the traditional Brahmanic norm is evident in the prominence, though not the dominance, of "wife" as a named kin relationship in several areas of women's donation inscriptions. What is of considerably more importance than this, however, is the great preponderance of kin relations in general as a way of self-designation for women among lay and renunciant Buddhist communities at Sāñcī and Mathurā, and for at least one Jain courtesan at Mathurā. The power of the extended family identification for matrons of all traditions—Buddhist, Jain, and Mughal—then, is evident throughout.

In the present examples, however, there is another feature shaping this identity as well: an affirmation of some economic autonomy and religious independence for women in the public endowing of religious institutions. This material agency is an especially accessible channel for religious activity by women, and becomes particularized not only in the kin titles of inscriptions but, if the interpretations are correct, in visually self-referential renderings as well. Here we note the case of the courtesan giver at Mathurā, as reflected in *yakṣī* figures, for example, and the case of Kambojikā as reflected in actual portraiture.

The royal matronage of Kambojikā and Nūr Jahān highlights two further themes: establishing the high status of the donor and expressing contemporary cultural syncretism. The very fact that the female figure from the Saptarṣi mound at Mathurā may be Kambojikā, donor of the *Guhā Vihāra,* suggests not only that it is a portrait statue, but also that such a representation might be made only of a figure of consequence. Moreover, the head wreath, the neck and arm adornments, and the complex draping of her robes signify a person of some importance. In the case of Nūr Jahān, the recognition of the *serai* as hers by the factor Francisco Pelsaert and the traveler Peter Mundy, and the notation that it belonged to a larger building program both consonant with Jahāngīr's and uniquely her own, aligned her matronage with that of other Indian queens in both physical scope and social consequence. In both cases, then, signs of the high status of the donors are evident, diversifying in this way the expressions used for self-representation found among women donors.

In all the cases of matronage examined here, we have noted the confluence of many peoples and influences at the sites. Several sites, Mathurā in particular, are urban centers where economic life is vigorous and complex, and where opportunities for women's donation are particularly varied and accessible. In the two cases of royal matronage, we note that the cultural confluence of the site is reflected in the object itself: in the case of the Kambojikā figure, a Śakan queen portrayed in Gandhāra style supporting a Buddhist institution, and in the case of Nūr Jahān, the collocation of Islamic arabesque and Hindu ornament, the latter showing, further, Mughalized tendencies and Persian, and perhaps European, influences. It may be that these two objects elucidate the role of women in synthetic processes, or that they underscore the role of high-ranking figures in inspiring or legitimizing the collocation of cultural trends, or that they mark the place of personal promotion in the donative tradition. It is certain, however, that in these two cases particularly, women are prominently visible as donors and that the very visibility of their donation spotlights both the unique person of the donor herself as well as the rich diversity of her time. Nūr Jahān's matronage of the Serai Nūr Maḥal, then, can be seen as consonant with other, somewhat earlier, examples of female giving in South Asia in which the donor is statedly a woman, using wealth appropriate to her status, for monumental art that reflects how she personally sees herself in the cultural matrix of the time.

## NOTES

1. Ellison Banks Findly, "The Pleasure of Women: Nur Jahan and Mughal Painting," *Asian Art,* "Patronage by Women in Islamic Art" issue, 6.2 (Spring 1993): 66–86.

2. Ellison Banks Findly, "Nur Jahan's Embroidery Trade and Flowers of the Taj Mahal," *Asian Art and Culture,* "Indian Trade and Textiles" issue, 9.2 (Spring/ Summer 1996): 7–25.

3. *Manusmṛti* (*Manu*), ed. Mahāmahopādhyāya Gangānātha (Calcutta: Royal Asiatic Society of Bengal, 1939) 8.29.

4. *Manu* 9.131, 195, 198, 200. See Pandurang Vaman Kane, *History of Dharmaśāstra* (Poona: Bhandarkar Oriental Research Institute, 1930–62), 3:788–801; A. S. Altekar, *The Position of Women in Hindu Civilization* (1938; 2nd ed., rpt., Delhi: Motilal Banarsidass, 1973), 229–50; Vijay Nath, *Dāna: Gift System in Ancient India (c. 600 BC. – c. AD. 300)*; *A Socio-Economic Perspective* (New Delhi: Munshiram Manoharlal, 1987), 72.

5. In which the wife is "half of the [husband's] own self" (*arddho ha vā eṣa ātmano yaj jāyā*). *Śatapathabrāhmaṇa,* ed. Ācārya Satyavrata Sāmaśramī (Calcutta: Baptist Mission Press, 1903–12) 5.2.1.10. See Stephanie W. Jamison, *Sacrificed Wife/Sacrificer's Wife: Women, Ritual, and Hospitality in Ancient India* (New York and Oxford: Oxford University Press, 1996).

6. *Taittirīyasaṃhitā,* ed. E. Roer and E.B. Cowell (Calcutta: Baptist Mission Press, 1860–99) 6.2.1.1–2; see *Manu* 9.11.

7. I. Julia Leslie, *The Perfect Wife: The Orthodox Hindu Woman according to the* Strīdharmapaddhati *of Tryambakayajvan* (Delhi: Oxford University Press, 1989), 183–93.

8. Kane, *History of Dharmaśāstra* 2.2:889–93.

9. Leslie C. Orr, "Women in the Temple, the Palace and the Family: The Construction of Women's Identities in Pre-Colonial Tamilnadu," in Karashima festschrift volume, ed. Kenneth R. Hall (forthcoming), 3–4, 9, 17, 21. See also Leslie C. Orr, "Jain and Hindu 'Religious Women' in Early Medieval Tamilnadu," in *Open Boundaries: Jains in Indian History and Culture,* ed. John E. Cort (Albany: State University of New York Press, forthcoming).

10. Gregory Schopen, "Doing Business for the Lord: Lending on Interest and Written Loan Contracts in the *Mūlasarvāstivāda-vinaya,*" *Journal of the American Oriental Society* 114.4 (October-December 1994): 535.

11. He does note, however, problems regarding Pāli disciplinary rules (Vinaya) in this light. Gregory Schopen, "Monastic Law Meets the Real World: A Monk's Continuing Right to Inherit Family Property in Classical India," *History of Religions* 35.2 (November 1995): 110, 122.

12. Orr, "Women in the Temple," 9.

13. Ibid., 21.

14. Ibid., 20.

15. Schopen, "Monastic Law," 122; see also Gregory Schopen, "Two Problems in the History of Indian Buddhism: The Layman/Monk Distinction and the Doctrines of the Transference of Merit," *Studien zur Indologie und Iranistik* 10 (1985): 9–10.

16. *Mātumattikaṃ itthikāya itthidhana,* "the mother's portion, the wife's property due her because she is a wife," in *Vinaya* 3.17; and *mattikaṃ dhanaṃ,* "the mother's property" in *Majjhima Nikāya* 2.63. All references to Pāli texts are to Pāli Text Society editions. These efforts, however, proved futile.

17. Ellison Banks Findly, "The Housemistress at the Door: Vedic and Buddhist Perspectives on the Mendicant Encounter," in *Debating Gender,* ed. Laurie L. Patton (New York: Oxford University Press, 2000).

18. Paul Dundas discusses this distinction in the case of the Jains (*The Jains* [London and New York: Routledge, 1992], 221).

19. See I. B. Horner, *Women under Primitive Buddhism: Laywomen and Almswomen* (London, 1930: rpt., Delhi: Motilal Banarsidass, 1975), 42, 55.

20. See Nancy Auer Falk, "Exemplary Donors of the Pāli Tradition," in *Ethics, Wealth, and Salvation: A Study in Buddhist Social Ethics,* ed. Russell F. Sizemore and Donald K. Swearer (Columbia: University of South Carolina Press, 1990), 124–43; Janice D. Willis, "Nuns and Benefactresses: The Role of Women in the Development of Buddhism," in *Women, Religion and Social Change,* ed. Yvonne Yazbeck Haddad and Ellison Banks Findly (Albany: State University of New York Press, 1985), 59–85; Janice D. Willis, "Female Patronage in Indian Buddhism," in *The Powers of Art: Patronage in Indian Culture,* ed. Barbara Stoler Miller (Delhi: Oxford University Press, 1992), 46–53.

21. Nath, *Dāna,* 75.

22. Ibid., 70.

23. Vidya Dehejia, *Early Buddhist Rock Temples: A Chronology* (Ithaca, N.Y.: Cornell University Press, 1972), plate 53, table 9; D. Jithendra Das, *The Buddhist Architecture in Andhra* (New Delhi: Books and Books, 1993), 1, 18–19, 39, 57; H. Sarkar, *Studies in Early Buddhist Architecture of India* (New Delhi: Munshiram Manoharlal Publishers, 1966), 77.

24. Vidya Dehejia, "The Collective and Popular Basis of Early Buddhist Patronage: Sacred Monuments, 100 BC – AD 250," in *The Powers of Art,* ed. Miller, 35.

25. See, for example, Walter M. Spink, "Ajanta's Chronology: Politics and Patronage," in *Kalādarśana: American Studies in the Art of India,* ed. Joanna G. Williams (New Delhi: Oxford & IBH Publishing Co., in collaboration with American Institute of Indian Studies, 1981), 109–26.

26. Das, *Buddhist Architecture,* 57; Sarkar, *Early Buddhist Architecture,* 55, 57.

27. Schopen, "Two Problems," 10, 23.

28. Dehejia, "Collective and Popular," 36; Manjushree Rao, *Sanchi Sculptures (An Aesthetic and Cultural Study)* (New Delhi: Akay Book Corporation, 1994), 184–214; John Marshall and Alfred Foucher, *The Monuments of Sāñchī,* 3 vols. (Calcutta, 1940; rpt., Delhi: Swati Publications, 1982, 1983); Vidya Dehejia, ed., *Unseen Presence: The Buddha and Sanchi* (Mumbai, India: Marg Publications, 1996).

29. Upinder Singh, "Sanchi: The History of the Patronage of an Ancient Buddhist Establishment," *The Indian Economic and Social History Review* 33.1 (January–March 1996): 15–18.

30. Dehejia, *Early Rock Temples,* 144–45.

31. Nath, *Dāna,* 81, 71–72.

32. Schopen, "Monastic Law," 106. See also Schopen, "Two Problems," 26; Gregory Schopen, "On Monks, Nuns and 'Vulgar' Practices: The Introduction of the Image Cult into Indian Buddhism," *Artibus Asiae* 49.1–2 (1988–89): 153–68; Gregory Schopen, "Deaths, Funerals, and the Division of Property in a Monastic Code," in *Buddhism in Practice,* ed. Donald S. Lopez Jr. (Princeton: Princeton University Press, 1995), 473–502.

33. Dehejia, "Collective and Popular," 38.

34. Alexander Cunningham, *The Bhilsa Topes; or, Buddhist Monuments of Central India* (London, 1854; rpt., Nepali Khapra, Varanasi: Indological Book House, 1966), 171.

35. Singh, "Sanchi," 9.

36. Nath, *Dāna,* 72. See also Rao, *Sanchi,* 208, and B. G. Gokhale, "The Early Buddhist Elite," *Journal of Indian History* 42.2 (1965): 391–402. For the *ghariṇīye* inscription, see Marshall and Foucher, *Sāñchī,* I (text): 315, no. 160.

37. Singh, "Sanchi," 11.

38. Singh, "Sanchi," 11, and on p. 20 Singh notes that while kinship is the critical marker for women donors, native place is an important one for male donors.

39. Given as in Cunningham, *Bhilsa,* 150–222, inscription nos. 4, 8, 37, 66, 80, 83, 85, 95, 105, 127, 148, 166; p. 222. For a longer list, see Marshall and Foucher, *Sāñchī,* I (text): 301–83, inscription nos. 31, 49, 60, 88, 108, 119, 124, 125, 136, 162, 217, 218, 336, 351, 352, 364, 367, 482, 495, 527, 567, 571, 625, 653, 701, 721, 728, 735, 770, 813. See also no. 347.

40. Given as in Marshall and Foucher, *Sāñchī,* I (text): 301–83, nos. 16, 41, 42, 44, 73, 75, 142, 172, 173, 193, 301, 321, 330, 368, 411, 490, 492, 493, 498, 500, 549, 804. See also nos. 583, 762. Compare the chart in Singh, "Sanchi," 12.

41. Given as in Cunningham, *Bhilsa,* nos. 16, 45, 46, 62, 96, 109 (sister-in-law); nos. 7, 18, 63, 64 (sister). See also Marshall and Foucher, *Sāñchī,* I (text): nos. 78, 79, 189, 597.

42. Cunningham, *Bhilsa,* nos. 118 (father); 121, 150, 190 (son); 135 (brother). See also Marshall and Foucher, *Sāñchī,* I (text): nos. 450 (father); 398, 479, 490, 592, 762 (son); 135, 769 (brother).

43. R. C. Sharma, *Buddhist Art: Mathura School* (New Delhi: Wiley Eastern Limited, New Age International, 1995), 6–7, 31, 35, 37; R.C. Sharma, *Mathura Museum: Introduction* (Mathura: Archaeological Museum, 1971), 2, 4.

44. Dehejia, "Collective and Popular," 42; Sharma, *Buddhist Art,* pp. 46, 53–55, 152, 167, figure 65; Sharma, *Museum,* 34–35, figure 28; J. C. Harle, *The Art and Architecture of the Indian Subcontinent* (New Haven and London: Yale University Press, 1986), 62–64, figure 43; Jack Finegan, *An Archaeological History of Religions of Indian Asia* (New York: Paragon House, 1989), 420, figure 13.1.

45. Schopen, "Image Cult," 162, 163.

46. Nath, *Dāna,* 70.

47. Heinrich Lüders, *Mathurā Inscriptions,* ed. Klaus L. Janert (Göttingen: Van den Hoeck & Ruprecht, 1961), inscription nos. 13, 93.

48. N. P. Joshi, "Early Jaina Icons from Mathurā," in *Mathurā: The Cultural Heritage,* ed. Doris Meth Srinivasan (New Delhi: South Asia Books, American Institute of Indian Studies, 1989), 347.

49. Lüders, *Mathurā,* nos. 15, 23, 93. See also D. C. Sircar, "Observations on the Study of Some Epigraphic Records from Mathurā," in *Mathurā,* ed. Srinivasan, 257, 258.

50. Lüders, *Mathurā,* no. 14, 17, 93.

51. Joshi, "Jaina Icons," 347.

52. Lüders, *Mathurā,* nos. 1, 24, 68, 74, 76, 81, 136, 143, 150, 151, 167, 172, 180; see also R. C. Sharma, "New Inscriptions from Mathurā," in Srinivasan, ed., *Mathurā,* 312.

53. Lüders, *Mathurā,* nos. 60, 61, 62; Sharma, "New Inscriptions," 312, 313, 314.

54. Examples from Jain inscriptions: Lüders, *Mathurā,* nos. 14, 17, 93.

55. Lüders, *Mathurā,* nos. 24, 67, 90. Orr finds "multiple kin" identification, that is, the process of identifying women by reference to more than one relative, to be a significant marker in tracking the changing trends of medieval Tamil inscriptions for women donors. Orr, "Women in the Temple," 10.

56. Orr, "Women in the Temple, 9.

57. For discussions of the status of women donors and renunciants in early Buddhism, see Findly, "Housemistress at the Door," and Findly, "Women and the *arahant* Issue in Early Pāli Literature," in *Journal of Feminist Studies in Religion,* 15.1 (Spring 1999): 57–76.

58. *Manu* 4.209, 219; 9.259, 260.

59. Horner, *Women,* 87–94. See Altekar, *Women,* 181–82 and Nath, *Dāna,* 71.

60. Moti Chandra, *The World of Courtesans* (Delhi: Vikas Publishing House, 1973), 48; see also 43–56.

61. Chandra, *Courtesans,* 85–91.

62. *Kāmasūtra* 6.5.25.

63. Kendall W. Folkert, "Jain Religious Life at Ancient Mathurā: The Heritage of Late Victorian Interpretation," in *Mathurā,* ed. Srinivasan, pp. 103–12; Sharma, *Buddhist Art,* 55–57.

64. Sharma, *Museum,* 24–26; Sharma, *Buddhist Art,* 14; Finegan, *History,* 243–45; B. C. Bhattacharya, *The Jaina Iconography* (Lahore, 1939; 2nd ed., rev., Delhi: Motilal Banarsidass, 1974), 142.

65. Harle, *Art and Architecture,* 61.

66. Joshi, "Jaina Icons," 333.

67. John E. Cort, "Art, Religion, and Material Culture: Some Reflections on Method," *Journal of the American Academy of Religion* 64.3 (Fall 1996): 620.

68. Dehejia, "Collective and Popular," 43–44; B. N. Mukherjee, "Growth of Mathurā and Its Society (Up to the End of the Kuṣāṇa Age)," in *Mathurā,* ed. Srinivasan, 65. A translation and discussion of many of the Jain inscriptions bearing the names of women donors can be found in Georg Bühler, "New Jaina Inscriptions from Mathurā," *Epigraphia Indica* 1 (1892): 371–93, and Bühler, "Further Jaina Inscriptions from Mathurā," *Epigraphia Indica* 2 (1894): 195–212.

69. Dehejia, "Collective and Popular," 43.

70. Bühler, "New Inscriptions," 380.

71. Sharma, *Museum,* 25; Finegan, *History,* 264. For an alternate version, see Chandra, *Courtesans,* 57. The designation of a professional lineage in this donation inscription of a *gaṇikā* woman is similar to the designation of teaching lineages in inscriptions of Jain religious women in medieval Tamilnadu. See Orr, "Jain and Hindu 'Religious Women,'" 12.

72. Finegan, *History,* 264; Sharma, *Museum,* fig. XIX.

73. Sharma, *Museum,* 25.

74. Cort, "Art," 616.

75. On Śvetāmbara Jain views, see Padmanabh S. Jaini, *Gender and Salvation: Jaina Debates on the Spiritual Liberation of Women* (Berkeley: University of California Press, 1991).

76. Chandra, *Courtesans,* 32; see also 32–42.

77. Dundas, *Jains,* 150–52, 164, 169–70.

78. Dundas, *Jains,* 171.

79. Nath, *Dāna,* 31.

80. Finegan, *History,* 263.

81. Sharma, *Museum,* 26–28; Sharma, *Buddhist Art,* 89–92, 122–31; Finegan, *History,* 254; Bhattacharya, *Jaina,* 29, 65–107; Gritli v. Mitterwallner, "Yakṣas of Ancient Mathurā," in *Mathurā,* ed. Srinivasan, 368–82.

82. Harle, *Art and Architecture,* 60; Sharma, *Buddhist Art,* 128; Mario Bussagli, *5000 Years of the Art of India* (New York: Harry N. Abrams, Inc., n.d.,), 97–101.

83. Chandra, *Courtesans,* 57.

84. Bhattacharya, *Jaina,* 86. For a discussion of *yakṣī* imagery in the Jain context in medieval Tamil Nadu, see Orr, "Jain and Hindu 'Religious Women,'" 4, 6–7.

85. The women in the harems of Kings Udena and Pasenadi in the Pāli Canon (*Vinaya* 2:290; *Jātaka* 2:23–26), for example, who give robes to the Saṅgha in abundance, Queen Nāganikā who gives support to the Nānāghāt cave complex, Queen Vāsiṣṭhīputrā who supports the Kanheri cave complex (Dehejia, *Early Rock Temples,* plate 53, table 9, series IV), and the chief queen of Khāravela who supports a temple and cave at Manchāpuri (Nath, 71).

86. Padma Kaimal, "Early Cōla Kings and 'Early Cōla Temples': Art and the Evolution of Kingship," *Artibus Asiae* 56.1–2 (1996): 33–66; Cynthia Talbot, "Temples, Donors, and Gifts: Patterns of Patronage in Thirteenth-Century South India," *The Journal of Asian Studies* 50.2 (May 1991): 308–40; Orr, "Women in the Temple," 5–6.

87. Sharma, *Museum,* 6; Sharma, *Buddhist Art,* 8–9, 24–25, 47, 61, 154–55, figure 12; B. D. Chattopadhyaya, "Mathurā from the Śuṅga to the Kuṣāṇa Period: An Historical Outline," in *Mathurā,* ed. Srinivasan, 21–22; J. E. van Lohuizen-de Leeuw, "Foreign Elements in Indian Culture Introduced during the Scythian Period with Special Reference to Mathurā," in *Mathurā,* ed. Srinivasan, 74–75; Sharma, "New Inscriptions," 309.

88. Sharma, *Museum,* 5, 29–30, figures XXIII-A, B; Sharma, *Buddhist Art,* 24, 61–62, figure 11; Bussagli, *Art of India,* 79, figure 81.

89. Chattopadhyaya, "Mathurā," 21.

90. Romila Thapar, *A History of India,* vol. I. (Baltimore, Md.: Penguin Books, 1966), 96–99.

91. Harle, *Art and Architecture,* 68–69.

92. Van Lohuizen-de Leeuw, "Foreign Elements," 74, 79.

93. Sharma, *Museum,* 30.

94. Van Lohuizen-de Leeuw, "Foreign Elements," 75.

95. Sharma, *Buddhist Art,* 154.

96. Sharma, "New Inscriptions," 309.

97. Sharma, *Museum,* 9.

98. See related artifacts in the Government Museum at Mathurā; Sharma, *Buddhist Art,* 24, 61.

99. Kaimal, "Early Cōla Kings," 55, 63–64.

100. Findly, "The Pleasure of Women."

101. For details, see Ellison Banks Findly, *Nur Jahan: Empress of Mughal India* (New York: Oxford University Press, 1993).

102. On the traditional Islamic *mahr* or dowry for Muslim women, see Robert Roberts, *The Social Laws of the Qorān* (London, 1925: new ed., London and Dublin: Curzon Press, 1971), 15–16, 28–33; Reuben Levy, *The Social Structure of Islam* (1957; rpt., Cambridge: University Press, 1971), 95, 97, 114; John L. Esposito,

*Women in Muslim Family Law* (Syracuse: Syracuse University Press, 1982), 24–26; Jane I. Smith, "The Experience of Muslim Women: Considerations of Power and Authority," in *The Islamic Impact,* ed. Yvonne Yazbeck Haddad, Byron Haines, and Ellison Findly (Syracuse: Syracuse University Press, 1984), 91–97.

103. Findly, *Nur Jahan,* 37–40. See also Irfan Habib, "The Family of Nur Jahan During Jahangir's Reign," in *Medieval India, A Miscellany* (Bombay: Asia Publishing House, 1969), 1:74–95.

104. H. Blochmann, trans., *Āʿīn-i Akbarī by Abū'l-Fazl 'Allāmī* (1873; 2nd ed., rev. by D. C. Phillott, Calcutta: Royal Asiatic Society of Bengal, 1927), 1:46–47. See also W. H. Moreland and P. Geyl, trans., *Jahangir's India: The* Remonstrantie *of Francisco Pelsaert (Cambridge: W. Heffer & Sons Ltd., 1925), 64; Niccolao* Manucci, *Storia do Mogor, or Mogul India, 1653–1708,* trans. William Irvine, 2 vols. (London, 1907; rpt., Calcutta: Editions Indian, 1965), 2:308, 310, 315–16, 319; Rekha Misra, *Women in Mughal India (1526–1748 A.D.)* (Delhi: Munshiram Manoharlal, 1967), 60–64.

105. Alexander Rogers, trans., and Henry Beveridge, ed., *The Tūzuk-i-Jahāngīrī, or Memoirs of Jahāngīr,* 2 vols. (1909–14; 2nd ed., Delhi: Munshiram Manoharlal, 1968), 2:228.

106. Pelsaert, *Remonstrantie,* 4–5.

107. Findly, *Nur Jahan,* 128–60. See also Findly, "The Pleasure of Women"; Findly, "Nur Jahan's Embroidery Trade."

108. J. I. Smith, "Experience of Muslim Women," 107.

109. H. M. Elliot and John Dowson, trans. and ed., *The History of India as Told by Its Own Historians: The Muhammadan Period* (London, 1875; rpt., New York: AMS Press, 1966), 6:399, 405.

110. See Vincent A. Smith, *A History of Fine Art in India and Ceylon* (Oxford: Clarendon Press, 1930), 180; Percy Brown, *Indian Architecture (Islamic Period)* (1956; 4th ed., Bombay: Taraporevala's Treasure House of Books, 1964), 83, 100–101; Khalid Mahmud, "The Mausoleum of Emperor Jahangir," *Arts of Asia* 13.1 (Jan.–Feb. 1983): 57–66; Catherine B. Asher, *The New Cambridge History of India,* 1:4, *Architecture of Mughal India* (Cambridge: University Press, 1992), 127–33.

111. *Tūzuk* 2:192–93.

112. Wayne E. Begley, "Four Mughal Caravanserais Built during the Reigns of Jahāngīr and Shāh Jahān," *Muqarnas* 1 (1983): 168. See also Sheo Narain, "Serai Nur Mahal," *Journal of the Punjab Historical Society* 11 (1931): 29–34.

113. Asher, *Architecture of Mughal India,* 128–29.

114. Pelsaert, *Remonstrantie,* 50.

115. Richard Carnac Temple, ed., *The Travels of Peter Mundy, in Europe and Asia, 1608–1667,* vol. 2 (London: The Hakluyt Society, 1914), 78.

116. Gulbadan Begam (Princess Rose-Body), *The History of Humāyūn (Humāyūn-Nāma),* trans. Annette S. Beveridge (1901; rpt., Delhi: Idarah-i Adabiyāt-i Delli, 1972), 7.

117. Rumer Godden, *Gulbadan: Portrait of a Rose Princess at the Mughal Court* (Twickenham, 1980; New York: Viking Press, 1981), 45, 48.

118. Godden, *Gulbadan,* 130; V. A. Smith, *History,* 178; Findly, "Pleasure of Women."

119. I note here as well that the right-hand panel of figure 6.6, showing arabesques with birds enclosed, is reminiscent of embroidery patterns traded internationally at this time and foreshadows arabesques with flowers enclosed used on the Taj. See Findly, "Embroidery Trade."

120. Orr, "Women in the Temple," 20.

7

# Gendered Patronage

## Women and Benevolence during the Early Safavid Empire

*Kishwar Rizvi*

The Safavid dynasty was founded by Isma'il b. Haidar (r. 1501–24) in Tabriz, Iran.[1] Upon his ascension, the new shah established Shi'ism as the state religion, thereby merging tribal, Sufi, and Shi'i concepts of authority into a unique imperial ideology. The Safavids traced their ancestry to the Sufi Shaykh Safi al-din Ishaq (d. 1334), whose order was based in Ardabil, in the northwestern province of Azerbaijan. The rulers' authority also relied upon their Shi'i lineage; in the sixteenth century, Shaykh Safi's biography *Ṣafwat al-ṣafa,* was re-edited with a fabricated family tree branching back to the prophet, Muhammad.[2] This distinction augmented their power base, much of which was composed of Qizilbash tribesmen of Anatolia and Syria.

The relationship between the Qizilbash followers and the Safavid shahs was the same as that between a Sufi shaykh (*murshid*) and his disciple (*murīd*). While founded on Turco-Mongol kinship ties, allegiances were framed within a fervent Sufi mode of Islam, with the head of the Safaviyya order as the supreme spiritual and political authority.[3] Loyalty to the visionary Safavid call to Islam (*da'wā*), was strengthened through blood ties and intertribal alliances such that it was not just the shah who was held in high regard, but his entire family, including the women. In the early years of the dynasty, the Safavids contracted matrimonial alliances mostly with high-born men and women of the Qizilbash tribes. The women, who came from devout and powerful families, brought with their dowries not only prestige, but also land and wealth.[4] They played an important role in the construction of a Safavid imperial image, one that chose selectively from tribal traditions and cloaked them in the rhetoric of Islam. In this overlay, both women and men defined equal and complimentary aspects of rulership. The settings they chose for the dissemination of this image were the shrines they embellished and the written histories they commissioned, both of which documented their aspirations and particular worldviews.[5]

The aim of this paper is to analyze the manner in which Safavid forms of authority and legitimacy were manifested by royal women during the formative period of the dynasty prior to the reign of Shah ʿAbbas (r. 1587–1629).[6] Study of the cultural environment, through contemporary texts and architectural patronage, reveals the language of power and piety utilized by the Safavid family. The site chosen for the analysis is the shrine of Fatima al-Maʿsuma (d. 817) at Qum, which was actively patronized by the women of the Safavid house. Their sponsorship of the building reveals the cultural significance of patronage in sixteenth-century Iran, and the place of architecture in it. The royal women emerge as autonomous actors in the context of familial relationships, while simultaneously furthering the common cause of the supreme dynastic rulership led by their male kin.[7]

Modern scholars have attributed the independence and political activism of the Safavid women to their Turco-Mongol ancestry.[8] According to Maria Szuppe, who has made a lengthy study of Safavid royal women, the Turkmen tribes from the time of the Seljuks retained their "pagan" social mores, which were not as restrictive as the Islamic ones. She argues that Turkmen tribal customs were based on nomadism, which accorded a great deal of importance to blood ties and the independence of women.[9] This conclusion is perceptive yet incomplete, for it does not take into consideration the influence of Islam, the presence of which is well documented in the culture of the provinces, as well as cities of northwestern Iran.[10] To assume that Safavid women were aberrations within the social structure of Islam is to present a monodimensional aspect of both the religion and of them. In addition, the nomadic Mongol customs of the thirteenth century cannot adequately explain the choices that defined society in the sixteenth century, of which the Turkmen elite were an integral component.

Previously, women who were part of the rulership in Iran had left their mark through institutions that were popularly and orthodoxly recognized. For example, when the Timurid princess Gawhar Shad (d. 1457) commissioned the famous addition to the Shrine of Imam Reza in Mashhad, and her own tomb complex in Herat, which was comprised of a mosque, *madrasa,* and dynastic mausoleum, she was exploiting codes of piety and politics that were standard to the cultural language of fifteenth-century Khorasan. Similarly, women at the beginning of the sixteenth century (both Iranian and Turkman), like their male counterparts, reinterpreted and made use of the dominant forms of religious expression, whether it was made publicly visible in the architecture of the shrines they visited or remained less visible in the form of their pious, charitable activities.

Building on earlier models of tribal and Islamic rulership, the Safavids also tapped into another source of authority, their ʿAlid ancestry.[11] Shahs like Ismaʿil and Tahmasb (r. 1524–76) were rulers propagating the Shiʿi version of Islam, as well as Sufi masters. Both of these roles were necessary components of their imperial persona, relying on orthodox and popular forms of devotion. Shiʿism was instituted as the religion of the land, and scholars and clerics were brought to Iran from traditionally Shiʿi enclaves, such as Jabal ʿAmil in Lebanon;[12] in coins issued by Shah Ismaʿil in 1501, to the Islamic profession of faith (*shahāda*), was added the Shiʿi slogan, *ʿAli walī Allah* (ʿAli is the friend of God).[13]

The royal household assumed an air of sanctity through their genealogical ties to the Prophet; Safavid men and women received respect and veneration, and their status was elevated almost to sainthood. Although never explicitly assuming the role of religious leaders of the Shiʿi, Shah Ismaʿil and his descendants manipulated popular belief to create an aura of holiness that surrounded the person of the shah. His family was identified as the *al-i Muhammad* (the family of Muhammad) and when Shah Tahmasb went forth among the people, men carrying steel drums would lead the procession, praising God and the Shiʿi imams and cursing symbols of Sunnism, the caliphs Abu Bakr, Umar and Uthman; they bore a lance with a copper circle, in the center of which was inscribed *ʿAlī walī Allah.*[14] The particularly messianic zeal and revolutionary spirit of the Safavid "movement" is reflected strongly in the poetry written by Shah Ismaʿil, under the *nom de plume,* Khataʾi. The poetry exhorts his followers toward devotion, obedience, *jihad,* and sacrifice for the young shah. In one verse, written in the Turkish language of his followers, Ismaʿil extols, "Know him to be God, do not call him human. . . . My name is Ismaʿil, . . . my mother is Fatima, my father ʿAli."[15] Thus, while the men modeled themselves after Shiʿi archetypal male figures such as ʿAli, the women found a role model in the person of Fatima al-Zahra, the daughter of the Prophet Muhammad.

In the Sufi and Shiʿi worldview there are five People of the House (*ahl al-bait*); Muhammad, his daughter Fatima, her husband ʿAli, and her sons Hasan and Husayn. As daughter, wife, and mother, Fatima al-Zahra was a pivotal character.[16] In the stories of the Prophet Muhammad and his family, Fatima al-Zahra is given the place of honor and the title, "Leader of Women (*sayyida al-nissa*)" as she was the closest to her father and would be the first from his family to rejoin him in Paradise.[17] As an ideal woman, Fatima al-Zahra was venerated by the Safavid elite. A prominent seventeenth-century Safavid cleric listed the names of Fatima al-Zahra in a hagiographic treatise. She was said to be made from light—hence the appellate, *al-zahrā'* (the radiant); her titles included *tahira* (pure), *zakīya* (intelligent), *razīya* (agreeable), *ṣadiqa* (true), *ma'suma* (innocent), and *pakīza* (clean).[18] The names are encountered again and again in sixteenth- and seventeenth-century descriptions of Fatima al-Zahra, as well as those of Safavid women. Thus, the daughter of Shah Tahmasb, Princess Pari Khan Khanum (d. 1578) was not only the "queen of the age" (*maleka-i zamāni*), but also the "Fatima of the age" (*Fatima-i zamāni*); Mahd-i 'Ala ("the lofty cradle," d. 1579), the mother of Shah 'Abbas, was called the "queen of the times," "the chaste" (*'afifa*)," "the radiant (*zahrā'*)," "the lawful progeny of the leader of the women (*dhariya tayiba sayyida al-nissa'*)" and the great Maryam (that is, Mary, mother of Jesus).[19]

The marriage of Fatima al-Zahra to her father's cousin, 'Ali, is a significant event in Shi'i hagiography. It is through this divinely inspired match, blessed by the Prophet himself, that the family of Muhammad was assured perpetuity and prosperity. The continuity of a family's lineage through the female heir is a pattern also shared by many Sufis. For example, there are several instances where the mantle (*khirqa*) of a Sufi master was passed on to the disciple and formalized through marriage with the master's daughter. In the case of the Safavids, bloodlines and spiritual lineage were simultaneously emphasized: in the Safavid genealogies, their Sayyid connections lead back to Fatima al-Zahra, while their Sufi source of authority (leading to 'Ali) was dependent on another woman, also named Fatima, who was the daughter of Shaykh Zahid (d. 1301) of Gilan.

The Safaviyya order, of which the Safavid rulers were supreme masters, was founded by a pupil of this Shaykh Zahid, Safi al-Din Ishaq. Safi's meeting with his spiritual master took place around the end of the thirteenth century, and he then followed the shaykh for twenty-five years, eventually becoming the head of his order.[20] Sixteenth-century Safavid court historians described the momentous event when the links between these two great families were solidified: after some years of meditation and contemplation, Safi was made Shaykh Zahid's spiritual successor, whereupon the great shaykh gave to his disciple in marriage a daughter, "of the same name as Zahra—peace be upon her (i.e., Fatima al-Zahra), who was nourished within the veil of chastity." Fatima was described as a gift (*'aṭīya*), which ignited a flame of envy in the hearts of the other disciples. An exalted daughter and devoted wife, she was praised as the ideal woman. When her husband died, she was struck by extreme grief, crying that she could not live another month without him. Eighteen days later she too passed away and was buried ceremoniously in the shrine of Shaykh Safi in Ardabil, in a tomb constructed by her son.[21] This Fatima, like the daughter of the Prophet Muhammad, had her own family prestige, independent of that obtained through marriage. In fact, it was the young shaykh who, through marriage to her, gained political and religious favor, a situation often repeated by sixteenth-century Safavid royalty.

The contemporary histories and chronicles reveal that Safavid women enjoyed considerable social importance at the court. Blood ties were solidified through marriage, and prominence for a woman could be achieved through the role of wife and mother, similar to women in contemporary Ottoman society. For example, the favorite wife of Shah Isma'il was Tajlu Khanum (d. 1540), who hailed from an influential branch of the royal Aqqoyunlu family, the Mausillu, and owned much land in central Iran and the Veramin district. Shah Isma'il's marriage with a woman of this powerful family was a strategic alliance, which solidified tribal loyalties and strengthened the Safavid hold on the region. This relationship between the Mausillu and Safavid houses continued for at least two generations afterward, for Shah Tahmasb was married to Khadim-i 'Ali Sultan Begum (d. 1593), who was the daughter of Musa Sultan Beg Mausillu, and his daughter from this alliance was married to another Mausillu, a chief of the Turkmen amirs.[22] That the latter marriage was a politically meaningful affair can been seen in the attention given to it by Safavid historians. In the accounts of the year 1580, Iskander Munshi relates the joyous event of this marriage, which was celebrated by three days of festivities in Tabriz. The initiation of the husband into the Safavid family was ritualized by the giving of a robe of honor and a jeweled crown, a scimitar and sword with their gem-studded sheath and hilt, a horse with a jeweled bridle, and luxury fabrics. The honor bestowed on him is further highlighted when Munshi points out that a rival from the Takkalu clan had also vied for the hand of this princess but was not considered suitable for "this magnificent gift" (*īn 'aṭīya-i 'āzimī*), Fatima Sultan Begum.[23]

The daughters and sisters of the shah were powerful women who often participated in the political arena. While Tajlu Khanum held considerable sway over the court of Isma'il, she was later in competition with her daughter, Mahin Banu "Shahzada Sultanom" (d. 1561–62) for the attentions of her son, Shah Tahmasb. It was Mahin Banu who exchanged diplomatic correspondence with the Ottoman queen, Hurrem Sultan, and was an intermediary in negotiations between Shah Tahmasb and the Mughal emperor Humayun.[24] She was portrayed as an accomplished woman, famous for her patronage of shrines and places of pilgrimage, and foundations that were set up with her income from properties in Shirvan, Tabriz, Qazvin, Ray, and Isfahan. She also established an endowment for the welfare of women, which aided the marriages of young orphan girls. At her death, her jewels and china collection were made into a pious gift.[25]

Tajlu Khanum's granddaughter, Pari Khan Khanum, was recorded in the Safavid histories as playing a causal role in the rise to power of her brother Isma'il Mirza and she was described by Iskander Munshi as an intelligent and great lady of the age.[26] While unmarried (and thus childless) women rarely appear in the histories of other Islamic societies, the Safavid writers give prominence to the unmarried daughter. Mahin Banu and Pari Khan Khanum were notable political players, and in the reign of Shah 'Abbas, his unmarried aunt Zaynab Begum (d. 1642—daughter of Shah Tahmasb) held great sway over the court politics.[27] The respect and power given to the pious, celibate sister in Safavid society was due to the strong blood ties that united the social and political culture of the time.[28] The unmarried daughter gained social legitimacy through her distinguished birth and lineage. In Safavid Iran, this attribute was augmented by the representation of two ideal daughters about whom the Shi'i scholars wrote: Fatima, the daughter of Muhammad, and Maryam, the daughter of Imran. These two women, Fatima and Maryam, are often conceptually conflated through their appellate *al-batūl,* the Virgin. Indeed, Shi'i hagiographers often took a quotation from the Qur'an concerning Maryam and substituted in it the name of Fatima: "O Fatima (Maryam) . . . Allah has chosen you. He has made you pure (*tāhara*) and exalted you above all women (*al-nissa' al-'alamīn*). Fatima (Maryam) be obedient to your Lord; bow down and worship with the worshippers."[29] The virtues exemplified by Fatima and Maryam, such as virginity, purity, and celibacy, were highly regarded traits in a woman of the Safavid court. However, this respect did not prevent the women from being given comparable attention and opportunities as their male siblings. Like the princes, they too were tutored by their Qizilbash guardian (*lālā*) and were taught the arts of calligraphy and horsemanship, along with religious doctrine.[30]

The educated and powerful Safavid women participated in the political and cultural arena, and were known as active patrons of art, architecture, and religious institutions. As mentioned earlier, Mahin Banu spent much of her wealth on charitable works, especially at the shrine of Imam Reza in Mashhad; similarly, Zaynab Begum built bridges and caravanserais along the Qazvin-Sava route. Pari Khan Khanum was not only a poet in her own right, but also a patron of poetry, having many poems dedicated to her by prominent contemporaries.[31] Moreover, she was influential in encouraging her father, Shah Tahmasb, to endow charitable institutions.[32] During his reign, in cities such as Mashhad, Qum, and Ardabil where Shiʿism was particularly strong, alms were distributed and feast days, such as the birthdays of Muhammad and Fatima al-Zahra, were celebrated regularly.[33]

The Safavids focused their attention on predominantly Shiʿi cities and popular shrines. In contrast to the Sunni Ottomans on their western borders who built Friday mosques, the Shiʿi state favored shrine worship, which typically venerated holy persons who played the role of intercessor between the supplicant and God. For the itinerant Safavid monarchs, shrines were the loci for political action and for the enactment of their dogma.[34] They were arenas in which social and cultural mores were established and disseminated. Emphasis was laid on pilgrimage to shrines such as that of Imam Reza in Mashhad, the shrine of his sister, Fatima al-Maʿsuma in Qum, and to the shrine of Shaykh Safi al-Din in Ardabil. These three buildings had different functions: Shaykh Safi's was a Sufi shrine, dependent on the services linked to such an institution; that is, it was a *zāwīya* (Sufi lodge) that served the community and its secondary buildings were originally for Sufi practice and ritual. In contrast, the shrines at Qum and Mashhad were both monuments built in veneration of a member of the Prophet's family and for the propagation of the Shiʿi dogma. The secondary institution linked to them was the *madrasa,* or theological college. The shrines of Sufi shaykhs and Shiʿi imams, while dissimilar in function, shared many similarities in terms of ritual, and hence, architecture. During the early Safavid period, the boundaries between Sufi and Shiʿi architectural types, which were already indistinct, were obscured even further. For example, in 1418 at Imam Reza's shrine, the Timurid princess Gawhar Shad had built a Hall of Readers (*dār al-ḥuffāz*) for Qur'anic recitation, a practice associated with Sufi worship. In the same manner, Shah Ismaʿil built a hall for hadith study (*dār al-ḥadīth*) at the shrine of Shaikh Safi for teaching orthodox Shiʿi theology.

Rituals of piety and benevolence were enacted at the shrines by both the humble and the rich. For example, Shah Tahmasb was commanded in a dream to thank Imam Reza for aiding the Iranian victory in Samarqand and to erect a dome in his name.[35] Shah ʿAbbas' reconquest of Khorasan from the Uzbeks in 1598 was also viewed not so much as a political event, but as a religious one, in which the objective was that of retrieving for the Shiʿi their holy site, the shrine of Imam Reza.[36] When Shah ʿAbbas saw the dome of the shrine, he was said to have wept and kissed the holy ground in thanks to the Imam for answering his prayers. As a sign of gratitude for this victory, Shah ʿAbbas bestowed upon the shrine chandeliers and candlesticks of gold and silver, and expensive carpets, and he ordered "the extension of the shrine complex, including lofty porticos and the buildings around them; (and) the painting and decoration of the sanctuary."[37]

The shrines of Shaikh Safi, Imam Reza, and Fatima al-Maʿsuma served as sites for the commemoration of victories as well as for enacting ceremonials of sovereignty, such as those of charity and largess.[38] For example, in 1526 Shah Tahmasb built the minaret at the northern entrance of the shrine of Imam Reza and replaced the tiles on the dome with plates of solid gold.[39] To the shrine of Fatima al-Maʿsuma in Qum, he gave a beautiful Qur'an.[40] Such benevolence was interpreted not only as a sign of piety, but also as the symbol of the Safavid political and religious ideology.

Since the Safavid shahs were heads of the Safaviyya order, their links to Ardabil were strong and many notable shaykhs and members of the Safavid family were buried within the precincts of the shrine of Shaykh Safi. This Shaykh's tomb was constructed in a room within his shrine where the Shaykh had performed his meditations and prayers. Situated between the tomb tower of Shaykh Safi and the mausoleum of his son and family members (including his wife and daughter) was the domed tomb of Shah Ismaʿil, built at his death in 1524 by Tajlu Khanum. When Fatima Sultan Begum, the daughter of Shah Tahmasb died in Tabriz, her body was taken to Ardabil for burial at the holy shrine of her great forefathers (*rawza-i mathra-i āba' o ajdād-i ʿāla*).[41] In the 1570 land register, *Ṣariḥ al-milk,* it is mentioned that the tombs of Shah Ismaʿil's mother and wife were also in the main shrine complex, although the location is unknown.[42] The shahs and their immediate family were buried within the precincts of the shrine, and the others were interred outside. The ancestral tombs of the Safavid family were venerated to such an extent that they were believed to provide blessings to whoever was buried near them. A Venetian visitor to the court of Shah Tahmasb wrote, "And if he was a man who was in the Shah's favor, he (Shah Tahmasb) orders him to be buried in the city of Ardabil . . . which would be three days from Tabriz, to the east."[43]

Whereas Ardabil was the dynastic shrine and associated primarily with Shaykh Safi, the shrine at Qum was perceived quite differently (fig. 7.1). An old and important city of Iran, at the beginning of the fourteenth century, Qum became a winter hunting capital for the Turkmen sultans.[44] The fifteenth-century historian, Ruzbihan Khunji recounts the time when Sultan Yaqub was at his winter quarters in Qum when Shaykh Haydar (the paternal grandfather of Shah Isma'il) sent his mother to the royal household there to get permission for a raid on Shirvan.[45] Her mediation on his behalf secured the order as well as assistance for the march. The involvement of his mother in Shaykh Haydar's political ambitions—she was, after all, the sister of the Aqqoyunlu sultan, Uzun Hasan—highlights her influence and also draws attention to the presence of women at the royal court in Qum.

Safavid shahs, such as Isma'il and Tahmasb, often wintered in or outside of Qum where game was abundant and the weather more clement than that of northern cities like Tabriz and Sultaniyya. Qazi Ahmad Qummi relates an episode of the year 1502, which is invaluable in reconstructing the imperial residence in Qum. The author's grandfather had been an architect (*mi'mār*) and state clerk for Shahrukh Mirza and for subsequent Turkmens sultans. After retiring, he returned to his birthplace Qum, and built a *zāwīya* there known as "Husayniyya." At Shah Isma'il's ascension, with the help of other builders, engineers, and architects, he repaired the old Imperial Palace (*daulatkhāna*) of Qum, which had earlier been the royal residence of Uzun Hasan and his son, Yaqub. Adjacent to this was built a new Residential Palace (*haramsarā*) of four storeys, with portals and balconies. This palace was decorated with carvings and beautiful paintings. A painting from the famous *Shāhnāma-i shāhi* of Firdawsi (the so-called Houghton Shahnama), completed c. 1527 during the reign of Shah Tahmasb, gives us an idea of what this imperial palace might have looked like (fig. 7.2). The scene "Dream of Zahāk," shows the king's chambers on the left, connected by an exterior corridor to the women's quarters on the right. Although illustrating a fictional situation, the visual similarity of this scene to Qazi Ahmad Qummi's written description allows us to imagine the appearance of Safavid royal residences in the early sixteenth century.[46] When the attention of Shah Isma'il turned to Qum, called the City of the

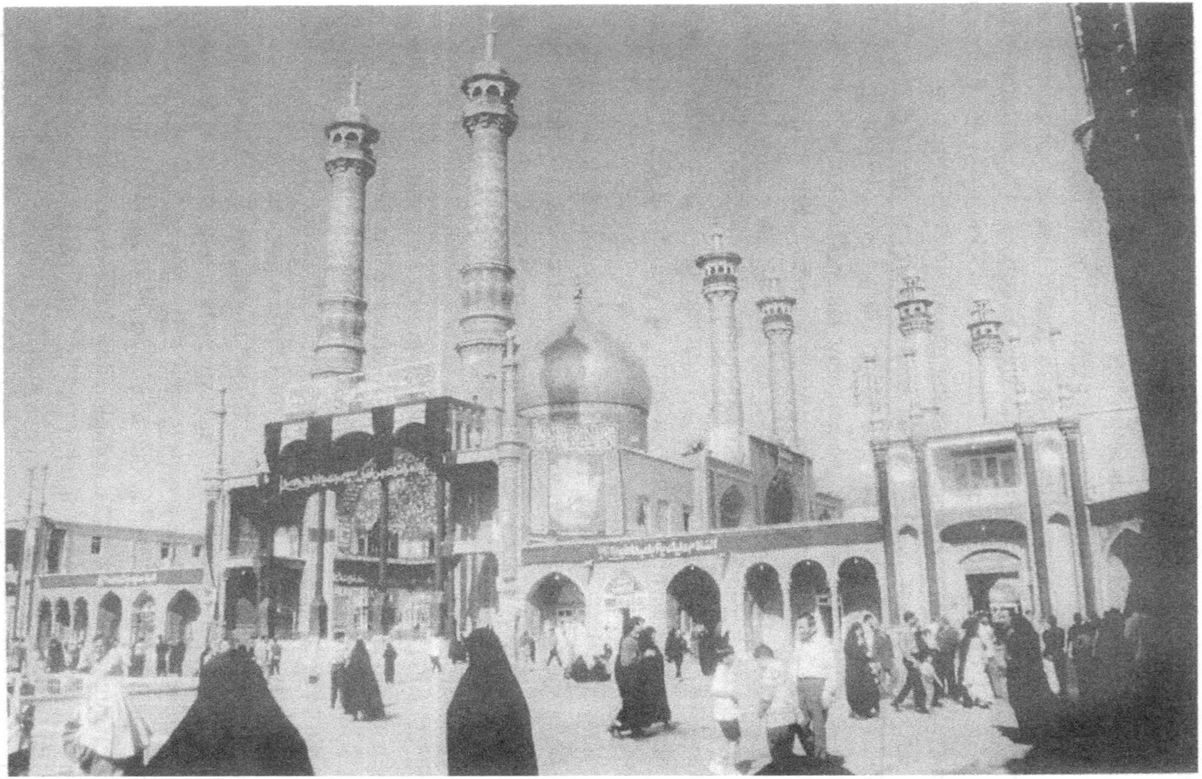

**Fig. 7.1.** The Shrine of Fatima al-Ma‘suma at Qum seen from the New Courtyard

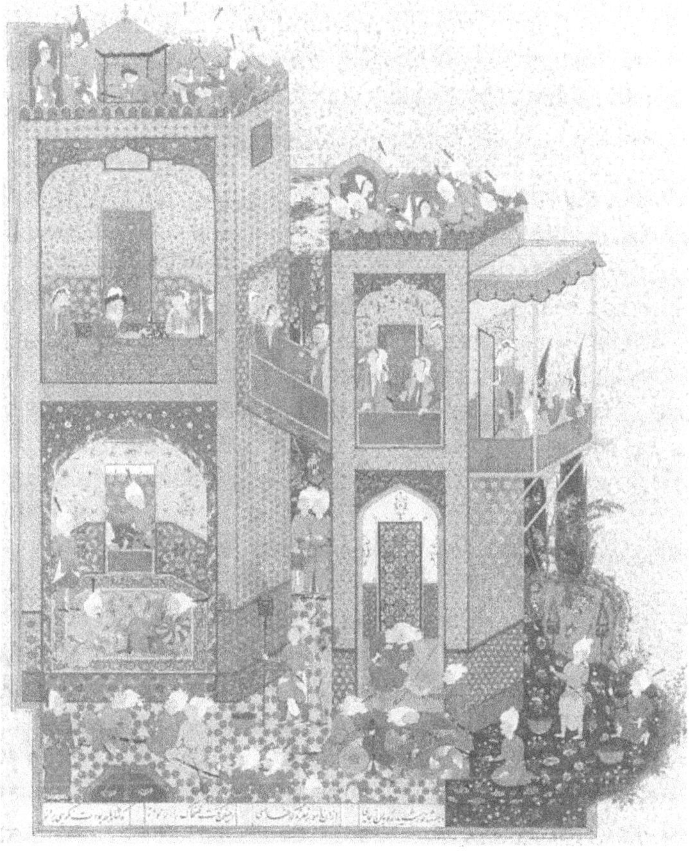

**Fig. 7.2.** "Dream of Zahāk," *Shāhnāma-i Shāhi* (1527) (Courtesy of the Arthur M. Sackler Museum, Harvard University)

Faithful (*dār al-mominīm*), all the nobles, patricians and Shiʿi aristocracy of the city were present in order to welcome him to his new palace.[47] It was here that the head-shaving ceremony of Shah Ismaʿil's son Sam Mirza took place in 1518,[48] and in 1536, the birth of Shah Tahmasb's son, Ibrahim Mirza, both amidst great rejoicing.[49]

The palace in the city of Qum was a surrogate, winter residence for the Safavids and also the site of retreat and exile from the court, especially for the women. After his mother had aided his brother Bahram Mirza against him, Shah Tahmasb sent her to Qum in 1528. In the account of 1578, Iskander Munshi recounts that when Sultanom Begum, the mother of Shah

Muhammad Khudabanda, sided against her son in a political intrigue, she was banished to Qum where she remained mourning the death of another of her sons, Ibrahim Mirza. He also writes that since Pari Khanum, the sister of Shah Muhammad Khudabanda had control at the court in Qazvin, the Shah had his loyal viziers come to Qum to pay allegiance to him, until his position was secure enough for him to go to Qazvin for his enthronement.[50] When the Shah's wife Mahd-i ʿAla gained too much control, and thereby offended his Uzbek amirs who were not pleased to take orders from a woman, the Shah made plans to send her away to Qum, just as his father before him had sent his mother.[51] The association of Safavid women with the city of Qum was a recurrent theme in the writings of the chroniclers and the City of the Faithful became a focus of female attention, particularly the shrine of Fatima al-Maʿsuma, located outside its walls. For the Safavid women, this shrine was not only a holy edifice deserving their benevolence but also a place where their physical inclusion as women was accepted.

The saintly Fatima al-Maʿsuma was seen as an intercessor on behalf of women and hence her shrine became a highly gendered space where acts of piety were performed. She is said to have arrived in Qum in 817, en route to visit her brother, the eighth Shiʿi imam, ʿAli b. Musa al-Reza, at Tus (Mashhad). On the way she fell ill and asked to be taken to Qum, which since the early eighth century had a reputation as a Shiʿi center. (According to Qazi Ahmad Qummi in the late sixteenth century, it had been an abode of Shiʿism for over seven or eight hundred years.)[52] After reaching the city, she died and was buried in the gardens of a cemetery belonging to a dignitary of Qum, Musa b. Kharaj, who subsequently made the cemetery *waqf* (endowed perpetuity) for the public. By the ninth and tenth centuries the shrine had become a popular place of pilgrimage and continued to attract many followers during the Timurid and Aqqoyunlu period.[53]

During the Safavid era the shrine was held in high esteem, and received two particularly interesting acts of benevolent endowment. The manner of patronage reveals the role played by royal women in the cultural and social dynamics of their time. In 1519 the dome of the shrine was rebuilt and the entire courtyard embellished in honor of Shah Ismaʿil. Four years later, Tajlu Khanum, his wife, made mortmain a large portion of her neighboring property and bestowed it to the shrine. The *waqfnāma* (endowment records) and the inscriptions on the entrance of the old courtyard are evidence of the religious and political significance of the shrine of Fatima al-Maʿsuma during the early sixteenth century.[54]

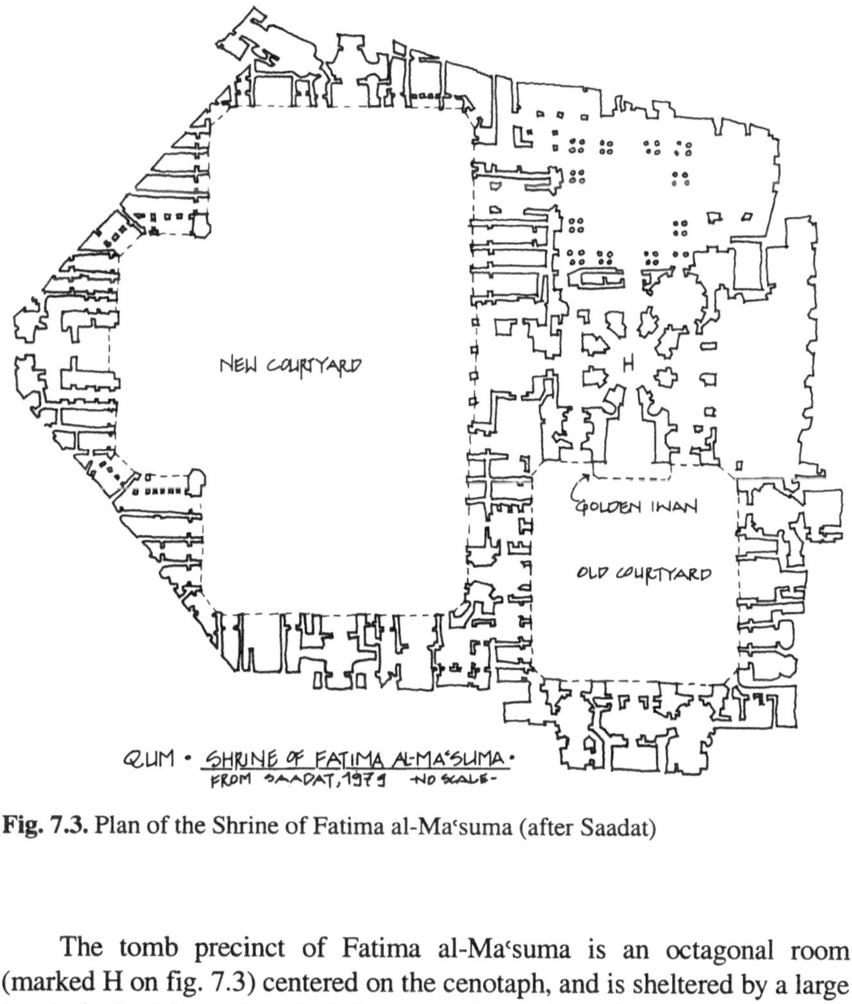


**Fig. 7.3.** Plan of the Shrine of Fatima al-Ma'suma (after Saadat)

The tomb precinct of Fatima al-Ma'suma is an octagonal room (marked H on fig. 7.3) centered on the cenotaph, and is sheltered by a large hemispherical dome. Attached directly to the tomb precinct is a deep portico, or iwan (fig. 7.4). Through an arched opening, this iwan leads to the old courtyard and to the original entrance of the shrine. The semidome of the iwan was decorated in the nineteenth century with golden *muqarnas* mirror-work, for which it is now called the Golden Iwan. The main portal is flanked by two secondary iwans. The facade and enclosures are decorated in tile mosaic with a wide palette of colors. The designs are of two types: the first is an accumulation of sinuous, floral motifs that cover broad surfaces of the wall; the second type is of fuller compositions, forming panels of either large floral medallions or of blossoming plants sprouting

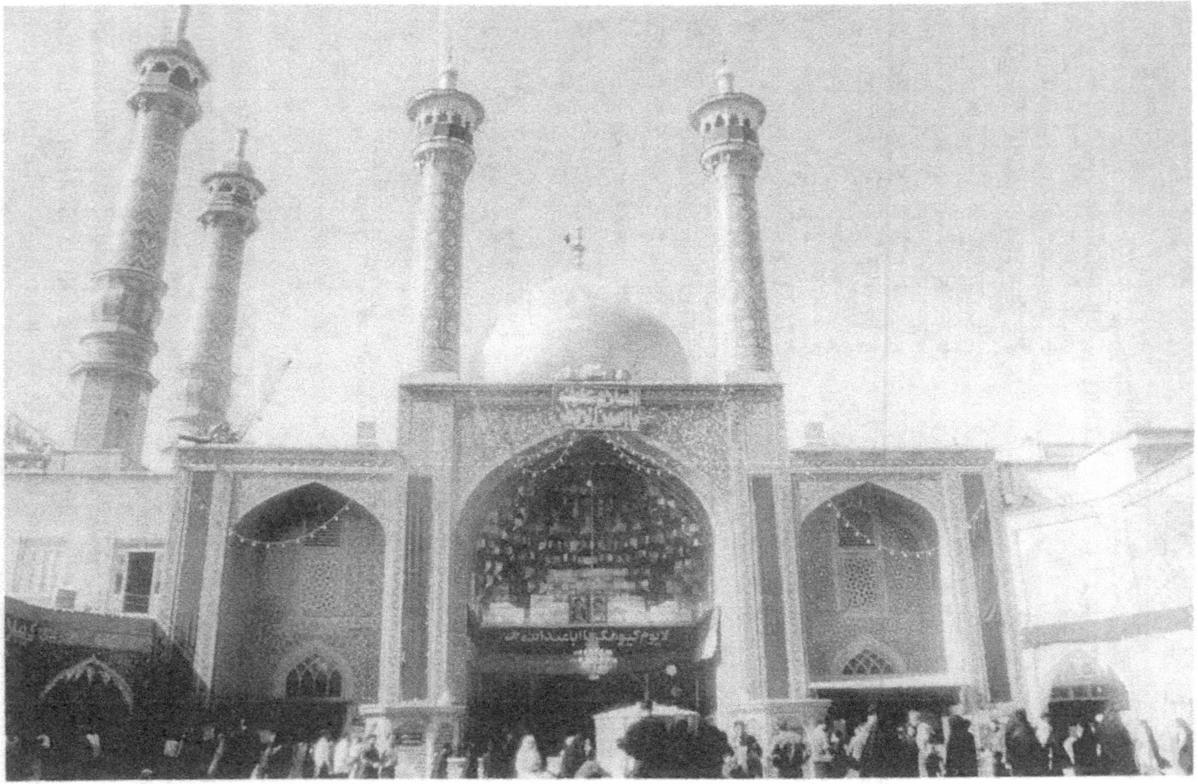

**Fig. 7.4.** Golden Iwan, entrance to the tomb precinct from the Old Courtyard

from vases, the whole framed in an ogee arch. There are three inscription bands adorning the iwan: a wide band below the *muqarnas* dome that envelopes the interior back and sides of the iwan; a second, lower band that is parallel to the first, but is also on the interior of the small iwan; and a narrow band that highlights the inside arch of the main iwan, consisting of the verses from the Qur'an, *surat al-nūr* (the Light verse).[55] In the pendentives of the secondary iwan are pairs of epigraphic medallions. There are six attributes written in white *naqshī* script: "the Merciful, the Proof, the Judge, the Glorious, the Compassionate, the Benefactor" (*yā raḥmān, yā burhān, yā dayān, yā subḥān, yā ḥanān, yā manān*).[56] This medallion was also mounted on the gateway of the Shrine of Shaykh Safi in Ardabil (in carved marble) and in the courtyard in the Shrine of Imam Reza in Mashhad (in tiled mosaic), in what might have been Safavid reembellishments.[57]

The first horizontal band, 0.60 meters wide, consists of white *thuluth* script, on a dark blue lajverdi background that starts from the lip of the arch and encircles the interior. Beginning with a Qur'anic verse, "Praise be to Allah who has guided us hither (7:43)," the inscription continues to document the construction of "this exalted building and insurmountable, holy precinct" which was built during the reign of the "just and all-knowing sultan," Shah Isma'il.[58] The name of the Shah occurs directly above the pinnacle of the arch and is rendered in a light blue mosaic, highlighting and differentiating it from the rest of the text. The titles of the king are standard, reiterating the Islamic image of the ruler as one who supervises the faithful, protects the land against tyranny, and who resurrects justice and benevolence. However, he is also depicted as "the Guide (*mahdī*)" who will lead all creatures to the great religion.[59] The position of this king is enhanced as he is cast in the role of proselytizer and master, taking on attributes often reserved only for God (for example, *al-malak al-manān*—"the Benefactor"). This was not unusual among the Safavids who posited the ruler as a semidivine godhead. The end of this foundation inscription bestows on his kingdom the eternal blessings of the Prophet Muhammad and is dated Rajab A.H. 925 (1519).[60]

The second inscription is divided in two halves, interrupted by the door into the tomb chamber. In style and embellishment, it is similar to the first, only slightly smaller. The white *thuluth* script is easily read as it is just above the dado and at a height of 1.80 meters from the floor. The body of this text contains a saying (*ḥadīth*) of the Prophet Muhammad. The first half of the repetitive verse is: "Whoever dies for the love of the family of

Muhammad, dies a martyr; whoever dies for the love of the family of Muhammad, dies cleansed/ . . . repentant/ . . . a perfect believer; . . . he meets the Angel of Death . . . (and) is conducted to Paradise like a bride to the house of her betrothed; . . . whoever dies for the love of the family of Muhammad, God makes his grave like a shrine of the Angels of Mercy." This last is at the entrance door of the tomb chamber, an appropriate site for such a verse, blessing the grave of Fatima al-Maʿsuma. After this there are warnings to those who die through hatred and opposition to the family of Muhammad, who would be denied the happiness of Paradise. The inscription ends with blessings on Muhammad, ʿAli, Fatima, her children Hasan and Husayn, and the remaining nine Shiʿi Imams, popularly called the Fourteen Innocent Ones.[61] The honorific title is given for each: *al-muṣṭafa Muḥammad, al-murṭada ʿAlī, al-batūl Fatima,* and so on. The emphasis in this inscription on the respect and allegiance to the family of Muhammad is striking but not surprising. On the one hand, it venerates Fatima al-Maʿsuma who, while not one of the Fourteen Innocent ones, is closely related to them; on the other hand, it reiterates the claim to religious authority of the Safavid shahs. One aspect of their rulership is revealed in the girdling inscription with the name of Shah Ismaʿil, which reinforces his duties as sovereign and pious leader, signaling his temporal supremacy as the *sultān bin al-sultān bin al-sultān,* that is, the scion of a family of kings (incidentally, the same title used by his Ottoman rival). Another aspect is unveiled in his title, *al-mahdī,* the honorific reserved for the twelfth imam, Muhammad, reinforced by the second inscription elliptically, which alludes to Ismaʿil's exalted ancestry through further transposing associations with the family of Muhammad by constantly reiterating the notion of *ahl al-bait.*[62] This theme is reiterated on the interior walls of the tomb chamber, below the dome, where there are sayings attributed to the Prophet Muhammad such as "The family of the Prophet is like the Ark of Noah; to ride it is to gain deliverance, to oppose it is to drown (in destruction)." In the sayings, the "people of ʿAli', (*shiʿiat ʿAlī,* that is, the Shiʿi) are depicted as the victorious ones, and the family of Muhammad is described as a tree in Paradise with its branches spreading over the earth.[63]

The highly charged ethos of idolization bestowed upon the family of Muhammad and the Safavid identification with them, as observed in the epigraphic program of the shrine, is also reflected in the *waqfnāma* of Tajlu Khanum, dated 1523.[64] The endowment deed makes mortmain properties around Qum and Sultaniyya for the Shrine of "Sitti Fatima, situated outside the Sava gate of the city of Qum." It begins with praises of God, Muhammad and ʿAli, and continues by expounding on the virtues of charity and almsgiving as ways of gaining blessings for the afterlife. After this, the donor of the endowment is identified as: "The great lady, the mistress, queen of the World, leader of the chosen (pure) people, . . . (she is) affluent, beneficent, pure, . . . the just, the ruler, the sultana of the chosen women. . . . Builder of great, charitable works, founder of benevolent foundations, the signs of sanctity and rectitude from the tent of her high position are brilliant (and) the lights of purity from the (bridal) canopy of her greatness are dazzling. The virtuous one of the World and of the Religion, Shah Begi Begum, daughter of the great Amir, Mihmad Beg, son of Hamza Beg Bektash Mausillu, may her greatness and chastity be eternal."[65] The endowment deed goes on to list the properties, gardens, and residences that were made mortmain, many of which lay outside the city of Qum.

Although the woman is here named Shah Begi Begum, she was identified by Qazi Ahmad Qummi as the previously mentioned Tajlu Khanum, favorite wife of Shah Ismaʿil.[66] According to him, she donated many of her numerous properties to the shrine of Fatima al-Maʿsuma. He also mentioned the presence of other buildings at the shrine which the architects of that "great Lady" built with her generous donations.[67] In addition to this, she was credited with building the dome of the Jannatsarā at the shrine of Shaykh Safi at Ardabil.[68] The manner in which Shah Begi Begum is described in the *waqfnāma* is interesting because, while most of her honorific titles credit her with purity and an exalted, sublime position, there are also those that point specifically to her role as the patron, builder, and founder of pious charities. Her important imperial position is alluded to by her identification as the just ruler (*ʿadila*) and sultana, feminized versions of the titles shared by her husband Shah Ismaʿil (as seen in the girdling inscription of the iwan).[69] And yet, it is not her husband's lineage that is mentioned but her father's, for she is introduced in the legal document as the daughter of Mihmad Beg Bektash Mausillu, a Turkman. Thus, although the parallel designation with her husband serves to identify her today, in her own time, the status and importance worth mention was her blood genealogy, which was not a function of her prestigious marriage but rather her birthright. Shah Begi Begum's ties to the Turkman elite was a source of distinction, as is acknowledged by the court historians.[70]

The Mausillu family's ties to Qum were considerable, judging by the amount of land and property owned by Shah Begi Begum in the town and its environs. As mentioned earlier, the Queen had a residence in Qum, where she had moved in 1528 with the rest of her entourage while Shah

Tahmasb was campaigning in Khorasan.[71] This trend of maintaining a primary residence in Qum continued with her daughter-in-law and cousin, Sultanom Begum.[72] These women of the Mausillu/Safavid houses who lived in Qum frequented the tomb of Fatima al-Maʿsuma. Moreover, that shrine became a focus of their charitable donations as living patrons and a site for their commemoration after death.

The *waqfnāma* of Shah Begi Begum postulated that a large portion of the endowment was for the shrine of Fatima al-Maʿsuma. The income from the numerous villages and properties outside the city of Qum were to be administered by the *mutawalli* (administrator) Sultan Ahmad al-Razavi. The terms of the endowment stated that the money was to be used by the *mutawalli* for the maintenance of the holy tomb and its environs (courtyards), and for the carpets, vessels and other necessities of the shrine. The building is identified with the woman who it commemorates, that is, the one with the same name as "the leader of the women of the world," Fatima al-Zahra. The shrine is described as divinely chosen, "the greatest of the great, the sublime, the pure, the magnificent, the radiant," and from whose canopies the people gain guidance and piety. The door of its great precinct would be made into a *qibla* from the desires of the nobility; the courtyard of its lofty resting place would become a Kaʿba for the wishes of the great and honorable ones. In the *waqfnāma,* a saying attributed to Imam Reza states that "whoever visits the shrine of my sister in Qum, is promised Paradise."[73] Veneration of the pious sister is also conspicuously evident in the *waqf* document of Shah Begi Begum, according to which the charitable act of endowment has been undertaken "with the desire that the blessings (*thawāb*) from it be upon the spirit of her ailing sister . . . , the crown of women and the queen of the angels of creation . . . , from the family of the joyous ones among the Muslims, . . . the deceased lady, the innocent, Beksi Khanum." The document is dated Safar A.H. 929 (1523).

In the same group of endowment deeds from Qum, there is one which mentions the *zāwīya* of Beksi Khanum.[74] While little is known about this sister of the queen, her immortalization by Shah Begi Begum's generous gift to the shrine of Fatima al-Maʿsuma highlights aspects of piety and patronage undertaken by the Safavid household in the early years of the dynasty. Primary clan relations at the turn of the sixteenth century, especially among the ruling elite, were shrouded in an air of religious adoration. Granting gifts to the shrines of holy men and women was a common practice through which aspects of the donors' religious commitment, as well as his or her financial and political power, was made public.[75] Another function of such charity was to make explicit one's own familial and social alliances. Endowing the *waqf* in such a way that the Divine favor gained by it would be conferred on a beloved relative, further accentuated the familial duty and serious intention of the founder. Who was chosen to receive the outward benefits of this charity was an expression of one's own loyalty. By donating the spiritual reward from her philanthropic *waqf* to the spirit of her sister, Shah Begi Begum was reinforcing not only her own familial ties, but also asserting her autonomy as a powerful political player in the Safavid court.[76]

The independence displayed by Shah Begi Begum in endowing the shrine of Fatima al-Maʿsuma brings to the fore the question of personal income. While the chroniclers document the considerable amount of wealth possessed by the Safavid queens and princesses, very little information is given as to how it was obtained. The identification of the famous and powerful wife of Shah Ismaʿil (Tajlu Khanum) through her own blood lineage (as Shah Begi Begum, daughter of Mihmad Beg Bektash Mausillu) may be construed as reflecting also the source of her wealth. The Qizilbash Turkmen and Safavids acquired status through cognate relationships, especially in terms of family recognition and allegiance, and wealth was similarly procured. Furthermore, adherence to Shiʿi laws and tribal customs allowed women greater equality in terms of inheritance. In Sunni law, outside of the rights given in the Qur'an, there are few provisions for female heirs to inherit; Shiʿi law as formulated in the eighth century, does not exclude women from sharing the family assets in company of male heirs. The closest relatives, irrespective of gender and from either the male or female side, inherit according to the Qur'anic divisions. This parity regarding inheritance (and also divorce) is attributed to the importance given to Fatima al-Zahra by the Shiʿi. As the sole link with the Divine lineage of Muhammad, without whom the Shiʿi imamate would not exist, she is revered and given rights comparable to those given a son.[77] Thus, the Shiʿi involvement with the family, beginning with that of the Prophet, gives a broad preference to the role of women, especially the daughter. In fact, one of the most cited events in the life of Fatima al-Zahra is that of the denial of her inheritance, which included the lands of Fadak and Khaybar. According to Shiʿi commentators, after the death of Muhammad, the Caliph Abu Bakr flatly refused to give to Fatima her share of the inheritance, saying that Muhammad had said that a prophet had no heirs and all his property was to be distributed as alms. The debate about the injustice done to the daughter of the Prophet and how she was denied her rights became a symbolic division between Shiʿi and Sunni scholars.[78]

In 1540, the substantial properties of Shah Begi Begum were confiscated by her son Shah Tahmasb, for treason against him, and she was banished to Shiraz. She died shortly afterwards, and was buried in the shrine of Bibi Dokhtaran (Lady of Daughters) in Shiraz.[79] Her position as the primary authoritative female figure was taken over by her daughter, Mahin Banu. This was the same woman whom Shah Tahmasb had earlier ritually betrothed to Muhammad al-Mahdi, the twelfth Shi'i Imam, insuring her celibacy and continued presence at his court.[80] Upon Mahin Banu's death in 1562, her properties were vested in Shah Tahmasb who managed the endowments made by this favorite sister in the name of the Fourteen Innocent Ones.[81] He instituted a *waqf* at the shrine of Fatima Ma'suma that included money for Qur'an recitation in her name, in order that the blessings from that devotion would benefit her spirit. Mahin Banu was buried in Qum, near the dome (*qubba*) of Fatima al-Ma'suma.[82]

Although Shah Begi Begum was herself buried in Shiraz, her daughter and at least one other female relation were buried at the shrine of Fatima al-Ma'suma.[83] The Safavid women were identified with this woman who, like themselves, shared the titles of Fatima al-Zahra and was associated with the family of the Prophet Muhammad. Ironically, even at this most venerated of feminine edifices, the most visible presence was that of a man: it is Shah Isma'il's name that is inscribed in the girdling inscription of the great iwan, not that of his counterpart, Shah Begi Begum, whose wealth most probably financed the construction. However, in both the epigraphy of the iwan and the *waqfnāma,* veneration is given to the family of Muhammad regardless of gender. In the iwan inscriptions, the Safavid claim is propagated by the image of the just ruler and godlike leader, Shah Isma'il. In the endowment deed, his consort's building and charitable donations provide a complimentary facet of religious authority, one of benevolence and generosity.

At the shrine of Fatima al-Ma'suma the women protagonists were mothers, sisters, wives, and daughters of the prestigious and wealthy families of the Safavid royalty. Taking advantage of their elevated status, these women affirmed their presence in the shrine, allowing us an insight into the cultural dynamics of the time. Kinship laws based on tribal codes were merged with Islamic perceptions of womanhood. As mentioned earlier, the prototype for the Safavid shah was variously Muhammad/'Ali/Husayn, or Mahdi, and the role model for womanhood was Fatima al-Zahra, daughter of Muhammad, wife of 'Ali, and mother of Husayn.[84] Thus, the Fatima depicted in the Shiʿi Safavid hagiographies is a woman with at least three familial aspects: daughter, wife and mother.[85] These are also attributes shared by Fatima al-Maʿsuma, Shah Begi Begum and her sister Beksi Begum in the 1523 *waqfnāma*.

Like the names of Muhammad, ʿAli and the other Imams, Fatima al-Zahra's is associated with one of the attributes of God, *al-fāṭir,* the Creator; as such, she is the symbol of earthly creation. In the Shiʿi hagiographies, Fatima al-Zahra is depicted as the grieved yet vengeful mother who stands to judgment before God, seeking divine retribution for the wrongdoing to her sons, Hasan and Husayn (who was martyred on the fields of Karbala).[86] Her *kunya,* or sobriquet, refers to her as *umm abīha* (Mother of her Father), a surprising and unusual term, suggesting once again a link with the Christian Mary, Mother of Jesus Christ. Like Mary, Fatima is seen as the "Mistress of Sorrows," mourning the death of her sons.[87] The mother figure was an important symbol for the Safavids and given a revered and elevated status. In Shah ʿAbbas' famous endowments of 1607, when his property and wealth in Isfahan was made mortmain in the names of the Prophet Muhammad, of the twelve imams, and of Fatima al-Zahra, a large portion of the spiritual reward went to his mother.[88] Writing about Shah ʿAbbas' building of the *sharbatkhāna* (a room for the distribution of sweet, perfumed water or milk, especially during religious feasts) at Ardabil in 1621, Jalal Munajjim also states that the building was endowed in the name of his mother, and this act was regarded as a highly religious event.[89] Here the veneration of the mother figure (like the idolization of the celibate sister Mahin Banu) represented a facet of male piety in which women became the vehicle for the dissemination of the Shah's religious persona. This secondary role played by the Safavid women reflects their recondite position in the social and religious milieu of their times, as the performers of charitable acts, and those in whose names such benevolence was undertaken.

While in the sixteenth-century sisters and daughters held privileged positions of power, by the seventeenth century, royal harem dynamics were transformed by the increased authority of the wife and mother. This was largely due to a change in marriage partners. Although Shah Tahmasb had begun the practice of contracting marriages to Georgian and Circassian women, when it came to succession, the sons who gained the throne were born of Turkmen mothers. During the reign of Shah ʿAbbas, however, shifts in the authority of royal women became more noticeable. The marriage alliances contracted for his daughters show a shift from Qizilbash followers chosen as husbands, to favoring the bureaucratic ʿulema and

Sayyids. As a result, the legitimacy of the Safavids as a tribal consortium began to change in favor of a more hierarchical and fixed patrimonial line of sovereignty. Fearing competition, Shah ʿAbbas had the royal princes confined to the harem where they were brought up away from the influence of tribal chieftains, in close association with the queens and princesses (much like the Ottoman system of family politics described elsewhere in this volume). Within the harem, concubine mothers gained greater control, overshadowing the Qizilbash guardian, who had earlier guided and reared the young princes.[90]

Changes in harem politics caused subtle displacements in attitude toward the Safavid family's patronage of the shrine of Fatima al-Maʿsuma. The women's authority was still veiled behind the actions of their male relatives, and the women from the family of Shah Begi Begum continued to frequent and make sizable donations to the shrine of their ideal. Although they did not leave permanent deeds such as that of Shah Begi Begum, their legacy is reflected in the burial and commemoration of four subsequent shahs of the Safavid dynasty: Shah Safi II, Abbas II, Sulayman, and Sultan Husayn were all buried in magnificent tombs at the shrine of Fatima al-Maʿsuma at Qum between 1629 and 1722. This marked shift in dynastic burial practice from Ardabil to Qum may have been due to increased orthodoxy or regional politics, but the most likely cause was the influence of the queen-mother. Her heightened political prestige in the court and sway over the young princes resident in the harem that she supervised must surely have contributed also to the great honor given to the shrine of Fatima al-Maʿsuma. As the institutional status of the queen-mother rose, so too did the status of Fatima al-Maʿsuma's shrine in Qum.

The early Safavid era has been described as one of "religious eclecticism" in which devotional attachment to the family of the Prophet Muhammad was widespread.[91] The Safavids benefited from the regard given to the *ahl al-bait* when they linked their own genealogy to that of the Shiʿi imams, and modeled their public personas after those of Muhammad, ʿAli and Fatima al-Zahra. Like their male kin, the women also participated in the propagation of the Safavid imperial image, that is, one dependent upon royal and religious authority. Shiʿi and Sufi devotion to the Safavid family was merged with Qizilbash tribal loyalty to produce a situation in which women had a complex and recondite position. Mistresses of their fortunes and active players in court politics, the Safavid women transcended gender inequality, yet often within fixed rules of social and religious expectation.

Like their predecessors, the Safavid family chose popularly venerated shrines in which to enact their vision of rulership, although their focus was particularly on those directly associated with the Shiʿi imamate. At the shrines, the Safavids disseminated an aura of sanctity and devotion, especially through the charity of women, or on their behalf. The buildings were embellished, money and food donated, and much land and property endowed for the prosperity of the shrines. In return, the rulers immortalized themselves and their loved ones; their names were inscribed in the architecture and their spirits forever blessed through religious foundations. At what was to become the dynastic shrine of the later Safavid shahs in Qum, the earliest interventions seen were those by women of the royal family. The shrine of Fatima al-Maʿsuma in Qum was a representative case in which the acts of piety undertaken by Shah Begi Begum in the name of her sister were a means of drawing attention to the extraordinary women of her family. Perhaps royal women enjoyed an economic autonomy and political agency greater than that available to less privileged women.[92] Their patronage was not indicative of the status of women in general, but gifts such as Shah Begi Begum's endowments to the shrine in Qum provide a rare and important window onto the cultural involvement of women of the Safavid house and their patronage during the early Safavid era.

## NOTES

I'd like to thank Gülru Neçipoglu and Nasser Rabbat for commenting on an earlier version of this paper, and D. Fairchild Ruggles for her editorial expertise. This paper is dedicated to my own role models, Doreen and Fateima.

1. H. R. Roemer, "The Safavid Period," *The Cambridge History of Iran,* vol. 6. (Cambridge: Cambridge University Press, 1986).

2. The familial genealogy was: Shaykh Safi al-din "Abu'l Fath" Ishaq bin Shaykh Amin al-din Gibrail bin al-Saleh bin Qutb al-din Abubakr bin Saleh al-din Rashid bin Muhammad al-Hafiz bin ʿAwaz bin [P]iroz al-Kurdi al-Sinjani "Zarin-kulah" bin Muhammad Sharfshah bin Muhammad bin Hasan bin Muhammad bin Ibrahim bin Jaʿfar bin Muhammad Ismaʿil bin Muhammad bin Ahmad al-ʿArabi bin Muhammad al-Qasim bin Abu'l Qasim Hamza bin Imam Musa al-Kazim bin Imam Jaʿfar al-Sadiq bin Imam Muhammad al-Baqir bin Imam Zain al-ʿAbidin ʿAli bin Imam Husayn bin Imam ʿAli bin Abi-Talib, in Ibn Bazzaz Ardabili, *Ṣafwat al-ṣafa* (759/1358), ed. Ahmad Karim Tabrizi (Bombay, 1911). Reprint (Ardabil: Danishga Azad Islami, 1990), p. 70; the version that circulated in the sixteenth century was edited by Abu'l Fath al-Husayni under orders of Shah Tahmasb in 1533.

3. I use the term Safaviyya to refer to the religious order prior to the imperial phase, after which the family will be called Safavid, in accordance with current scholarship. Kathryn Babayan, "The Safavid Synthesis: From Qizilbash Islam to Imamate Shiʿism," *Iranian Studies* 27 (1994): 135–62, esp. 138. For a more detailed analysis on the Qizilbash, see Babayan's "The Waning of the Qizilbash: The Spiritual and the Temporal in 17th-Century Iran" (Ph.D. diss., Princeton University, 1993). See also, Michel Mazzaoui, *The Origins of the Safawids: Shiʿism, Sufism and the Gulat* (Wiesbaden: F. Steiner, 1972).

4. The precedent for contracting political alliances had been set much earlier, for Ismaʿil's great grandfather Junayd was married to the sister of the Aqqoyunlu king, Uzun Hasan, with a great deal of fanfare and honour; Fadullah bin Ruzbihan Khunji-Isfahani, *Tārīkh-i ʿālamʿāra-i amīnī (Persia in AD 1478–1490),* trans. V. Minorsky (London: Royal Asiatic Society, 1992), 267. For an exhaustive documentation of women at the Safavi court, see Maria Szuppe's "La participation des femmes de la famille royale à l'exercise du pouvoir en Iran Safavide au XVIe siècle" in two parts, *Studia Iranica* 23 (1994): 211–58, and 24 (1995): 61–122.

5. For example, Mir Ghiyas al-din Muhammad Husayni Khwandamir, *Ḥabīb al-siyar fī akhbār afrād al-bashār* (Tehran, 1334/1954). Volumes 3 and 4 translated by W. Thackston Jr. as *Habibu's Siyar, Tome Three: The Reign of the Mongol and the Turk* (Cambridge, Mass.: Department of Near Eastern Languages and Civilizations, Harvard University, 1994). This was completed in 1524; Qazi Ahmad Qummi, *Khulasat al-Tavarikh,* ed. Ehsan Ishraqi, (Tehran: University of Tehran, 1984) completed in 1590; Iskander Munshi, *Tārīkh-i ʿālamʿāra-i ʿabbāsī,* ed. Iraj Afshar (Tehran, 1971), written during the reign of Shah ʿAbbas. Although Munshi's work is later than the period under consideration, it is based mainly on the earlier histories; the language for the description of the royal family is also in keeping with the general reverence bestowed on them by his predecessors.

6. This is an important turning point in the history of the Safavid rule, as it was during the reign of Shah ʿAbbas that a number of socioeconomic and religious reforms were undertaken that effectively also altered the role of the harem and its women inhabitants. Changes included transformations in the bureaucracy and shifting authority from Qizilbash tribesmen to the more urban Persian elite. Although these changes in policy had begun during the lifetime of Shah Ismaʿil himself, it was the transfer of power from Qazvin to the central Iranian city of Isfahan that made them irrevocable. On the urban elite, see Kathryn Babayan, "The ʿAqaʾid al-nisaʾ: A Glimpse of Safavid Women in Local Isfahani Culture," *Women in the Medieval Islamic World: Power, Patonage and Piety,* ed. G. R. G. Hambly (New York: St. Martin's Press, 1998).

7. Howayda al-Harithy suggests that women in Mamluk Egypt were participants in the political agenda of their male counterpoints, in that their patronage of religious buildings was a form of meditation between the "foreign" military

aristocracy and the civilians. This argument can also be applied to the case of the Safavids, where the royal women and men were part of a larger sociopolitical agenda in which the conquerors had to find ways of legitimizing their power and dogma. Howayda al-Harithy, "Female Patonage of Mamluk Architecture in Cairo," *Harvard Middle Eastern and Islamic Review* 1.2 (1994): 152–74.

8. Guity Nashat, "Women in Pre-Revolutionary Iran," in *Women and Revolution in Iran,* ed. Guity Nashat (Boulder, Colo.: Westview Press, 1983), p. 13.

9. Szuppe, "La participation des femmes de la famille royale" 23:213. When she cites the cases of the thirteenth-century Ayyubid/Mamluk queen Shajar al-Durr (d. 1250) and her contemporary in India, Razia Sultana (d. 1240) she reminds us of their Turkic origins.

10. See for example, Ann K. Lambton, *Continuity and Change in Medieval Persia, Aspects of Administrative, Economic and Social History* (Columbia Lectures on Iranian Studies 2, 1988).

11. Ann K. Lambton, "Concepts of Authority in Persia: 11th to 19th Centuries A.D.," *Iran* 26 (1988): 95–103, p. 100.

12. Rula Jurdi Abisaab, "The Ulama of Jabal ʿAmil in Safavid Iran, 1502–1736: Marginality, Migration and Social Change," *Iranian Studies* 27 (1994): 103–22.

13. Munshi, *Tārīkh,* 28. ʿAli, the fourth Caliph after Muhammad, was an important figure in Shiʿism as the reason for the split between Sunnis and Shiʿis. The Shiʿi contend that as the son-in-law and cousin of Muhammad and thus one of the venerated *al-i Muhammad,* ʿAli should have succeeded the caliphate upon the death of Muhammad, instead of Abu Bakr. See Moojan Momen, *An Introduction to Shiʿi Islam* (New Haven: Yale University Press, 1985).

14. Michele Membre, *Mission to the Lord Sophy (1539–42),* trans. A. H. Morton (London: School of Oriental and African Studies, University of London, 1993), 20.

15. Wheeler Thackston Jr., "The *Diwan* of Khataʾi: Pictures for the Poetry of the Shah Ismaʿil I," *Asian Art* 1.4 (1988): 37–63.

16. Moojan Momen, *An Introduction to Shiʿi Islam,* 14.

17. The Timurid eulogist, Kashifi devotes an entire section to Fatima. Husayn Waiz al-Kashifi, *Rawḍat al-Shuhudāʾ* (Tehran: Kitab-faroshi Islamiyya, 1952), 117–45.

18. Muhammad Baqir Majlisi, in his popular Persian treatise on the lives of the Fourteen Innocent Ones. Muhammad Baqir Majlisi, *Jalaʾ al-ʿayun* (Tehran: Intesharat Rashidi, 1983), 81.

19. Szuppe, "La participation des femmes de la famille royale," 23:241; Munshi, *Tārīkh,* 248. Women in the Mughal courts were also given titles elevating them to the status of Maryam; for example, Akbar gave his mother the title Maryam makani (Mary of both worlds) and Jahangir's mother was called Maryam al-zamani (Mary of the age); see Ellison Banks Findly, *Nur Jahan: Empress of*

*Mughal India* (Oxford: Oxford University Press, 1993), 94. The titles suggest an association of the queen-mother with the archetypal Christian mother, Mary.

20. Roemer, "The Safavid Period," 192.

21. For example, Qummi, *Khulasat al-Tavārīkh,* 415. Most events narrated by the Safavid historians are based on the biography of Shaykh Safi by Ibn Bazzaz Ardabili, *Ṣafwat al-ṣafa.* The story of envy and initiation in this event is similar to that describing the marriage of Fatima Sultan Begum, daughter of Shah Tahmasb. Iskander Munshi identifies her with the titles of *sabiyya-i qudsīa, Fatima, zuhrā-i zahrā;* Munshi, *Tārīkh,* 13. Also in Amir Mahmud bin Khwandamir, *Irān dar rūzgār-i Shāh Isma'il va Shāh Tahmasb Safavī,* ed. Iraj Afshar (Tehran: Kitabkhana Khayyam, 1370/1991), 38.

22. Szuppe, "La participation des femmes de la famille royale," 23:234. The biography of Amir Khan Mausillu is given in Munshi, *Tārīkh,* 140.

23. This section in Munshi is very revealing concerning the dynamics of marriage contraction. He mentions the marriage of another daughter of Tahmasb's, Shahrbanu, to Salman Khan, the leader of the Ostajlu tribes, who was then given the governorship of Shirvan. Munshi, *Tārīkh,* 260.

24. Szuppe, "La participation des femmes de la famille royale," 24:70, 77. Earlier Aqqoyunlu women had also held the position of intermediary and "diplomat," such as Uzun Hasan's mother Sara Khatun, who was sent to the Ottoman court of Mehmed II. See Leslie P. Peirce, *The Imperial Harem: Women and Sovereignty in the Ottoman Empire* (New York: Oxford University Press, 1993), 219.

25. Qummi, *Khulasat al-Tavārīkh,* 429.

26. Munshi, *Tārīkh,* 138. A fair amount of misogyny is noticed in Munshi's writing, where he credits the failure of the prince to his listening to the advice of feebleminded and intellectually limited women—"*zanān-i nāqis 'aql kutāh khard*"—however when he refers to the women of the Safavid household directly, it is with the utmost respect.

27. Szuppe, "La participation des femmes de la famille royale," 24:100.

28. Superficially, this construct is visible also in Mughal cases, for example, Jahanara Begum, the sister of Akbar; Gulbadan Begum, the daughter of Humayun; Nur Jahan, wife of Jahangir and mother of Shah Jahan.

29. For example, Ibn Babawaya (d. 381/991), *Al-amalī wa al-majālis,* quoted in Mahmoud Ayoub, *Redemptive Suffering in Islam* (The Hague: Mouton, 1978), 239. The original verse is from the Qur'an, Surat al-Imran (3:42–43). Fatima, like Maryam, also remained pure, a virgin, giving birth mystically from her left thigh, whereas Mary gave birth from her right. L. Veccia Vaglieri, "Fatima" in *Encyclopedia of Islam,* 2nd ed., 847.

30. Szuppe, "La participation des femmes de la famille royale," 23:243.

31. Such as Maulana Muhtasim Kashani.

32. Shohreh Gholsorkhi, "Pari Khan Khanum: A Masterful Safavid Princess," *Iranian Studies* 28 (1995): 143–56, p. 147.

33. Munshi, *Tārīkh,* 123.

34. I borrow the term "itinerant monarch" from Charles Melville, who has convincing shown that during the early phases of Safavi rulership, the notion of a capital "as the permanent center of government and administration" does not really apply. C. Melville, "From Qars to Qandahar: The Itineraries of Shah ʿAbbas I (995–1038/1587–1629)," *Études Safavides* (1993): 195–224.

35. Shah Tahmasb, *Tazkira-i Shāh Tahmāsb: sharh-i vāqayi va ahvālāt-i zindigāni-i Shāh Tahmāsb biqalam-i khudāsh,* Abd al-Shukur (Berlin-Charlottenburg and Tehran: Intesharat Sharq, 1343/1964), 23.

36. Munshi, *Tārīkh,* 566.

37. Ibid., 377.

38. Although Ardabil in the early period, and Qum in the later period, developed strong dynastic associations for the Safavids, the case of Mashhad is different. Very interesting chronological links can be formed between the military campaigns of Shah ʿAbbas and his building programs at Mashhad, where the political dynamics are seen. For example, Shah ʿAbbas' victory over the Uzbeks in 1598 was celebrated by generous endowments to the shrine of Imam Reza. Another famous pilgrimage of Shah ʿAbbas in 1601 from Isfahan to Mashhad corresponds to the end of successful campaigns in the northeast, which resulted in a large exodus of Uzbek princes into Iran, who were welcomed and settled in Isfahan. It was at this time that Shah ʿAbbas had the gold tiles of the dome replaced (which Shah Tahmasb had installed in 1526 and which were looted by the Uzbeks in 1589). At the shrine of Imam Reza, ʿAbbas gave burial spaces to his favorite government personel; for example Hatem Khan, his vizier who died in Tabriz (d. 1609) and is buried in a mausoleum (*gunbad*) which he had himself restored, and the renowned general Allahverdi Khan (d. 1613) who had also built his mausoleum (*gunbad*) during his own lifetime. Munshi, *Tārīkh,* 827, 871, respectively. Only one member of the Safavi family is buried in the immediate precincts, Maryam Sultan Begum (d. 1608), the daughter of Shah Tahmasb.

39. Munshi, *Tārīkh,* 123.

40. Modaressi Tabatabai, *Turbat-i Pākān,* 2 vols. (Qum: Chapkhana Mehr, 1390/1976), I:141.

41. Munshi, *Tārīkh,* 293.

42. Zain al-ʿAbidin ʿAbidi, *Ṣariḥ al-mılk* (Shawwal, A.H. 977). Ms. 3598, microfilm 10; Iran Bastan Museum, Tehran, n.p.

43. Membre, *Mission to the Lord Sophy*, 40. This is affirmed by the existing sixteenth-century gravestones in the graveyard of the shrine.

44. J. Calmard, "Kum," *Encyclopedia of Islam,* 2nd ed., 371.

45. Khunji-Isfahani, *Tārīkh-i ʿalamʿāra-yi āmīnī,* 280.

46. For more on this manuscript, see Martin B. Dickson and Stuart Cary Welch, *The Houghton Shah-nama* (Cambridge: Harvard University Press, 1981).

47. Qummi, *Khulasat al-Tavārīkh,* 79.

48. Khwandamir, *Ḥabīb al-Siyar fī akhbār afrād al-bashār,* 510.

49. Qummi, *Khulasat al-Tavārīkh,* 266.

50. Munshi, *Tārīkh,* 224–25.

51. Ibid., 250.

52. Ibid, 79.

53. Bijan Saadat, *The Holy Shrine of Imam-zadeh Fatima Maʿsuma,* 2 vols. (Shiraz: Asia Institute, Pahlavi University, 1977), I:24; Calmard, "Kum," 371.

54. The *waqfnāma* of Shah Begi Begum is reproduced in Tabatabai, *Turbat-i Pākān,* 131.

55. "[This lamp is found] in house which Allah hath allowed to be exalted and that His name shall be remembered therein. Therein do offer praise to Him at morn and evening. Men whom neither merchandise nor sale beguileth from remembrance of Allah and constancy in prayer and paying to the poor their due; who fear the day when hearts and eyeballs will be overturned; that Allah may reward them with the best of what they did, and increase reward for them His bounty. Allah giveth blessings without stint to whom He will. As for those who disbelieve, their deeds are as a mirage in a desert. The thirsty one supposeth it to be water till he cometh unto it and findeth it naught, and findeth, in the place thereof, Allah Who payeth him his due; and Allah is swift at reckoning" (24: 36–39).

56. As not all of the names are God's attributes, such as "the Proof" and "the Glorious (Majestic)," the question becomes "to whom do they refer?" The presence of this medallion in the most prestigious Safavid shrines hints at a self-referential Safavid identification. However, similar (but not exact) medallions are also present in the Blue Mosque in Tabriz, and appear in earlier fifteenth-century manuscripts.

57. In Mashhad two more attributes are added, "the Imam, the Forgiver" (*yā imām, yā ghufrān*).

58. Modaressi Tabatabai, *Turbat-i Pākān,* 64.

59. *Hadi al-khalāʾiq ilā ashraf al-adyān.* The same designations of the king, the precedent having being set here, are copied later in another section of the courtyard, on an inscription dedicated to Shah Tahmasb, dated A.H. 950.

60. Written by Vali al-Husayni, who is no doubt the same Sayyid Vali Qummi mentioned in Qadi Ahmad Qummi's *Gulshan al-Hunar,* as being a master of the *thuluth* script. Qazi Ahmad mentions that the inscriptions on the *suffa* and the doorway of Hazrat Maʿsuma are in his hand. Apparently the inscriptions on the inside and outside of the dome of the same edifice were written by Maulana Haydar Qummi, another master calligrapher. Qazi Ahmad Qummi, *Calligraphers and Painters: A Treatise by Qadi Ahmad, Son of Mir Munshi (1015/1606),* trans. V. Minorsky (Washington: Freer Gallery of Art, 1959), 74.

61. Reference to the "Innocent Imams" is also made in a 938/1531 inscription in the Isfahan congregational mosque, dedicated to Shah Tahmasb; see Lutfallah Hunarfar, *Ganjīna-i āthār-i tārīkh-i Isfahān* (Isfahan: Sagafi, 1965).

62. For a study of Qur'an exegesis on this subject, see Moshe Sharon, "*Ahl al-Bait*—People of the House," *Jerusalem Studies in Arabic and Islam* 8 (1986): 169–84.

63. "*Mathal ahl al-bait kamathal safinat nūh, min rakab fiha naja wa min takhaluf ʿanha gharq.*" These verses are very common during the Safavid period, appearing as epigraphy in the Qum and Ardabil shrines; they were also often repeated by the Safavid chroniclers to reinforce the Safavid genealogy. See Khwandamir, *Ḥabīb al-siyar fi akhbār afrād al-bashār,* 459, and Qummi, *Khulasat al-Tavārīkh,* 15. The theme is taken up also in Safavid miniatures; for example a famous image of the *ahl al-bait* is in the *Shāhnāma-i shāhi* of Firdawsi (Houghton Shahnama), "The Ship of Shiʿism," folio 18 verso; reproduced in Stuart Cary Welch, *A King's Book of Kings* (New York: Metropolitan Museum of Art, 1972).

64. Tabatabai, *Turbat-i Pākān,* 131–41.

65. "*ʿAlīa hazrat makhdūma-i ʿazamī bānu-i kubrī, malaka-i malkāt ʿalam sarwar-i matharāt-i umm, manaʿma-i, muḥsana-i makthara-i makrama-i maʿzama-i rafiʿa-i jalīla-i hakima, ʿadila sultana al-khawātīn al-matharat muhzara-i anwah al-saʿdat wa insāf al-makarmāt, . . . bānīa-i mubarāt-i ʿazima, mo'assa-i asās-i khairāt jasīma, asār-i taharāt wa salah az khayām-i rafiatash tabān . . .ʾasmat al-dunyā wa al-dīn, Shāh Begī Begum,*" ibid., 135.

66. The name Tajlu Khanum is a pet name, sometimes given to more than one person in a family. Morton in Membre, *Mission to the Lord Sophy,* 82.

67. According to Tabatabai, Tajlu Khanum is responsible for the iwan and dome reconstructions of A.H. 925, which is quite plausible, given her connections to the shrine and her other charitable works; however, I was unable to find any specific architectural or programmatic evidence either in the epigraphy or other texts I consulted.

68. Qummi, *Khulasat al-Tavārīkh,* 290. In the *Ṣariḥ al-milk* of ʿAbidi it is mentioned that a Begi Sultan, known by (Qalajlu/Tajlu?) bint Hamza Agha bin Murad Agha Rumlu had endowed the tomb of Shah Ismaʿil in Ardabil.

69. The title "*al-sultān al-ʿadl*" was also shared by the Ilkhanid princess, Sati Beg Khan (daughter of Uljeitu); see Gavin R. G. Hambly, "Becoming Visible: Medieval Islamic Women in History and Historiography," in Hambly, *Women in the Medieval Islamic World: Power, Patronage and Piety,* 13.

70. For example, after her husband's death in 1524, she was consulted along with the male tribal leaders, regarding the coronation of her son Tahmasb. Qummi, *Khulasat al-Tavārīkh,* 176.

71. Ibid, 186. Also mentioned in Szuppe, "La participation des femmes de la famille royale," 24:72.

72. Munshi, *Tārīkh,* 224.

73. This is also found in a book of *ḥadīth* attributed to Imam Reza, collected by the tenth-century scholar, Ibn Babawiya, *ʿAyvān al-akhbār al-riḍa* (Tehran, 1977), 713. Muhammad Baqir Majlisi also repeats this *ḥadīth* in a section devoted

to pilgrimage to the shrine of Fatima al-Maʿsuma, in his *Tuhfat al-zāirīn* (Tehran, 1897), 543. Interestingly, the prayers for this pilgrimage include sisters, aunts, and mothers of the imams!

74. Tabatabai, *Turbat-i Pākān,* 133.

75. This is, of course, not novel or specific to the Safavid case. Earlier and similar examples can also be found in India, Iran, Turkey, and Egypt. See also Richard M. Eaton, "Political and Religious Authority of the Shrine of Baba Farid," in *Moral Conduct and Authority: The Place of Adab in South Asian Islam,* ed. B. D. Metcalf (Berkeley: University of California Press, 1984) 333–56; Eva Maria Subtelny, "Socio-Economic Bases of Cultural Patronage under the Late Timurids," *International Journal of Middle East Studies* 20.4 (1988): 479–505; Raymond Lifchez (ed.), *The Dervish Lodge: Architecture, Art and Sufism in Ottoman Turkey* (Berkeley: University of California, 1992); Lenore Fernandes, "The Evolution of the Khanqah Institution in Mamluk Egypt" (Ph.D. diss., Princeton University, 1980).

76. A point proven in the histories and chronicles. See Szuppe, "La participation des femmes de la famille royale," 24:71. In his article on the 1604 and 1614 *waqfs* of Shah ʿAbbas, Robert McChesney makes the argument that the main motivation there was politcal legitimacy concerning the Safavid dynasty. R. McChesney, "Waqf and Public Policy: The Waqfs of Shah ʿAbbas, 1011–1023/1602–1614," *Asian and African Studies* 15 (1991): 165–90.

77. Wilfred Madelung, "Shiʿi Attitudes toward Women as Reflected in Fiqh," in *Society and the Sexes in Medieval Islam,* ed. A. L. al-Sayyid-Marsot (Malibu, Calif.: Undena Publications, 1979), 74–75. Also see Moojan Momen, *An Introduction to Shiʿi Islam,* 183. Some of these rights were curtailed in the late seventeenth century by the likes of Muhammad Baqir Majlisi. For an analysis of Majlisi's writing on the rights of women, see Adele K. Ferdows and Amir H. Ferdows, "Women in Shiʿi Fiqh: Images through the Hadith," in Nashat, *Women and Revolution in Iran.* These authors depict the scholar as an extreme misogynist. For our analysis, however, distinction must be made between royal Safavid women and their nonaristocratic counterparts.

78. Vaglieri, "Fatima," 844.

79. Qummi, *Khulasat al-Tavārīkh,* 290.

80. Morton, relying on Qummi's *Khulasat al-Tavārīkh,* writes: "Her piety and purity were such as to enthrall Tahmasb, who dedicated her by vow to the Mahdi or twelfth imam, consulted her in all state affairs and did not act without her approval, making her the 'Queen of the Age, the Mistress of the time.'. . . Her place as the Mahdi's wife to be was later taken by one of Tahmasb's daughters." Membre, *Mission to the Lord Sophy*, 80.

81. On Shah Tahmasb's behalf, the actual administration was undertaken by Mir Kalantar, a Sayyid from Astarabad. Munshi, *Tārīkh,* 150.

82. Her coffin remained there until 1584, when it was removed to Karbala. Qummi, *Khulasat al-Tavārīkh,* 431.

83. There is a gravestone found at the Shrine of Fatima al-Ma'suma, dated 941 (1535), which records the death of another female relative of Shah Begi Begum: Aga Shah Khatun, the daughter of Hamza Beg bin Bektash Beg Mausillu. Tabatabai, *Turbat-i Pākān,* 133.

84. For other important female role models in Shi'ism, see David Pinault, "Zaynab bint 'Ali and the Place of the Women of the Households of the First Imams in Shi'ite Devotional Literature," in Hambly, *Women in the Medieval Islamic World: Power, Patronage and Piety.*

85. Shaykh al-Mufid does not devote any specific chapter to Fatima al-Zahra, but she is always an important and crucial adjunct to the narrative, her role shifting according to her relationship with her male kin; Shaykh al-Mufid, *Kitāb al-irshād,* trans. I. K. A. Howard (New York: Tahrik-i Tarsil-i Quran, 1981). The seventeenth-century theologian and historian Muhammad Baqir Majlisi devotes the second chapter of his Persian hagiography to Fatima, giving it as great importance as the Prophet, Muhammad (but, of course, most of the emphasis is on Husayn!). Muhammad Baqir Majlisi, *Jala' al-'ayun.*

86. Mahmoud Ayoub, *Redemptive Suffering in Islam,* 212.

87. Barbara Freyer Stowasser, *Women in the Qur'an: Traditions and Interpretation* (New York: Oxford University Press, 1994), 80.

88. McChesney, "Waqf and Public Policy: The Waqfs of Shah 'Abbas," 170.

89. Jalal al-Din Munajim, *Tārīkh-i 'abbāsī, yā rūznāme-i mullā jalāl,* ed. S. Vahidniya (Tehran: Intesharat Vaheed, 1965), 301. In an administrative manual written in the beginning of the eighteenth century, the belongings of the royal *sharbatkhāna* are listed: "vessels of gold, silver, china, glazed ware (*kashi*) and copper, as well as crystal sugar, candy (*qand*), medicinal herbs (*'aqaqir*), coffee, tobacco, glass; tops, tubes (*sar-na-nay*) and other accessories of hookahs; *halila, amula,* and other preserves; lemon juice, rose-water, etc., spirits (*'araq*?), *turshi* (pickles), perfumes, etc.." *Tadhkirat al-Muluk: A Manual of Safavid Administration,* trans. V. Minorsky (London: Luzac, 1943).

90. Kathryn Babayan, *The Waning of the Qizilbash,* 80; see also her article, "The 'Aqa'id al-nisa': A Glimpse at Safavid Women in Local Isfahani Culture," in Hambly, *Women in the Medieval Islamic World: Power, Patronage and Piety;* Roemer, "The Safavid Period," 278.

91. S. Amir Arjomand, *The Shadow of God and the Hidden Imam* (Chicago: University of Chicago Press, 1984), 106.

92. In the *Ṣariḥ al-milk* of 'Abidi many transactions are undertaken on behalf of women, from as early as the fourteenth century. Here, women are portrayed as business partners, owning stores and property, as well as patrons, endowing money and donations to the Shrine of Shaykh Safi al-Din in Ardabil. Many of the women in the later (sixteenth century onwards) periods belonged to the extended Safavid-Zahidi family.

8

# Public and Private for Ottoman Women of the Nineteenth Century

*Nancy Micklewright*

Defining the terms public and private, and developing an understanding of the implications of these concepts for the study of society has occupied feminist scholars from a number of disciplines for the past two decades. Traditionally, historians have explained the apparent absence of women in European history by differentiating between the well-documented public life of men and the minimally recorded lives of women that occurred behind closed doors, away from the historian's scrutiny. Because there are such apparently clear boundaries between public and private life and space in Islamic societies, scholars of the Middle East have been quick to apply theoretical models developed for the study of other societies to their own work, and just as quickly have realized that this was unsatisfactory. As the body of historical research on gender issues in the Middle East has slowly grown, various definitions or redefinitions of public and private in an Islamic context have been proposed.[1]

A particularly cogent analysis for the concepts of public and private for the Ottoman world of the sixteenth and seventeenth centuries is presented in the 1993 ground-breaking book, *The Imperial Harem,* by Leslie Peirce. Her work is based on an extensive examination of a variety of written records, among them archival documents and contemporary histories. She demonstrates that the practices of seclusion assumed to govern the lives of imperial women also applied in many cases to men, and were understood as demonstrating social and political status, rather than marking gender. In this paper, I will examine similar issues but will draw on a more visual category of evidence, women's dress in nineteenth-century Istanbul. My scope of analysis, instead of public and private in the Ottoman court of the sixteenth and seventeenth centuries, will be the households of the elite of nineteenth-century Istanbul.

Although costume has long been recognized and used as a historic document in the history of European and North American art, and in other disciplines as well, it is less common in Middle Eastern studies.[2] I will therefore begin by laying out the conceptual framework of my research. My first, and most basic premise, is that the body, male or female, is a primary site for the negotiation of social identity. Dress, which is at once pervasive and personal, is intimately and inextricably involved in the negotiation process. Clothing choices demonstrate the identification, real or desired, with particular groups within the social universe of the wearer, and should be understood as operating within several social networks at once. At any particular historical moment, clothing—or as Roland Barthes has called it, the fashion system—is an intricately nuanced system of communication by which individuals may signal their gender, class, occupation, nationality, and religion, to name only the most obvious of social groupings. Specific modes of dress are understood by those within a fashion system to signal power and status, and access to these modes of dress is contested, especially at times of political or social unrest. Finally, clothing and what it signals is acutely sensitive to the slightest alterations in the human condition. Thus costume reflects individual taste, serving to distinguish one person from another, while at the same time providing shared visual signals that proclaim the wearer's membership in particular social groups.

Although scholars of European or North American dress, particularly contemporary fashion, are quick to acknowledge the pace and significance of change, many of these same scholars, when they turn their attention to so-called ethnic costume, erroneously assume a static form of traditional dress. In some cases, this assumption can be blamed on a lack of surviving evidence, so that in the absence of surviving garments or other documents recording changes, it is assumed that change simply did not occur. Additionally, there is also a premise that nonwestern or non-modern society is somehow ahistorical or unchanging.[3]

Clothing serves as a barrier between a person and the rest of the world, and in one sense is the ultimate delineator of public and private (as these terms are understood in the West): that which is not seen (the body) is private, and that which is seen (the clothing) is public. Historians of visual culture typically regard walls as the principal separator of public from private spaces, but dress is a far more fundamental agent of separation. Although dress was a form of display that operated behind the protective walls of the home, where elite Ottoman women spent much of their lives, it was also meant to be seen by others and thus was, to some degree, "public." Looking at their dress is a material means of studying Ottoman women that provides information not available from written sources.[4] A study of the dress of Ottoman women allows us to understand how women perceived or wished to present themselves in their world, and how they used costume to signal their membership in certain social groups.

My study of women's dress is based on a variety of sources, first and foremost of which are the costumes themselves.[5] From collections in Turkey, North America, and Great Britain, I have been able to identify twenty garments that have enough accompanying information concerning date and provenance to be useful. Close analysis of other materials such as contemporary writing and photographs allows me to contextualize the costumes. These additional primary sources included the writings of European women and some men travelers, missionaries, diplomats, and residents in Istanbul. In the last decade a great deal of research has been done, in publicizing, analyzing, and in some cases republishing the work of a number of writers, and in assessing the value of this genre of literature for various projects. The work of women writers in particular, with greater access to the domestic environments where clothing was displayed, and generally more useful as observers of dress, has received a fair amount of attention.[6] Julia Pardoe, the British woman whose 1837 account of her visit to the Ottoman Empire in the 1830s, *The City of the Sultan*, is one of the most detailed and useful of the travel accounts for the study of costume, gives this description of the dress of a wealthy woman, and provides a good example of the kind of information available from these sources,

> Her costume was an odd admixture of the European and Oriental. She wore trousers of pale blue cotton flowered with yellow; and an antery of light green striped with white and edged with a fringes of pink floss silk; while her jacket, which was the production of a Parisian dress-maker, was of dove-colored satin, wadded, and furnished with a deep cape and a pair of immense sleeves, fastened at the wrists with diamond studs.[7]

Another important source is autobiographical writing by Ottoman women, such as the writings of Zeyneb Hanoum, published in 1913, Emine

Foat Tugay's family history, published in 1963, Halide Edib's memoirs of 1926, and the autobiography of Leyla (Saz) Hanımefendi, written in 1920/1921.[8] Leyla (Saz) Hanımefendi, born in about 1850, spent her most of her childhood and adolescence at the palace as a companion to the royal princesses, as well as becoming one of the first well-known female composers and musicians. Her memoirs are a treasure trove of information about life at court, full of description and detail. For example, here is part of her account of the celebrations that took place at court upon the return of Sultan Abdül Aziz from Europe in 1867:

> The *sultanes* wore green dresses,[9] quite light, and trimmed with beautiful white lace. They had long trains and they wore big diadems along with rather simple necklaces. The older *kalfas* also wore green dresses, some plain, some striped and some even with polka dots. The youngest girls wore light green dresses mixed with white and some wore white dresses, trimmed with green, along with small flowered patterns or small green ribbons. At this period, the young ladies and young girls had completely abandoned the old dresses with three tails or trains and the baggy pants underneath; fashion now demanded skirts with a single train which was caught up and attached to the belt—there were now petticoats instead of *şalvars* or the baggy pants previously worn. The headdresses had also changed with the times and now usually matched the costumes; there were earrings with jewels, medallions and elaborate hairstyles, garnished with precious stones. (p. 162)

The writings of other Ottoman women include similarly detailed accounts of aspects of their lives. While the focus of the accounts differ from author to author, all provide useful information for understanding the dress of the women of the Ottoman elite of Istanbul.

In the nineteenth century, there was an active foreign language press, with its fashion columns and business advertisements, which included the *Journal de Constantinople, La Turquie, The Levent Herald, The Oriental Advertiser/Le Moniteur Oriental,* and *Le Temps.* All of these newspapers included news of social events, politics, and business, from the vantage point of the European community. *The Oriental Advertiser,* for example, ran a column every Thursday called "Courrier de la Mode," describing the latest Parisian fashions. The newspapers are extremely useful for noting the availability of European goods and services in the city, since they took advertising and also marked the comings and goings of commercial vessels and all sorts of people. The ads were of two kinds—private, for instance a seamstress or governess advertising for clients, and commercial, which included among other businesses, importers of sewing machines, and shops selling ready-made clothing and fabric imported from France and England.

With regards to visual representation, costume manuscripts are a useful source because they illustrate the dress worn by various members of Ottoman society, but they are problematic since little is known about their purpose or the workshops that produced them.[10] A particularly valuable, but hugely difficult body of material are the many photographs of Turkish women from the nineteenth century that have been published in some number from the late 1970s onward. Although a number of early publications treated these images as though they provided a true and unmediated view of the nineteenth-century world, more critical studies have addressed the serious issues of representation, misrepresentation, and manipulation that the photographs foreground. The historical photographs are indeed a valuable source for cultural study but are not necessarily useful as unmediated documents of what they purport to illustrate.[11] Two extremes in the kind of information presented by historical photographs are illustrated by the image (half of a stereo view) marketed by the successful international firm of Underwood and Underwood, entitled Favorites of the Harem, from circa 1900, and the portrait by the Ottoman photographer Ali Sami of his sister at home circa 1880–90 (figs. 8.1 and 8.2). The Underwood and Underwood image, produced most probably in a New York studio, evokes an image of the harem popular at the time, complete with five scantily dressed women whose poses invite the viewer's gaze. While we can not say for sure if consumers at the time would have recognized this image as a fabrication, modern photo historians certainly can, thanks to its complete lack of resemblance to actual Ottoman interiors or dress. Unfortunately, there are many other photographs of Ottoman women that are equally as constructed but in much more subtle ways, and are thus much more misleading as documents for the study of costume. Photographs produced by Ottoman photographers (as opposed to the Europeans who dominated commercial photography in Istanbul) of their friends and family give us a different view of women. Ali Sami's view of his sister shows us a woman dressed in a skirt and blouse similar to what would have been worn by a woman at that time in London or Paris. She is standing near furniture of European design and paintings, of a sort that would not have been available in Istanbul several decades earlier, are displayed on the wall. While this photograph may be equally as constructed as the previous example, its very constructedness gives us useful information about the cultural aspira-

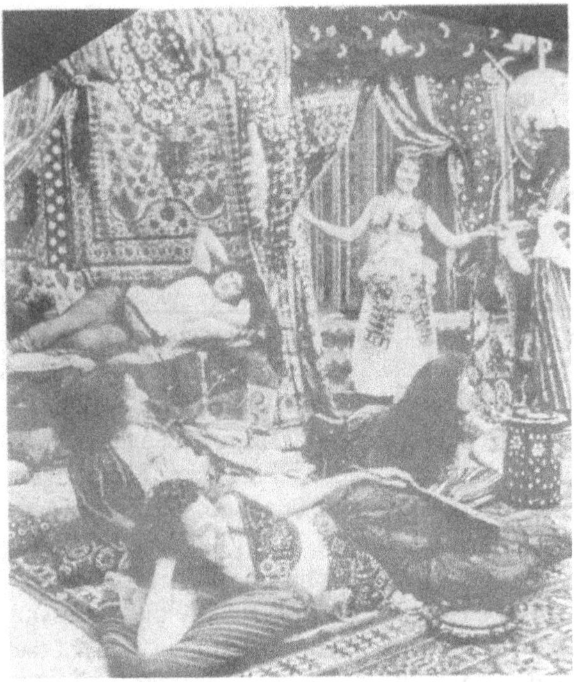

**Fig. 8.1.** Half of stereo view, *Favorites of the Harem* (marketed by Underwood and Underwood, c. 1900). The fantastic view of harem life offered by this photograph is an excellent example of why historical photographs cannot be treated as unmediated "windows on the past."

tions, expressed through dress and interior furnishings, of this member, and perhaps by extension, this family of the Ottoman elite.

A last group of visual documents is the work of painters, both Europeans (or other foreigners) and nineteenth-century Ottoman artists. Like historical photographs, the work of Orientalist painters raises a number of complex, interrelated issues focusing on colonialism, the role of art in defining and perpetuating cultural stereotypes, and the relationship between art, commerce and government, to name only a few.[12] *Shopping in the Harem,* the work of a Baghdad-born Hungarian painter, S. A. Swoboda (fig. 8.3), gives us a detailed and engaging view of three harem women examining the wares of an itinerant female merchant. Of interest for details of costume as well as gaining an understanding of how business was conducted from the harem, it is impossible to place much faith in the facts of the painting since there is

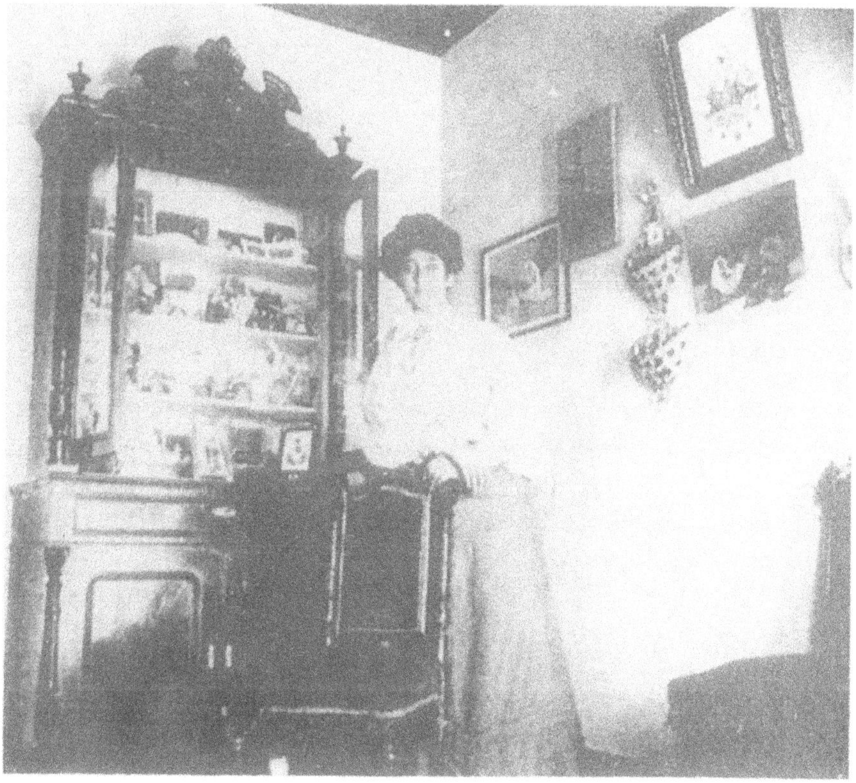

**Fig. 8.2.** Portrait of his sister by the Ottoman photographer Ali Sami. Family photographs such as this are useful sources for costume history, but they are difficult to obtain, since most are still hidden in the albums and private collections for which they were originally made.

no evidence that the artist was actually able to observe his subjects in real life, or indeed that an accurate depiction of the subjects was his intent.

Each of these categories is a problematic source, yet each can provide essential information for the study of costume history. The Ottoman women's press that emerged in the last decades of the nineteenth century lies outside the frame of the present study (due primarily to the late date of most of the publications); however, it is a very rich source of fashion and other information, as the work of Elizabeth Frierson in this volume and elsewhere has shown.[13]

Now, what can we learn from this disparate group of dresses, newspapers, photographs, paintings, and books? It is essential to acknowledge

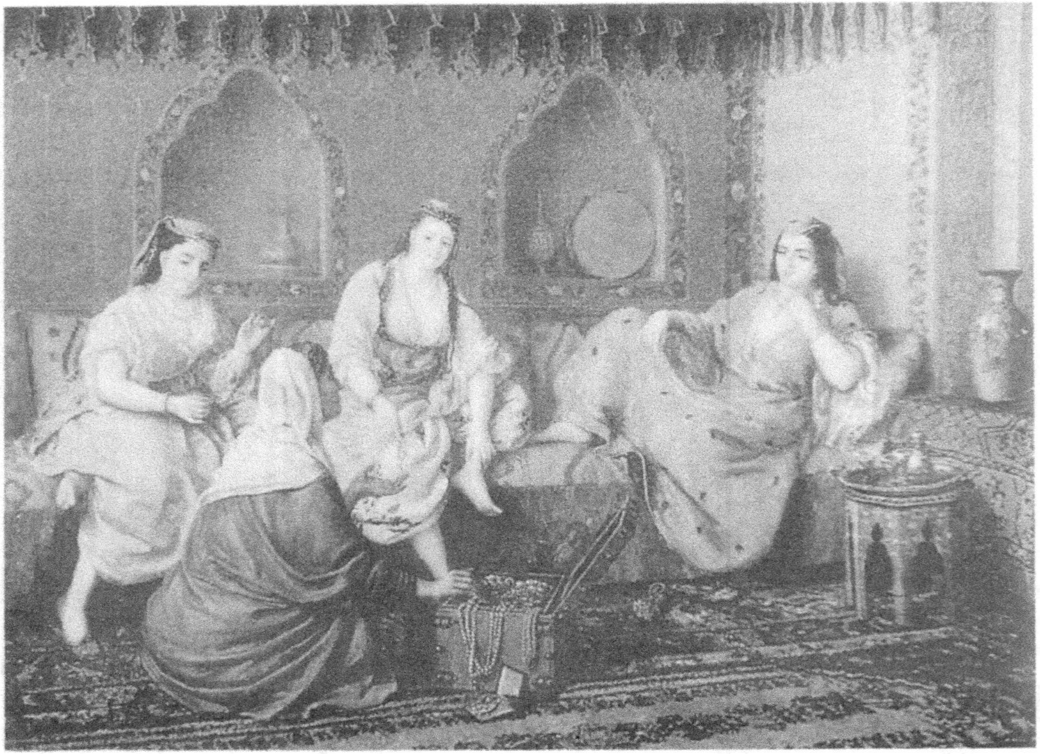

**Fig. 8.3.** Oil painting on canvas, *Shopping in the Harem,* signed by Sandor Alexander Swoboda, c. mid-19th century (Dolmabahçe Sarayı collection, courtesy of the National Palaces, Istanbul). It is not clear that Swoboda had access to the type of scene he recreates here, although many of the details of the furnishings seem accurate.

at the outset that my work focuses on the women of the elite, since it is their costume that has been saved in family trunks and private collections. It is they who attracted most of the attention of visitors, photographers and painters, and they who wrote, both for themselves and for one another. It is virtually impossible to study the lives of poor women through the medium of costume, since their clothing has completely disappeared and is rarely documented by other sources.

The problem that I originally addressed in my research was how to understand the dramatic change in women's dress that took place in Istanbul in the course of several decades, reflected in a representation of a harem woman from a late-eighteenth-century costume manuscript in the German Archaeological Institute (fig. 8.4), and Osman Hamdi Bey's portrait of Naîle Hanım, from the end of the nineteenth century (fig. 8.5). The harem woman wears a version of the loosely tailored, layered costume in several pieces that was typical of Ottoman dress for both men and women, while Naîle Hanım's dress is a closely fitted, one-piece garment produced by a tailor or seamstress conversant with European fashions. These two images span nearly a century, but most of the changes in dress took place in the thirty-year period between about 1830 and 1860. The construction of historical periods from a span of years is always an arbitrary exercise, whose exact parameters are determined by the particular matters under consideration. In this case, although a period of transition, such as the fashion change discussed here, is by definition a process and thus difficult to pinpoint with dates, there are a few historic events that were significant in the process and serve as convenient brackets. One was the 1829 decree of Sultan Mehmed II regulating men's dress; another was the royal visit of both the French Empress Eugenie and the Prince and Princess of Wales to Istanbul in 1866. The royal visits generated intense social activity among both the expatriate foreign communities and the court, details of which were reported in the press. Both royal women paid visits to the Ottoman women of the court, and the French empress in particular was considered to be the epitome of fashionable elegance. There are numerous references to the impact that the Empress Eugenie in particular had on women's fashion at the court, of which the following is typical:

> During the reign of Sultan Abdul Aziz, when the Empress Eugenie came on a visit to Stamboul, she caused a revolution in Harem fashions. She was then in the heydey of her beauty, and the Sultan admired her openly. . . . Little by little, European styles of dressing, of arranging the hair crept into the palace. . . . By 1870 the old fashions had been forgotten.[14]

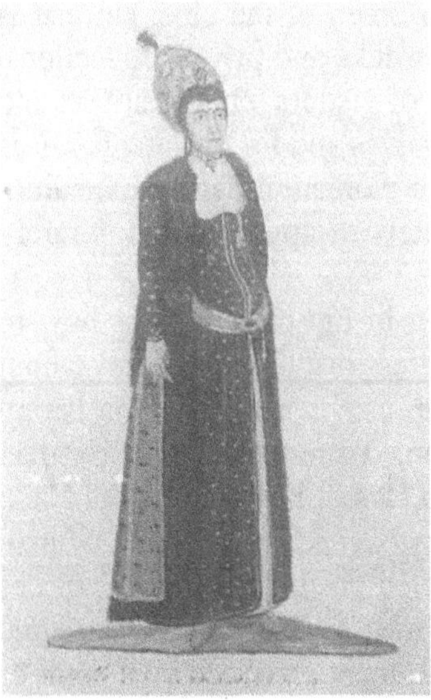

**Fig. 8.4.** Page from a costume manuscript, late eighteenth century (courtesy of the German Archaeological Institute in Istanbul). The woman in this painting, identified by the caption at the bottom of the page as a Turkish woman in winter dress, wears a long white undershirt (*gomlek*), baggy trousers (*şalvar*), an *entari* held closed by buttons and a belt, with a sleeveless, fur-trimmed *entari* on top. She wears jewellery and her headdress is decorated with a plume and a jewelled ornament.

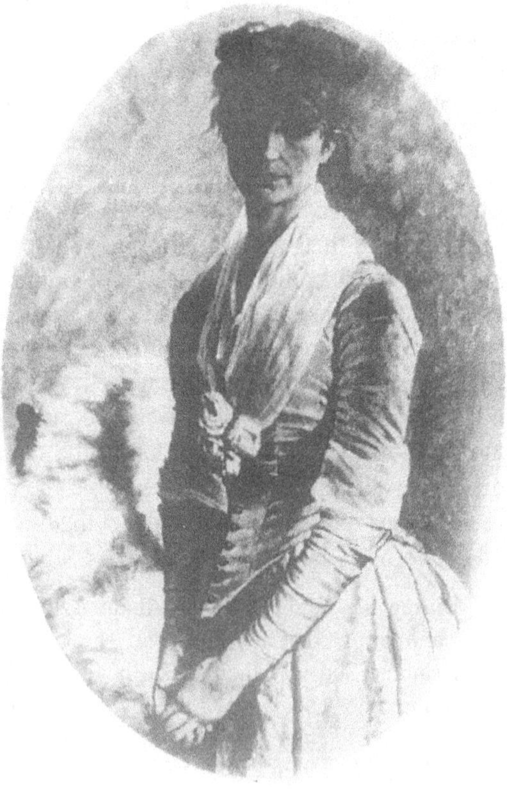

**Fig. 8.5.** Portrait of Naîle Hanım, by Osman Hamdi Bey, late nineteenth century (courtesy of the Istanbul Museum of Painting and Sculpture). Osman Hamdi Bey was the first director of the Istanbul Archaeological Museum and a prominent painter of Orientalist themes as well as portraits of the Ottoman elite.

The decades between 1830 and 1860 were a particularly tumultuous time for the people of Istanbul. The numbers of Europeans present in the city and the availability of European goods increased dramatically as a result of improvements in steamship service across the Mediterranean, developments in the economic relations between the Ottoman Empire and Europe, and political events such as the Crimean War (1853–56). Political and social change kept pace with demographic changes and as the century progressed, began to have far-reaching effects on Ottoman society.[15] While the most dramatic costume transformations took place within these years, they proceeded at different rates among different social groups. Indeed the process of change has not ended; fashion continues to be used today in Istanbul, as it is everywhere, as a social marker.

The nineteenth-century fashion changes among the women of Istanbul followed a pattern observed elsewhere, in which individual elements of a foreign costume tradition are adopted first before the embracing of entire ensembles.[16] In the Ottoman example, it was parasols, gloves, and slippers, mostly imported from France. In fact, parasols became an important and relatively long-lived fashion accessory for Ottoman women, as numerous paintings and photographs indicate. Another way of experimenting with the new costume was the substitution of a foreign garment for a similar familiar one. A costume in the Topkapı Sarayı collection (which contains garments originally made for members of the harem) provides a good example of this practice, which is also reported by European women observers, including Julia Pardoe, as quoted above. The three-piece ensemble should be dated between about 1825 and 1835, based on construction similarities between the jacket and other dated examples. The costume consists of the three typical pieces: oversized trousers or *şalvar,* a robe-like garment called the *entari,* and a short jacket, or *cepken* (fig. 8.6), all meticulously handsewn from the same fine mauve wool twill. As the drawing indicates, the jacket has been constructed using European-style tailoring and decorative techniques, in sharp contrast to the less tailored traditional style, which would not have had set in, gathered sleeves, or cuffs, or tucks. While this fashionable jacket is functionally equivalent to a traditional *cepken,* its shape looks completely foreign. The familiar *entari* incorporated a new style reflected in a garment now in the collection of the Yapı ve Kredi Bankası in Istanbul (fig. 8.7). Here the normal construction, carried out in a blue compound weave with a floral design in yellow, green, red, and purple, is modified to include the addition of cuffs on the sleeves and the beginnings of a waist. Two garments from the Topkapı Sarayı collection

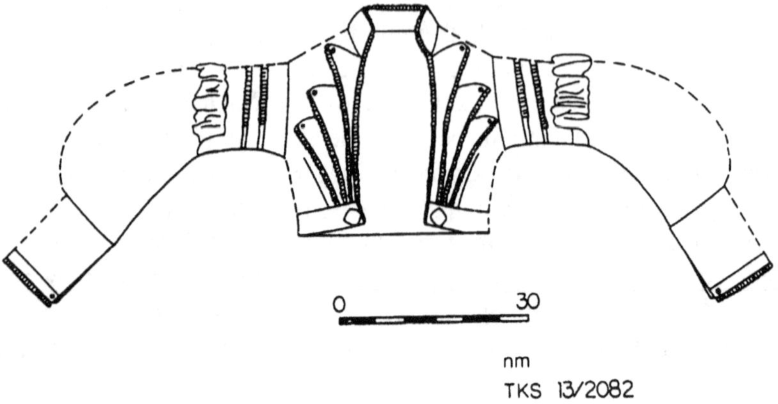


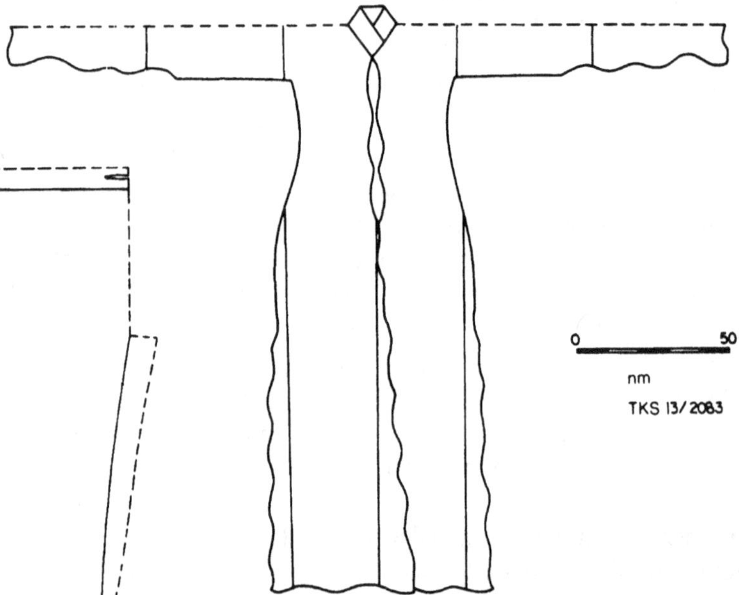


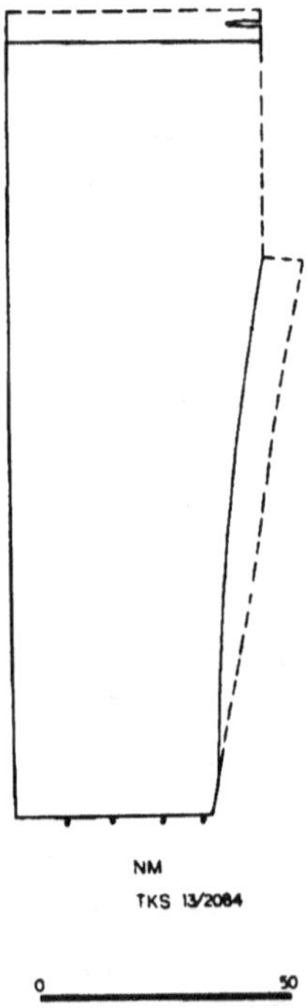


**Fig. 8.6.** *Şalvar* (lower left), *entari* (lower right), and *cepken* (upper), parts of a three-piece costume of mauve wool twill, in the collection of the Topkapı Sarayı, 13/2084, 13/2083, and 13/2082 (author's drawing). While the other two pieces in this ensemble are traditionally constructed, this jacket is avoids the traditional decoration of elaborate trim or embroidery and instead features oversized sleeves, tucks, and ruffles.

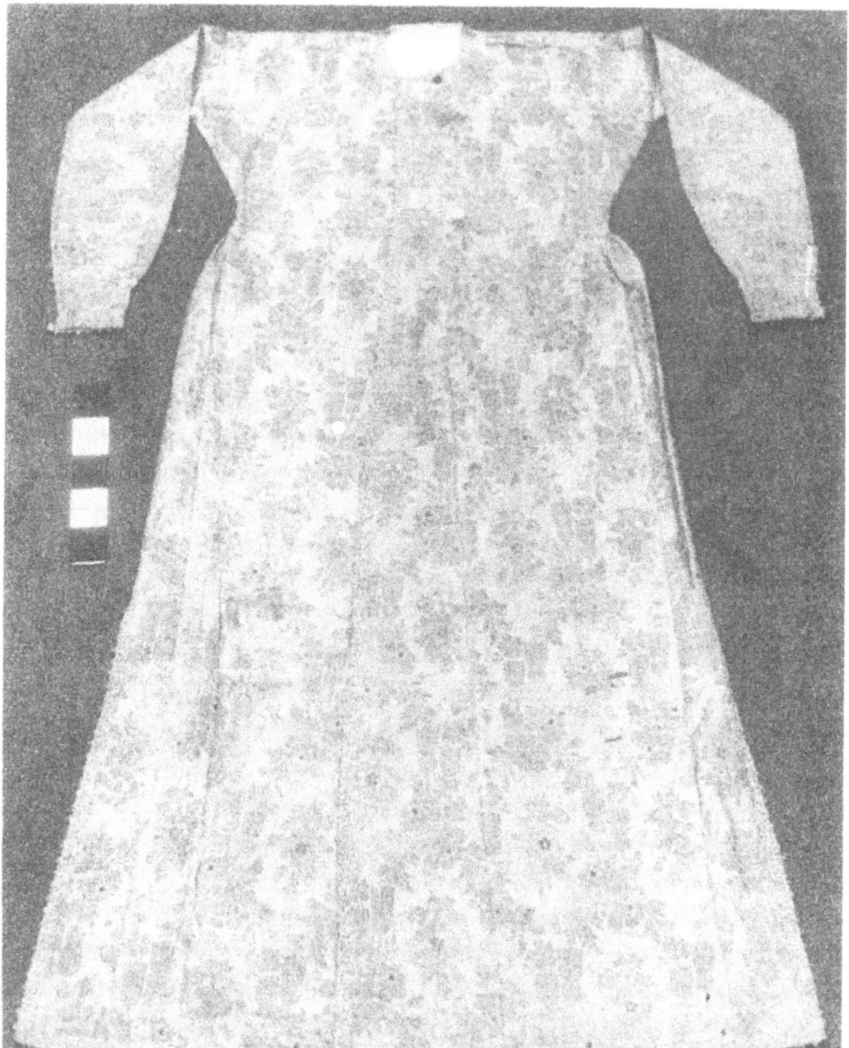

**Fig. 8.7.** Nineteenth-century *entari* with cuffed sleeves and a slightly gathered waist (no. 102, courtesy of the Yapı Kredi Vedat Nedim Tör Museum Collection, Istanbul).

indicate continued experimentation with the older Ottoman construction to achieve something of the look of European dresses. In the first example a waist has been incorporated in an otherwise standard *entari,* and in the second (fig. 8.8), a simple but meaningful change in construction, the modification of the front opening, changes the lavishly embroidered purple silk *entari* into a dress. From here, it was a relatively easy transition to garments which were indistinguishable from those worn by women in London and Paris in the same period, and indeed the records show that just such a change occurred. Despite the similarities in appearance between the garments worn by elite women in London or Paris, and what women in Istanbul may have worn, it is important to remember that the social contexts in which these clothes would have been viewed was quite different. Ottoman women were dressing for much more circumscribed social groupings in domestic settings, while their European counterparts attended public events at museums, theaters, concert halls, gardens, and so on, where their clothing would have been seen and appreciated by large numbers of friends and strangers, both women and men.

The way in which the elite women of nineteenth-century Istanbul modified their traditional dress to include elements of European costume demonstrates a pattern of change well known in fashion history. A more uncommon pattern involves the wholesale adoption of a new style, without the long period of transition in which elements from two traditions were combined. This more unusual mode of change is generally indicative of a fashion change imposed on one group by another. An example of this is the replacement of traditional native dress by European-inspired costume that took place under the influence of colonial or missionary groups in some parts of Africa in the nineteenth century. An example closer to our topic is the replacement of traditional Ottoman military dress with a completely new European-style uniform as a part of the military reforms of Mehmed II in the 1820s. The baggy *şalvar,* robes, sashes, and distinctive headgear that delineated every level of rank within the military were abandoned in favor of serge trousers, looser in fit than those worn by European men at the same date, but completely different in cut than the *şalvar*, with a broad-cloth vest and jacket, and a red wool head covering that soon evolved into the fez.

What does it mean that in the case of nineteenth-century Ottoman women, the more gradual fashion change takes place? Here it is significant that although the Ottoman government regulated the street wear of women, their indoor clothes were not subject to government legislations.[17] The

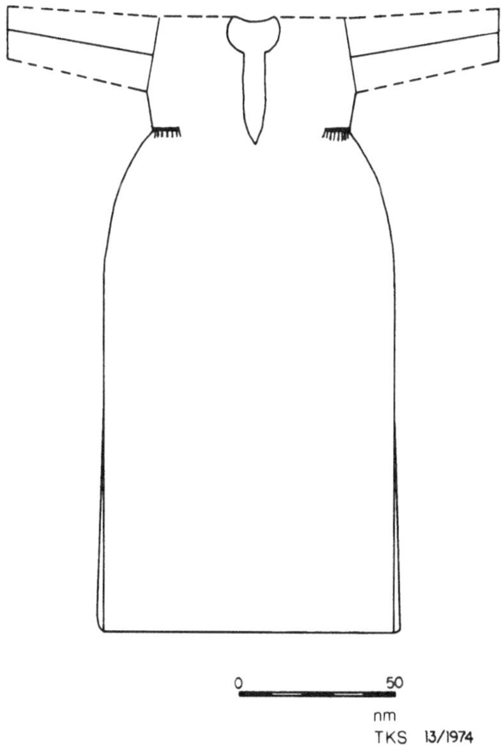


**Fig. 8.8.** Dress made of purple silk heavily embroidered with gold. Constructed of pieces of similar shape to those used in an *entari,* the long center opening here is modified to a neck slit, thus transforming the garment to a dress, the basic element of clothing among European women. Although worn with matching *şalvar* by Ottoman women, the widespread use of this kind of garment was an early step in the adoption of a European vocabulary of dress (Topkapı Sarayı collection, 13/1974; author's drawing).

experimentation with aspects of European costume that occurred during the course of the nineteenth century indicates a growing familiarity with the foreign tradition on the part of women. Their costume choices were made to signal their membership in certain social groups, based on criteria such as wealth, education, marital status, and religion. Wearing European-style clothing, and carrying accessories such as parasols or gloves, particularly in the earlier part of the nineteenth century, was an indication of the wearer's closer familiarity with European customs and wealth. Greeks and Armenians had easier access to such information, although wealth was an equally important factor in the adoption of the new costume. Jewish women seem to have been outside of the fashion community for the most part, and the women of religiously conservative Muslim families were particularly slow to abandon their traditional dress. The fact that costume change took place at different rates among Greeks, Armenians, Jews, and Muslims, to name only the most visible social divisions in the Ottoman populace, indicates the level of choice that was operative. Rather than having their style of dress forced upon them, Ottoman women were making deliberate choices about their costume, exercising personal taste and creating markers of social identification.

In this summary of my research, I have presented the point of view of what we could call fashion technology. I could have discussed other aspects: the means by which fashion information was disseminated, the economic implications involved in the new fashion and the attendant tailoring and materials involved, the political ramifications of choosing to wear European-style clothing, and so on. The study of costume is by definition multivalent, but for our purposes in this brief essay, technology is an accessible entry point into the complexities of fashion, tracking change in a tangible way while touching on many less tangible aspects of the topic.

These garments and their related documentation provide a view of nineteenth-century women difficult, if not impossible, to obtain through other sources. Women, unless they stepped onto the political stage as major players in dynastic politics, were rarely written about by contemporary historians. They seem to have led largely undocumented lives, sequestered by walls both architectural and social from the world of the street and marketplace. But the keen interest in European style evidenced in the material documentation of the garments worn by these women demonstrates that, while perhaps unseen themselves, Ottoman women were close observers of the dress and other customs of the European women around them. Mostly omitted from the written record, Ottoman women reveal themselves through their clothes, an important primary and material source that compensates in part for lack of other forms of documentation.

The view of Ottoman women that appears in the writing of most nineteenth-century European authors as well as in many more recent works is that of passive or powerless prisoners of the home, victims of a social system based either on Islamic or Ottoman precepts concerning the proper place of women.[18] According to these views, the women, whose concerns were limited to those of indulging their own vanity and raising children, have no power of self-determination and no avenues for independent self-expression. But just as western assumptions of public and private do not fit well in the Ottoman context, so too assumptions of what constitutes power do not account very well for how women functioned in Ottoman society. Since they did not participate overtly in the business of government, in the judicial system other than as plaintiffs, or in the expanding educational system, to name only a few arenas of "public" life, women are assumed to have been without agency. While many aspects of women's lives were left out of the historical record, it is nevertheless becoming clearer as more research is carried out, that women were in fact active agents in many different arenas of Ottoman society. For example recent research indicates that women could be patrons of significant public architecture and could wield considerable political influence.[19]

It has been more difficult to come to an understanding of women as patrons of objects, as wielders of economic influence on a personal level. Ottoman women had some control over their own economic situation since under Islamic law, women are allowed to inherit property, to own and operate a business, and upon marriage are entitled to *mehr,* a sum of money paid to the bride from the groom or his family, over which she has control.[20] In terms of textiles, we know that women were informed consumers of some extremely expensive garments, that they made relatively extensive purchases of fabric, gold thread, and other accessories, both from the home and in the local shopping districts. In her memoirs, Leyla Hanımefendi includes a chapter, "Purchases of the Imperial Harem," in which she describes how women of different social ranks in Istanbul carried out their shopping.

> The princesses and the ladies of the Imperial Harem were allowed to go there [the Great Bazaar] and they did go from time to time, but it was not considered suitable to stop in front of the shops, much less to enter them. They would install themselves in the mosque of Nurosmaniye. . . . The shopkeepers, advised by the people of the suite of the princess, would bring their merchandise to them and in turn, these would be presented to the princesses by the eunuchs. The princess would then make her choice. . . .
>
> The ladies of the great konaks also did their shopping in the Bazaar just like the princesses. . . . Those who lived near the Bazaar would send the eunuch or woman in charge of their household to pick out samples of material so they could make their choice at home. . . .
>
> The ladies of the small bourgeoisie would generally do their shopping in the weekly markets of their own quarter where they could buy all the things that they needed. (pp. 115–17)

Women of the elite were small- or larger-scale employers of seamstresses, jewellers, milliners, shoemakers, embroiderers, and others involved in the fashion business. They were also, as the women's press and foreign newspapers indicate, participants in a discourse centered on the social, political, and economic implications of their own fashion choices and purchases.[21] The economic influence that women wielded as patrons and consumers of clothing may well have extended to other areas of personal and domestic consumption—jewellery, household furnishings, and so on, but this is an area in which more research is needed.

The newly embraced European-style clothing, which generated intense debate among the elite women of Istanbul, whether as a result of their political concerns or their fashion concerns, was not visible on the street.[22] It would have been seen only by those among whom they visited and by members of their own extended families, contexts defined in the western usage as private. The importance given to clothing visible exclusively within this so-called private context argues for a redefinition of public and private for Ottoman women. For women, domestic settings were the arenas in which business such as the exchange of political or social information, or the establishment of family alliances was conducted. Within their homes and in the homes in which they visited, women interacted with male relatives and with other female members of the elite to pursue particular social, economic, or political goals, to enhance their own status or financial security, and to further the careers of their male relatives in which they had a vested interest. The attention paid by women to matters of dress and other aspects of personal display (hair and jewellery) visible only to other women and male relatives reflects their understanding of the significance of the activities conducted within the "privacy" of their own quarters.

For the earlier Ottoman period, class and social status were the determining forces for establishing practices of seclusion that applied to both men and women, and within this social structure, women as well as men could exert considerable political power.[23] While this model provides an important starting place for looking at nineteenth-century social practices and for exploring the profound importance of harem politics, I would suggest that it requires certain modifications to incorporate the far-reaching political and social changes that took place during the nineteenth century. The impact of these changes differed sharply for men and women: while the public venues in which men operated, such as theaters, banks, offices, and restaurants, became much more numerous and varied, women did not experience a concomitant loosening of their socially sanctioned seclusion.

They continued to remain secluded when outside of their own homes and to operate within strictly defined social networks comprised of other women and male relatives. Yet recent studies have shown that, despite these constraints, women were able to negotiate a considerable amount of power as political, economic, and social actors. In this analysis of the collections of women's costume that survive today and the visual and written descriptions of mid-nineteenth-century Ottoman dress, we find women making decisions about financial expenditures and choosing modes of self-representation that reveal a great deal of themselves and the rapidly changing society in which they lived.

## NOTES

Nick DeCaro, Lianne McLarty, Reina Lewis, and Leslie Peirce, colleagues at the University of Victoria and elsewhere, have all given me very helpful suggestions about this paper at one stage or another. I am very grateful to them, and also to D. Fairchild Ruggles for her careful editing of my work.

1. For a good introduction to the discourse on public and private among feminist historians, as well as additional bibliography, see the various essays in D. Helly and S. Reverby, eds., *Gendered Domains. Rethinking Public and Private in Women's History* (Ithaca, N.Y.: Cornell University Press, 1992).

2. For a discussion and current bibliography of the study of costume in the Middle East, see Y. Stillman and N. Micklewright, "Costume in the Middle East," *Middle East Studies Association Bulletin* 26 (1992): 13–38.

3. The role of dress in forming and signaling social identity has been the subject of many works, but for a particularly interesting discussion of this subject, see Kaja Silverman, "Fragments of a Fashionable Discourse," in *Studies in Entertainment: Critical Approaches to Mass Culture,* ed. Tania Modleski (Bloomington: Indiana University Press, 1986), 139–54. A more extensive treatment of the topic may be found in Anne Hollander's oft-cited work *Seeing Through Clothes* (Berkeley: University of California Press, 1978). Of the many studies of costume in the nonwestern world, Sidney Mead's work *Traditional Maori Clothing* (Sydney: A. H. and A. W. Reed, 1969) is an outstanding example of a study in which the linked issues of dress and social change are foregrounded.

4. We have virtually no reliable representations of nineteenth-century Ottoman women at home, and the contemporary documents that concern women generally reveal their legal or economic activities. For women in the economic sphere, see particularly the work of Donald Quataert, "Machine Breaking and the Changing Carpet Industry of Western Anatolia, 1860–1908," *Journal of Social History* (1986): 473–89; "Ottoman Women, Households and Textile Manufacturing, 1800–1914," in *Women in Middle Eastern History,* ed. Beth Baron and

Nikki Keddie (New Haven: Yale University Press, 1991), 161–76; and "Clothing, Laws, State and Society in the Ottoman Empire, 1720–1829," *International Journal of Middle Eastern Studies* 29 (1997): 403–29. For recent work on women in Ottoman history more generally, see Madeline Zilfi, *Women in Ottoman History* (Leiden: E. J. Brill, 1997).

5. The discussion of Ottoman costume that follows is based on research carried out for my Ph.D. dissertation, "Women's Dress in Nineteenth Century Istanbul: Mirror of a Changing Society" (University of Pennsylvania, 1986).

6. Given the quantity of publications that now exist, it is not surprising that their quality varies. It is impossible to provide a full bibliography here, but a useful starting place is Billie Melman's excellent work, *Women's Orients: English Women and the Middle East, 1718–1918* (Ann Arbor: University of Michigan Press, 1992).

7. Julia Pardoe, *The City of the Sultan and Domestic Manners of the Turks in 1836* (Philadelphia: Carey, Lea and Blanchard, 1837), 179.

8. Zeyneb Hanoum, *A Turkish Woman's European Impressions* (Philadelphia: J. B. Lippincott, 1913); Emine Foat Tugay, *Three Centuries: Family Chronicles of Turkey and Egypt* (London: Oxford University Press, 1963); Halide Edib, *Memoires of Halide Edib* (New York: The Century Co., 1926); and Leyla (Saz) Hanıimefendi, *The Imperial Harem of the Sultans: Daily Life at the Çirağan Palace during the Nineteenth Century* (Istanbul: PEVA Publications, 1995). There are certainly many other Ottoman women who wrote about their lives, and their work is becoming increasingly well known as it receives more scholarly attention. For example, Muge Galin at Ohio State University is currently examining the life and writing of Fatma Aliye Hanım, an important figure in the late Ottoman period whose work has been relatively little studied until recently.

9. In the previous paragraph the author states that "green was considered to be the colour of satisfied hopes and wishes as well as joy."

10. These sources, illustrating the costume worn by men and women of the Ottoman empire, usually organized by social or military rank or geographic location, exist in some number and have been published from time to time. They are a puzzling group of manuscripts, since little is known of the circumstances surrounding their production, and even less of their artists. A dissertation nearing completion by Leslie Meral Schick of Harvard University will no doubt answer many of the questions that arise concerning these manuscripts.

11. For more extended discussion of the issues involved in the study of historical photographs from the Middle East, see Paul Chevedden, "Making Light of Everything: Early Photography in the Middle East and Current Photomania," *Middle East Studies Association Bulletin* 18 (1984): 151–74, and Micklewright, "Dervish Images in Photographs and Paintings," in *The Dervish Lodge. Architecture, Art and Sufism in Ottoman Turkey,* ed. Raymond Lifchez (Berkeley: University of California Press, 1992), 269–83, and "Teaching with Historical Photographs," *The Turkish Studies Association Bulletin* 19 (1995): 78–80. For

general bibliography, see Chevedden, "Making Light," and Nissan Perez, *Focus East. Early Photography in the Near East, 1839–1885* (New York: Abrams, 1992).

12. Since the publication of Edward Said's *Orientalism* in 1976, a whole body of scholarship has emerged that addressed aspects of these issues. Few studies focus specifically on Orientalist painting, and fewer still do so with the intent of looking at the painting in its complex cultural context. Linda Nochlin's early, but still useful article, "The Imaginary Orient," *Art in America* 71 (1983): 119–31, and a recent book by Reina Lewis that examines the work of women Orientalist painters, *Gendering Orientalism: Race, Femininity and Representation* (London: Routledge, 1995), are two of the most useful. Turkish Orientalist painters have received some scholarly attention, mostly in the form of exhibition catalogues. An exception is Osman Hamdi Bey, who has been the subject of at least one book (Mustafa Cezar, *Sanatta Batıya Açılış ve Osman Hamdi* [Osman Hamdi and Western Trends in Art] (Istanbul: Türkiye İş Bankası Yayınları, 1971), and a number of articles. From the point of view of costume history, the most important issue to consider in this body of work is the accuracy of representation. For the most part, it is impossible to rely on the paintings since we can not know that the artists were able to see the scenes they recreate in their work. Nor can we assume that the intention of most Orientalist painters was a faithful recreation of life around them, despite the very realist style of many of their works. As with the other visual material already discussed, Orientalist painting must be used very cautiously in reconstructing costume history.

13. See Elizabeth Frierson, "Hanımlara Mahsus Gazette: State, Press and Gender in the Late-Ottoman Empire, 1895–1909" (Ph.D., Princeton University, 1996).

14. Princess Musbah Haidar, *Arabesque* (London: Hutchinson and Co., 1944), 89.

15. There is an extensive bibliography of recent scholarship devoted to the political, social, and economic history of the nineteenth-century Ottoman Empire. An excellent entry into this topic is provided by H. Inalcik and D. Quataert, *An Economic and Social History of the Ottoman Empire, 1300–1914* (Cambridge: Cambridge University Press, 1994).

16. The process of costume change outlined here is described in more detail in my article, "Tracing the Transformation of Women's Dress in Nineteenth Century Istanbul," *Dress* 13 (1987): 33–42.

17. For the sake of modesty, the Ottoman women of Istanbul, of all ethnic groups, covered their indoor clothing with additional garments when they were on the street. Their street wear of course changed over time, but for the Muslim women of Istanbul for most of the nineteenth century, it consisted of a *ferace,* or long coat, and *yashmak,* or veil covering the hair and lower half of the face. From time to time, government regulations were announced that legislated certain details of this costume, for instance the thickness of the fabric used for the *yashmak.* See

Donald Quataert, "Clothing," for a discussion of the sumptuary regulations in this period.

18. Recent scholarship, much of it already cited here, has begun to challenge this construction of Ottoman women. See for example, Alan Duben and Cem Behar, *Istanbul Households: Marriage, Family and Fertility 1880–1940* (Cambridge: Cambridge University Press, 1991), various work by Donald Quataert, ("Machine Breaking," "Ottoman Women"), and Elizabeth Frierson, "'Is There Any Future for Us in Trying to Be Ladylike?' The Ethnic Politics of Late-Ottoman Dress and Manufacture" (unpublished paper, used with permission of the author, 1995), and "Unimagined Communities: Women and Education in the Last-Ottoman Empire," *Critical Matrix* 9 (1995): 57–92. Frierson, "Unimagined Communities," provides references for additional work on this topic.

19. Recent publications on Ottoman women as patrons of architecture include Peirce, *Imperial Harem,* and Ülkü Bates, "Women as Patrons of Architecture in Turkey," in *Women in the Muslim World,* ed. Lois Beck and Nikki Keddi (Cambridge, Mass.: Harvard University Press, 1978), 245–60, and, "The Architectural Patronage of Ottoman Women," *Asian Art* 2 (1993): 51–65. The recent exhibition catalogue edited by Günsel Renda, *9000 Years of the Anatolian Woman* (Istanbul: Ministry of Culture, 1993), discusses Ottoman women as patrons of the arts generally and provides examples of objects produced or commissioned by women. It also has an excellent bibliography. For women as producers in the textile industries, see Quataert, "Ottoman Women."

20. For a discussion of how the institution of *mehr* operated in Ottoman Istanbul, see Duben and Behar, *Istanbul Households,* 114–21.

21. See Frierson, "Is There Any Future?" for an extended analysis of the ongoing discussion by Ottoman women in the women's press about the connections between fashion and politics.

22. It is clear from the sources quoted by Frierson in her recent work that streetwear for women was also a subject of heated debate (Frierson, "Is There Any Future?").

23. See Peirce, *Imperial Harem* for this analysis.

9

# Mirrors Out, Mirrors In

## Domestication and Rejection of the Foreign in Late-Ottoman Women's Magazines (1875–1908)

*Elizabeth Brown Frierson*

At first glance, it would seem that late-Ottoman readers were obsessed with foreigners. Translators did a brisk business bringing the works of Tolstoy, Jane Austen, and Dumas Père et Fils into Turkish for serialized or cheap paperback publication. Feature articles in magazines gave nonstop lessons in geography or cultural ethnography, while biographies of such Europeans as Lady Mary Wortley Montagu alternated with biographies of Muslim luminaries such as Fatma bint Abbas as exemplars in education or morals for Ottoman readers. Advertisers touted the foreign origins of their goods to draw customers, along with illustrations of foreigners using the products to become educated, productive, or to earn respect as professionals. The short-items section alone could contain a dozen or more reports from around the world in any given issue.

Some magazines were almost entirely filled with foreign news, foreign fiction, and ethnography. For example, one popular women's magazine opened its September 1, 1901 issue with the following items: a moral tale, translated from the French, a feature article on Siamese women, part three of a serialized novel by Tolstoy, statistics on American women's progress in various careers, and short items about a Brooklyn woman, European royalty, and Prague as the city of gloves, comprising in all over eleven of the eighteen columns of text not given over to advertisements, puzzle contests, or masthead.[1] While this issue presents a range of materials dealing with foreign topics, it far from exhausts the possibilities.

Mahmud Celâleddin, editor of *İnsaniyet,* titled the first feature article for his magazine, "An Excerpt from a Conversation Which Took Place between a Foreigner and an Ottoman."[2] *Mehâsin* presented such topics as "A Great Woman: The British Queen," "Parisian House Décor," "The Women of America," and features on Sarah Bernhardt, Edmond and Rosemonde Rostand, and a Countess Dunway.[3] In *Hanımlara Mahsûs Gazete,* readers learned that Sarah Bernhardt was recovering from an operation, that the wife of the ruler of Korea had died, that a women's cycling club had been founded in Paris,[4] and that British women had increased their representation in several careers.[5] A woman in Paris stabbed another in a fight over a man;[6] a sixteen-year-old girl was marooned with Amazonian savages and befriended them by teaching them modern agricultural techniques.[7] French schoolgirls apparently outperformed boys on national exams. Rumanian girls were forbidden to wear the corset because of its harmful effects. In India, children's names were chosen on the thirteenth day after their birth.[8] A Hungarian girl was buried alive after thieves cut off her fingers to steal her rings.[9] In a rare mention of contemporary Arab women, the editors expressed their horror that a women in Egypt had been burned alive by her brother (*şahs-ı denî,* a lowly or despicable person) because she was pregnant.[10]

One wonders what Ottoman readers made of all this piecemeal information being presented to them under the rubric of the foreign (*ecnebî*), European (*avrupadan* or *avrupalı*), and American (*amerikalı*). It is clear that this was not evidence of a desire to adopt wholesale the qualities of the West, as these writings contained both positive and negative perspectives on foreigners and their behaviors. Readers were guided to accept as well as to reject various Western influences, and to adapt the acceptable influences into Ottoman and Muslim norms. Moreover, these images functioned as mirrors wherein readers could find reflections of Ottoman identity: attitudes toward education, morals, public activity, and new civic and social duties for women, such as taking over some part of funding schools, care of orphans, and war relief.[11] Further, in their discussions of criminal behavior among Ottoman gypsies and women in Paris, these features were highly evocative of Ottoman urban realities. Their percussive prose and raucous actors made modern shadow-plays out of ethnic conflicts marking the breakdown of the empire. Ultimately, discussions of the foreign abroad were also critiques of the foreign within, both in the minority populations at the heart of European access to Ottoman state and society, and in the selective westernization carried forward by the state and its subjects.

## Press and Society in the Hamidian Era

The popular press had expanded significantly from its origins at mid-century, thanks largely to three factors. First, the sultanate of Abdülhamid II from 1876 to 1909 was notable for its expansion of public education at all levels, and literacy rates and readership grew as a consequence. Second, the state had found cheap serials useful early in the century for publicizing such basic information as market days and bureaucratic promotions, and later in promoting its version of reformist ideologies. Third, the empire daily became more tightly linked by rail, sea, and telegraph with the world beyond its borders to the west and east. Private and state publishers of the popular press expanded the production of cheap serials as guides to encompass the changing physical, mental, and economic conditions of Ottoman life in their daily papers, magazines, paperback essays and fiction, pamphlets, and almanacs. For the historian today, these publications are vivid guides to meeting points between state and society, where Hamidian publishers, editors, writers, readers, and censors struggled over the founding debates of Islamic modernity. As the press expanded, so too did the scope of these discourses, as Ottoman readers became aggressive readers and writers of letters to editors or specific authors. In so doing they took hold of aspects of modernity and actively crafted them into local productions of culture, and by the turn of the century, women were in the thick of it.

Illustrated scientific and literary *gazetes* generally sold at very low prices of one or two *guruş,* making them a rough analogue for the European penny press. They did not necessarily constitute a mass-circulation press, as there were many low-priced publications with small audiences or local distribution, surviving only because they were heavily subsidized by the state or by an individual high in the state apparatus. Though the Ottoman *guruş* press was initially, like these, created and supported by government officials and used to bring ideology to the level of middle-class and then popular culture, by the 1890s readers began to play influential roles through their letters to editors and through their responses to advertisements. Ultimately, the Hamidian women's press constituted a key element in an Ottoman political public sphere, because of the highly flexible praxes of censorship, the cheapness of serial publications, their illustrated sections to aid unsophisticated readers, the high numbers of participants in the production of a cheap popular press, as well as the topics discussed.[12] The critical thrust of this popular press was not, like Habermas' *politische Öffentlichkeit,* aimed at the indigenous monarch but rather aimed at loci of power and secrecy in the empires of Europe, which were formally external to the Ottoman polity but by the late nineteenth century deeply interwoven into its daily political, social, and commercial life.[13] As the *guruş* press expanded, Europeans both external to and resident within Ottoman territories, and their clients among non-Muslim communities within the empire, came to play central roles in these critiques in their popular constructions of new Ottoman identities.

The women's press at first glance might seem peripheral to the great questions of state and social transformation in the nineteenth and early twentieth centuries, but in fact it leads us directly to the most basic and intimate site of modernization: the household. At the turn of the century, the Ottoman household was no longer a private domestic sphere of extended family within Mediterranean traditions of interiority defining social space, but was instead a highly fraught, intensely scrutinized matrix of morality and modernity, tradition and progress, production and consumption.[14] In these respects Ottoman households were much like households in any other modernizing European or Asian society at this time, as they were increasingly legitimate fields for state intervention in people's private lives, and for education of a populace into a modern patriotism. The periodical press as it expanded became less a creature of the state designed to forward these goals, and more a place where state policies were promulgated and then discussed, refined, and adapted to work out those features of daily life that would become distinctive of Islamic modernity. Further, by the 1890s hundreds of women used the popular press to lay claim to a public identity as loyal subjects of the sultan, taking upon themselves the task, as writers, of defining Ottoman identities. The Hamidian women's popular press is both evidence of this process, that a public sphere could arise in a non-European culture, as well as a guide to how this public sphere, with early participation by women in significant numbers, took shape in a time of growing literacy, the ripening of educational reform, refinements in protectionist industrial and commercial policy, and spiraling ethnic compartmentalization.

## Women's Serials

Although women's supplements to magazines were published as early as the 1860s, it was not until the late 1880s and 1890s that they became popular enough to be published on their own. By that time, it had become a key element of liberal thought to argue for women's education and economic contributions as hallmarks of a modern society; and to encourage these trends, publications entirely for women were founded with increasing frequency, most folding after a short run. For example, *Hanımlar* (*Ladies*) published only one issue in 1882, while *Mürüvvet* (*Munificence*) published nine issues in 1887. As state educational reforms took root and potential female readership expanded, however, these journals became more commonplace, and journalists began to address concerns of middle-class and working readers, such as schoolteachers, seamstresses, and entrepreneurs, and themselves became more entrepreneurial, taking up the new opportunities presented by Hamidian state support of Muslim commerce and manufacture. Family magazines such as *Resimli Gazete* (*The Illustrated Paper*) were also inexpensive, and illustrated to facilitate comprehension for newly or marginally literate readers. These magazines pursued explicitly didactic missions, describing themselves as either supplementing the curricula of the schools, or picking up where schooling left off for adult readers. Women's magazines, produced by both men and women for a female readership, were written for wives and mothers, or to train young girls to become modern wives, mothers, and teachers. The successful serials attracted advertising, subscribers, and sales at kiosks and bookstores; their publishers and editors also learned to negotiate the legal terrain of press laws, rules, regulations, and more importantly, patterns of enforcement.[15]

In their pages we can trace the results of Hamidian reforms in education as well as changes in the economic and social environment. Earlier historians have generally dismissed a women's press before the Young Turk revolution of 1908 as an upper-class phenomenon, severely restricted by supposedly stiff Hamidian censorship, and in any case not readable as the vast proportion of women were presumed to be illiterate. In fact, while the first writers for the Ottoman women's press were indeed wives and daughters of high civic officials, by the late 1890s women's magazines had been taken over almost entirely by hundreds of professional journalists and schoolteachers drawn from non-elite sectors of society. In addition, the press revealed changing patterns of production and consumption through the presence of European and East Asian advertisers, as well as of such Ottoman entrepreneurs as one publisher's wife who ran an atélier producing European fashions interpreted for the Ottoman market.

While the founding goals of most Turkish-language women's magazines in this period were to enable women to continue their education after leaving school, and more fundamentally to train women to be good Muslims, wives, and mothers of loyal Ottoman subjects, their scope rapidly exceeded this goal, or perhaps expanded the parameters of what being a good Muslim and a good mother entailed. Writers and readers of the women's press gave themselves legitimacy as public figures by tying questions about women and the family to the most vexing and pressing issues of the late-Hamidian era, and the dilemmas presented by foreign influence exerted from without and from within the borders of the empire were tailor-made for this purpose. Ottomans in late-Hamidian society sought simultaneously both to fight off that influence and to turn it to their advantage in their struggles collectively and individually for survival. As a result, discussions of the foreign could be used to express Muslim propriety, Ottoman loyalties, ingenuity in adapting western forms, wit in satirizing western and westernized behaviors, and through all of these, to forge a patriotic identity for women in their domestication and mastery of the foreign.

Women's journals presented, in nearly every issue, short items about foreign women entering professional life, qualifying as doctors, forming unions, being invited to join professional honorary associations. The editors of the most successful women's magazine, *Hanımlara Mahsûs Gazete* (*The Ladies' Own Gazette*), were especially active on this front, frequently including statistics on the numbers of western women in various professions, such as secretarial, accounting, architecture, publishing, and advertising. At the same time, these exemplars of western progress were set against frequent discussions of Ottoman and Muslim women's productive and reproductive capabilities as framed in an anticolonial rhetoric, presenting critiques of capitalism and western mores, and aiming these critiques increasingly at minority communities within the empire. In addition, the greatly expanded public education system under Abdülhamid II trained and employed women, primarily Turkish Muslim women, as schoolteachers and as skilled workers, and as foot soldiers in the front lines of economic warfare over markets and manufacture. The women's press shows how the aims of encouraging motherly, wifely, and religious virtues expanded into the far more ideologically charged enterprise of redefining Ottoman womanhood for a consciously modernizing age.

## Creation and Uses of the Foreign

Journalists used foreign women as a warning and spur to Ottoman women's own advancement, presenting them ethnographically as cultural curiosities whose differences were used to legitimate discussions of public life, domestic relations, work, seclusion in the home, headcoverings, and loss of traditions as a means of working out the specifics of modernity. In many articles on foreign topics, Ottoman women found their own concerns played out in the setting of a different society, and used to define what was ambivalent, what was negative, and what was positive in foreign and indigenous models. A woman who read the magazine could then use these definitions to set parameters for her own views and behavior both toward the foreign, and toward herself and her splintering society.

At the same time, journalists did not hesitate to take over some western ideas in order to reject others. One of the intellectual trends imported from Europe was social Darwinism, which both fed and worked against the selectivity of selective westernization. In arguments for educating women and strengthening their moral authority in the home, writers and reformers commonly pointed to the West as a model for social change by calling attention to its higher status among "civilized regions of the world" relative to the Ottoman Empire. Equally common were cautions against women becoming too free, too ambitious, and too visible in the pursuit of modernity, *alafranga*.[16] Writers constantly attempted to circumscribe western patterns of reform and behavior and say to their readers, "this far, and no farther"; yet the belief that Ottomans, and especially Ottoman Muslims, stood one rung below Europe in an evolution toward unconstant civilization dissolved these lines of demarcation. Individual writers often made conflicting arguments in the same issue of a given magazine, one attempting to exclude a western fashion, for example, while another recommended ways to wear it, an incoherence that was mimicked in the varieties of fashion seen in urban street scenes. This heterogeneity of opinion was a leading characteristic of discussions of foreign practices, most graphically demonstrated by the frequency with which illustrations, patterns, and advertisements for corseted fashions appeared side-by-side with fervent arguments against the corset as a hazard both to a woman's health and to her moral fiber.

This inability to be absolute in excluding western influence has become familiar in historiography of colonial states and societies, where the daily mixing of ruler and ruled left few areas of life untouched on either side.[17] The Ottomans had successfully avoided colonization in the heartlands, however, and recent studies of the late-Ottoman economy make it clear that colonial paradigms at various points fit perfectly and at others do not fit the Ottoman case even informally.[18] As in Japan, where the byword for many Meiji reformers was "western science, eastern ethics," Ottoman thinkers sought to preserve their cultural identity while absorbing western scientific advances and work habits, to create a compound that was intrinsically modern, an Ottoman rather than a purely western modernity. In 1904 for example, one author wrote in the women's press that the Japanese "preserve completely their customs, ethics, and ways, and accept only the commercial and industrial aspects of European civilization."[19] The very act of preserving tradition, however, required the creation of a heritage in discarding some traditions and maintaining others.

## Domesticating the Foreign

A woman looking east or west of Ottoman territories in the nineteenth century saw dangers encroaching from all directions. To the west and north stood states and cultures that showed alarming abilities to affect the future of the Ottoman Empire, and which had proven themselves to be the sources of beneficial and harmful innovations. Ottomans looking eastward saw cautionary tales of colonization among a panoply of dissimilar cultures and faiths, and they drew out of these compounds potential models for resistance to the West. Scattered throughout the world as well could be found cultures that the press presented as primitive, thereby confirming the Ottoman Empire's place within the civilized world. Seeing other cultures as primitive may have provided a palliative for Ottomans who found their own faiths and cultures portrayed as primitive in European literature and politics.[20] These divisions appear within the pages of the popular press for women, where foreigners included all those outside the Ottoman Empire and its successor states or suzerains in Egypt and North Africa, thus including any women outside the *dar ül-İslâm.* Foreign women featured primarily as lessons in cultural geography, with each lesson containing a second, implicit, moral tale. It is in the implicit lesson, and in the ambiguities shown by conflict between the two narratives, that late-Ottoman realities can be glimpsed.

By the late nineteenth century, western foreigners had lost much of their exoticism in the eyes of urban Ottomans. This was nowhere more evident than in the great port cities of Salonica, Izmir, and Istanbul. Westernizing reforms and capitulations had infiltrated all levels of Ottoman life, from the water one drank in Istanbul to the uniforms worn by the sultan's guards, bureaucrats, and students (fig. 9.1). The reorganization of the imperial capital along the lines of French prefectures in mid-century, and subsequent aggressive programs of infrastructural improvement, had made

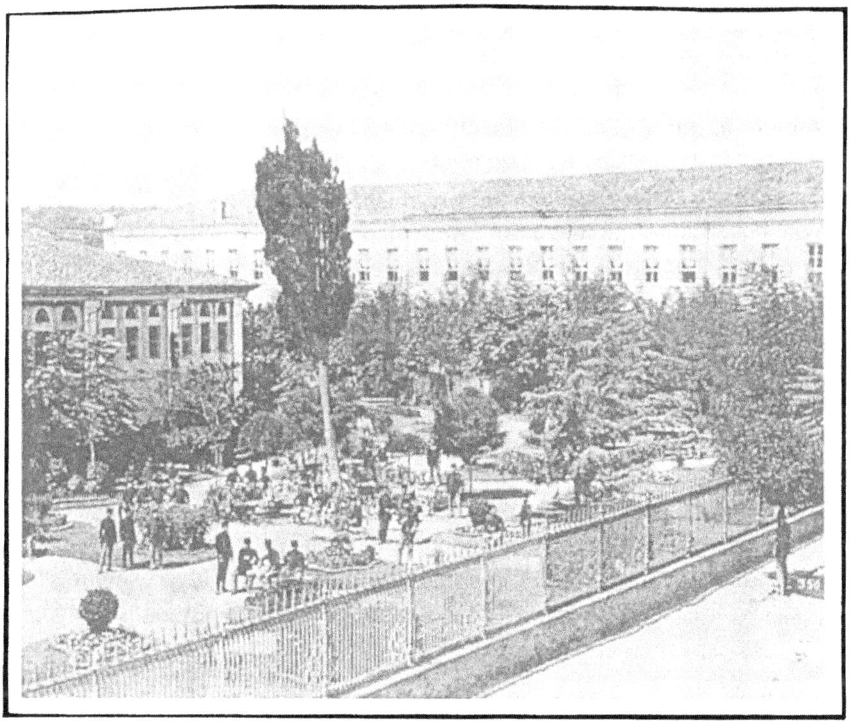

**Fig. 9.1.** Garden of the Imperial School of Artillery and Civil Engineering Abdullah Frères, 1880s (Library of Congress Abdul Hamid Collection Album 9542, no. 8)

such standard elements of European life as steam ferries, tramways, trains, gaslight, police bureaus, theaters, and meeting halls equally standard elements of Istanbul life in some quarters.[21] The popular press had kept pace with these changes, incorporating the latest European trends in publishing.

The large number of resident foreigners and protected minorities within Istanbul makes the retrospective identification of foreign and *indigène* intricate and highly inflected. The municipality of Galata, with consular offices, department stores, and many resident foreigners, was both a model of European advancement in its wide boulevards and stone architecture, and a model of European depravity in its quayside wine shops, prostitution, gambling, and high crime rate. Galata constituted a rich mix of foreign and westernized identities on display just across a short bridge from the heart of the old city. Its elite population consisted of bankers, merchants, and diplomats of all nationalities, and at the street level of

Ottoman minority, Maltese, Ionian, and other Mediterranean and northern European translators, traders, skilled labor, petty merchants, and criminals. The port cities of the empire all held such quarters, constituting syncretic frontiers of varieties of citizenship, subjecthood, and national identity that defied easy definition then, and continue to do so now.

It is not surprising, then, that women's magazines ostensibly dedicated to the construction of a modern Ottoman, Muslim motherhood devoted vast numbers of column inches less to Islam, to Ottoman history, to news of the provinces, or even in significant numbers to eminent women in Islamic history, than to the foreign. Foreign women figured prominently in the pages of the women's press, overlapping with every other long-running topic including education, fashion, economics, household affairs, and cultural identity. In addition to discussions of the lives of foreign women, foreign expertise or fiction, and advertisements for foreign products, the featured illustration often depicted a Western woman, a Western city, an East Asian city, or a more far-flung locale, such as the southernmost tip of Africa or a sunset over the South Pole. Fashion illustrations and advertisements also presented images of Western women in social and professional settings.

## Europe and Asia as Both Kindred and Inferior

Most feature articles on foreign women served as simple instruction in geography and ethnography. These fit in with many popular journals' stated mission to educate their readers in the sciences, and might more readily be grouped with didactic articles on new medical treatments or recent inventions. Still, in most of these pieces, there is a rhetorical twist or spin, a use of foreigners to reflect positively or negatively on Ottoman and Muslim practices. Some titles give a hint of this agenda, as in "the dangers of the corset," or "Chinese foot-binding."[22] In others, the message was embedded in the text of the article itself or appeared as a direct comparison of conditions at the conclusion of the piece. "The Life of Woman" was a frequent column in *Hanımlara Mahsûs Gazete,* generally comprising pagelong articles on women of a particular country. From these pieces, readers would learn the physique of women of a certain country, their domestic habits, and perhaps some hobbies and curious social customs. While writers constructed these features to be of interest for Ottoman readers, highlighting points of similarity or difference relevant to their lives, the tone was generally light and dispassionate, and free of the intricacies of polemic that characterize directly topical essays.

For example, an article on the women of Holland described them as generally blonde, plump, and sweet-faced, as the most zealous housewives in Europe, and as not running about in search of outside entertainment "to the point that even today Dutch women confess to not understanding a single thing about the ways of life of French, Italian, or Spanish women." They were preoccupied with decorating their houses but despite their extreme domesticity, Dutchwomen were advanced in the sciences and arts. They had also apparently taken great care to preserve their national dress, especially headdresses. "But you must not think that these women do not have their own amusements. When Dutch women have finished their work, they hide behind their windows two mirrors forming an angle, and facing opposite the window they pass the time in this fashion, watching the behaviour and promenades of passersby in the street."[23] Dutchwomen by this account would have struck an Ottoman woman sympathetic to the goals of *Hanımlara Mahsûs Gazete* as kindred in several respects: their devoted housewifery and love of flower gardens, their personal cleanliness and attention to appearance, their lack of activities outside the home, and their custom of watching the street from behind shutters, an eloquent image of confinement and observation.

Articles about Japan, on the other hand, made a serious project of assessing the impact of the West on a traditional culture self-consciously trying to modernize. Readers were led to compare themselves with the women of a distant empire facing a distinctly similar set of conflicts between tradition and modernity. Like others struggling to survive European domination, Ottomans saw the Japanese victory in the Russo-Japanese War of 1904-05 as a corrective to relentless pressures from the west and north. Ottomans had been watching Japan closely for some time prior to the Russo-Japanese War, since the similarities in political structure between Japan and the Ottoman Empire were not lost on Ottoman observers, especially after mid-century attempts to join parliamentary innovations and imperial tradition in the Meiji and Tanzimat eras.[24] The surge in interest after 1904–5 was merely a change in degree in the Ottomans' intense curiosity about how the Japanese were balancing their own traditions with the forces of modernity surging through every level of their society. Like other countries in Europe and Asia, Japan was presented in terms of its traditions, but these traditions were presented as curious behaviors that were being abandoned. An article written in 1901 compared the women of Japan to European and Asian women in several respects: they did not tend to get fat like Europeans, their fingers were the size of European children's fingers, their skin color was contrasted with that of Europeans and Indians. Much was made of how Japanese women presented themselves to the world, their use of cosmetics to achieve pallor, their cleverness in arranging their hair, and notably for Ottoman readers, the use of a headcovering when going out in public, also featured in illustrations in other magazines (fig. 9.2).[25] The theme of discarded traditions is clear: Japanese women had abandoned the custom of blackening their teeth, and they did not bind their feet like the Chinese, yet their posture was described as very unhealthy from stooping over to convey humility, a statement sure to raise the eyebrows of readers who followed Ottoman magazines' consistent exhortations to exercise and stand up straight.

The article stated further that Japanese girls at the age of nineteen began to be secluded, and when in public to behave with extreme decorum, and at marriage became extremely obedient and loyal wives, to the point that a sailor returning after fifteen years absence "will find the family honor in a stainless condition. Even if husbands are debauched and vicious, their wives do not consider the idea of taking revenge with the same behaviour."[26] They were devoted mothers, thinking only of their children, and were primarily responsible for childrearing since the husband spent most of his time outside the house. Japanese wives traditionally walked behind their husbands in public, but recently some couples had begun to walk side by side, and they chose between European-style hats and traditional headcoverings when going out. As in Istanbul, it was most rare for husband and wife to walk arm in arm, and such behavior in the street would have been a cause for people's derision.

In the final paragraph the author broke out of this expository mode into a positive critique of Muslim custom by way of Japan, giving credit to a Muslim legal practice for strengthening rather than weakening the social position of women:

> In Japan, in a comparison of women with men, the man is always shown respect and honor. Even though the women of Japan are superior to men in terms of sharpness of intelligence, government and power are in the hands of men. The sole most important reason for this is that women do not bring a dowry at the time of marriage. In Japan, women are always seen as contemptible.[27]

The author linked Japanese women's inferiority to their lack of dowry (*mehr*), which to an Ottoman bride represented a measure of financial security as well as ties to her natal family. The dowry to this author was

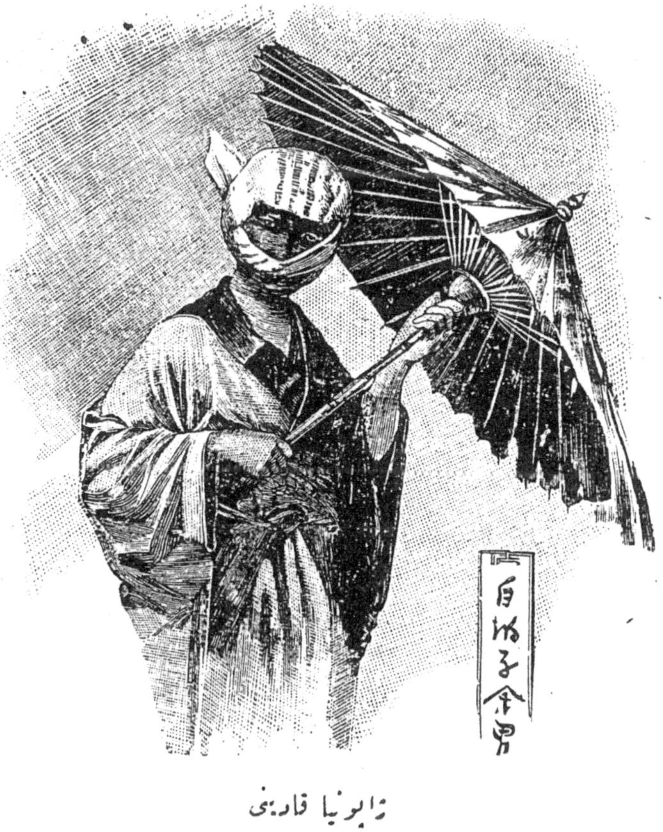


**Fig. 9.2.** Women of Japan. *Hanımlara Mahsûs Gazete* 50 (11 March 1903), p. 1176.

not, as European critics would have had it, a mere commodification of woman but rather her guarantee of worth, status, and protection.

In the aftermath of the Russo-Japanese war, the question of Japanese domestic relations was dealt with in more detail in women's magazines, along with the question of when Japanese women wore the kimono and when they wore Western dress.[28] For the women of Istanbul, Japanese women were both familiar and alien, a rough mixture of qualities to be exclaimed over, seen as kindred, and in some ways pitied. As Japanese women moved up to walk beside their husbands, while still being perceived as lowly and contemptible, Ottoman women may have seen their own movements forward and back in the public and private negotiations of status in a rapidly changing society.

Illustrations in this series on the life of women tended also to focus on distinctly foreign aspects of non-Ottoman culture and in general, whether describing Eskimo nightshirts or Siamese baldpates, these armchair adventures left their readers with a firmer grip on their membership in "the world of Islamic and western civilization." Articles on their neighbors in this civilized world, however, evinced extreme anxiety and ambivalence about their exact position with respect to women of Europe and America. Editors used vignettes of European and American women to depict women both positively and negatively, pushing at or breaking through boundaries of oppressive precedent, of propriety, and of legality.

## Reinventing Women's Work

> In America, when people get out of bed in the morning, they say to each other, "I wonder what Edison will discover today?"
>
> —Bahtiyar, *Hanımlara Mahsûs Gazete*[29]

Adherents of United States exceptionalism would have delighted in the coverage of American invention, hard work, and eccentricity in the popular press. Writers equated "America" with the United States, while Canada, Mexico, and Central and South America fell on the periphery of Ottoman writers' interests. As the home of the Singer sewing machine, which had a highly sucessful market in Ottoman cities, America was associated in Ottoman households with innovation, practicality, speed, and efficiency. In September 1903, the editors of *Hanımlara Mahsûs Gazete* translated a statistical table from a European women's magazine, showing a remarkable growth in female participation in careers in the United States between 1870 and 1890. These statistics gave the impression that American women led the world in breaking new ground in the professions:

| | 1870 | 1890 |
|---|---:|---:|
| Engineer | 0 | 127 |
| Accountant | 0 | 27,777 |
| Architect | 1 | 22 |
| Lawyer | 5 | 208 |
| Beautician (*Te'niktris*) | 7 | 21,185 |
| Dentist | 24 | 337 |
| Journalist | 35 | 888 |
| Theatre director | 100 | 634 |

| | | |
|---|---|---|
| Scientific & literary writer | 159 | 2,725 |
| Printer and sculptor | 411 | 10,810 |
| Official | 414 | 4,875 |
| Doctor and surgeon | 527 | 4,555 |
| Actress | 692 | 3,949 |
| Musician | 5,753 | 34,518 |
| Clerk | 8,016 | 64,048 |
| **Total** | 16,212 | 177,893[30] |

There is no editorial comment on these statistics, which is unusual, given that editors and writers did not ordinarily hesitate to condemn foreign women whom they perceived to be overly public or active. This lack of comment on such short items left it to the reader to determine her own opinion of American women's apparent rush to work. In the context of other articles and illustrations over the years, such as the citation of female patent-holders in the United States to refute Möbius' *Über den physiologischen Schwachsinn des Weibes* ("On the Physiological Feeblemindedness of Females"), further, this neutral presentation takes on the strong possibility of a positive valence.[31]

Innovation was not limited to American women, morever. Following immediately on the statistics of American women reinventing themselves as qualified professionals was a tale of Venetian commercial savvy put into practice by a twenty-three-year-old fitter:

> One of the most tedious things for women is the great amount of time prolonged by clothes fittings, and during this time a thousand kinds of formalities (stand straight, take one step, raise your arm, bend your elbow, turn your neck) must be tolerated while standing on one's feet for hours.
>
> Lately in Venice a large tailoring store set up a competition to see whether or not fitting times could be reduced. A fitter named Mademoiselle Minna, only twenty-three years of age, fitted a very intricate ball gown on a girl in twenty minutes and fifteen seconds.[32]

In 1895, an article such as this would have been addressed to the elite group of readers whose lives were made tedious by submitting to fittings more often than most. By 1903, however, the reader could well have been on the other side of tedium, either tailoring for her own family, or tailoring for pay. In this light, the article fits into the trend of admiring Western efficiency and innovation, and an Ottoman modernist promotion of "zeal and endeavor," qualities also promoted in illustrations of skilled workers in various home, atélier, and factory settings (figs. 9.3 and 9.4).

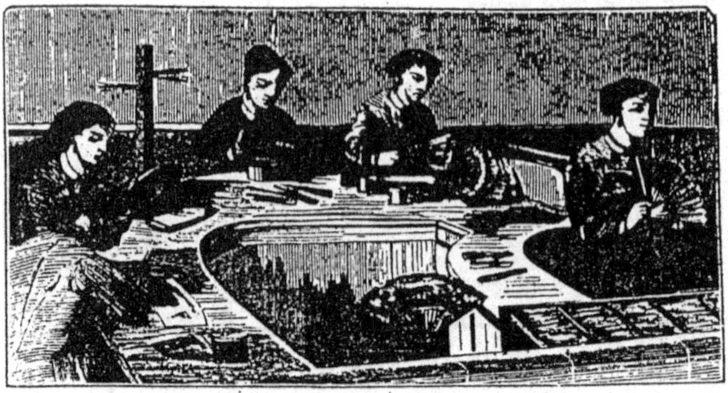

پارسده یلپازه اوزرینه رسم یاپمغه مخصوص ایش محلی ؛ ورسم یاپان قادینلر..

**Fig. 9.3.** Parisian atélier for making fans. *Hanımlara Mahsûs Gazete* 66 (18 June 1896), p. 2

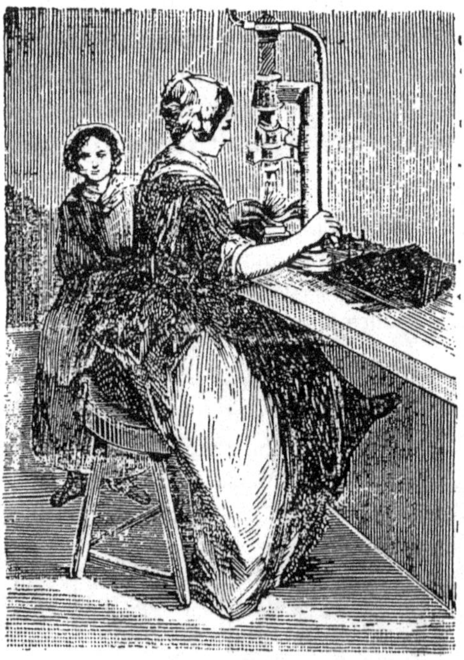

ایکنه اعمالاتی حقنده‌کی رسملریمزدن :

ایکنه‌نك دلنمسی

**Fig. 9.4.** Making holes with needles. *Resimli Gazete* 20 (27 February 1895), p. 205.

Foreigners who succeeded in education and the professions also received either neutral coverage or praise. In December 1898, A. Rasime reported somewhat ambiguously on "a new success for women in France": female lawyers had gained the right to appear in court as lawyers.[33] While it is true that Muslim as well as minority women had for centuries been appearing in court on their own behalf in inheritance and other property cases in traditional *şeriat* courts, it is not yet clear what the relationship of any Ottoman woman was to the new civil courts and the new attorneys graduating from the Imperial Law School founded in 1838.[34] Rasime was unwilling to make a definitive statement for or against women in the professions, arguing that it was more important at the moment to achieve a general level of sophistication in the arts and sciences for the majority of women, rather than to promote one or two female lawyers and doctors. The possibility of Ottoman female lawyers and doctors in the future, though, was left open when Rasime suggested in a social Darwinist vein that in time, women might be able to bring glory "to Islam and to Ottoman womanhood . . . the professions of doctor and lawyer are things which will be known by time and evolution (*tekâmül*)."[35]

Professional European women were frequently praised, moreover, as when the readers of *Hanımlara Mahsûs Gazete* were told in 1904 that in Paris, each neighborhood police station was required to have a doctor on staff, living nearby and receiving a civil stipend. One year after the first appointment of a woman as staff doctor, the government replaced her with a male doctor. Several police chiefs apparently wrote in protest, saying that women doctors worked faster, were at home when needed, instead of at a club or the theater, and were overall more loyal to their jobs.[36] Foreign women resident in Istanbul were given coverage as well, both as in advertisements for Mme. Valentine, a dentist,[37] and in brief announcements, as when it was reported that Mme. Gross, former director of the European telegraph office of the Agence de Constantinople, had returned to Istanbul.[38]

Finally, authors such as Madame de Sévigné and Jane Austen were constantly praised, translated and serialized in Ottoman journals along with their male counterparts, occasionally with a tableau or even an entire series of cartoons to illustrate the plot. While at first the literary writers for the Ottoman press were primarily poets such as Nigâr Hanım and Leylâ Hanım, from the 1890s onward schoolteachers, professional journalists, and other women of the pen such as Emine Semiye and Makbûle Leman presented *adab* essays, short stories, fictionalized fables and vignettes, and serialized novels.[39] This adaptation of European and Russian literary forms to Ottoman narratives has left a record of translation and syncretism too rich to explore here in the detail it merits. For the moment, suffice it to say that the world of literary production produced the least problematic foreign exemplars in the act of publication, though censorship records show that content remained fraught with difficulty. While in 1895 the famous author Fatma Âliye felt it necessary to warn her readers against gaining a reputation for nagging and perpetual outrage like European blue-stockings, she and hundreds of others argued for Ottoman women to take up the pen. Adding to these arguments, there were hundreds of articles promoting female literacy and female professional writers and educators, supplemented by instructional articles on diction, language, and style in speech and performative reading, all as skills to be practiced.[40]

Despite such encouragement, the issue of women's right to write was by no means settled. Emblematic of the mixed messages were illustrations such as one in which a woman was depicted on the front page of a magazine in a pose of concentrated attention to her writing, wondering "What shall I write?" (fig. 9.5), or one extravagantly praising a woman for her hard work and thought as she sat hunched over papers and pen with the caption "Imagine what beautiful works she is creating!" At the same time, the frank frontal gaze of the novel reader in figure 9.6 stands out from the majority of illustrations in this era that showed women gazing into the distance, slightly to the side of the observer, or in profile (fig. 9.6). Fiction is less complicated only by comparison to the compound of front-page condemnation of women defeminized by pursuing higher education, and of women who neglected their households to pursue a profession, offset continually by subversive short items in the back pages that celebrated or at least did not condemn the professional successes of women abroad. Indeed, the roles of women as spectators and leisured readers seem in retrospect more complicated than that of women as producers of entertainment.

## Derelictions of Duty

Hamiyet Zehra minced no words in her condemnation of frivolous women in her 1895 article "The Duty of Women!":

> There are some women who devote most of their time to chasing after amusements. There are some people who, watching these women, are struck with distraction and bewilderment. How is it possible for this woman continually to be going out into the street and wandering around? That woman is charged with any number of duties.[41]

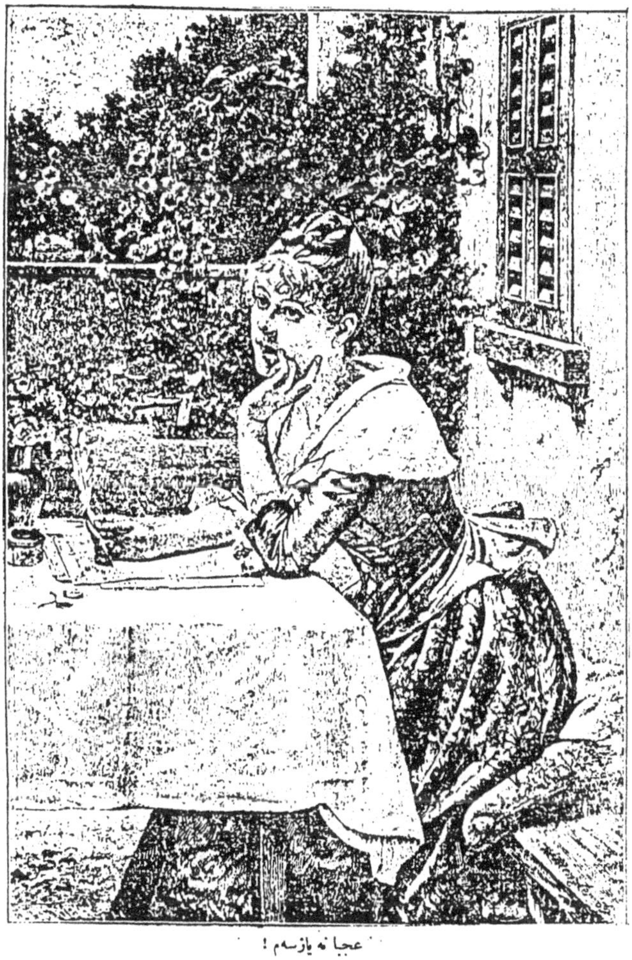


**Fig. 9.5.** "I wonder, what shall I write?" *Hanımlara Mahsûs Gazete* 134 (28 October 1897), p. 1

In her emphasis on hearth and home as the place where women could be mistresses of all the treasures in the world, Hamiyet Zehra argued that women in America and Europe had lost touch with their true duties by pursuing higher education and amusements. She was irked as well by those who attempted to make a show of their erudition, stating that they could only meet with ridicule and disbelief. Curiously, after criticizing American and European women for such behaviors in the main body of the article, in the

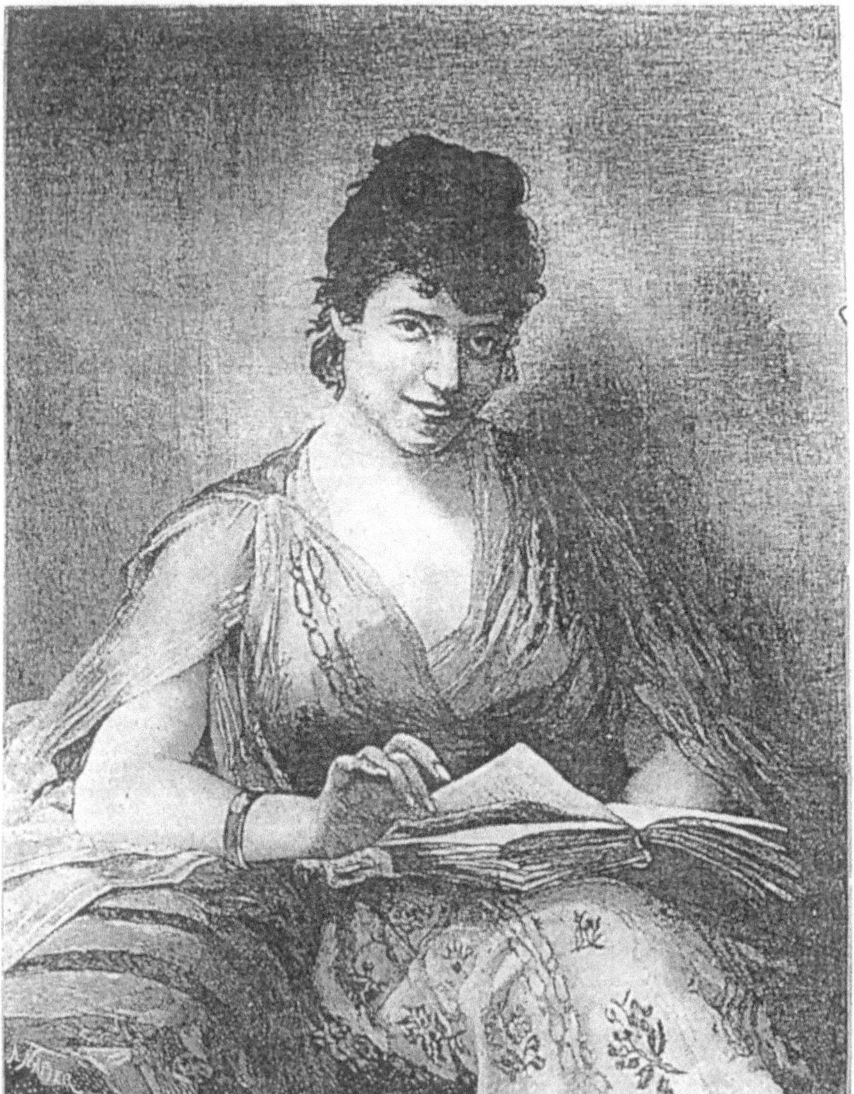

**Fig. 9.6.** A novel reader. *Hanımlara Mahsûs Gazete* 139 (2 December 1897), p. 4

last two paragraphs of the piece from which the excerpt above was taken, she described women chasing after amusement only vaguely as "some women" of no particular regional identity. Further, when she posed her rhetorical question about these frivolous women, she put the women directly in her, and her readers', line of vision and sphere of judgment. Moreover, she concluded her article by inflecting her critique with contempt: "We can only look with pity on this addiction to going out to plays three or four times a week."

This move from distant Americans to women more near at hand put Hamiyet Zehra in company with the satirizers and critics of Ottoman life *alafranga;* her targets at this point were evidently not women abroad but Ottoman women, whether Muslim or not, who neglected their household responsibilities, and were too visibly and frequently present in the streets. In a similar vein but from another angle, when Bahtiyar wrote her article on the kinetoscope, which occasioned the notion that Americans woke up in the morning with Edison on their minds, she celebrated the kinetoscope primarily for allowing people to bring the theater into their own homes, rather than going out into the streets for entertainment.

More than simply arenas for impropriety and entertainment, however, city streets were scenes of depravity and crime, almost universally committed in the universe of the most successful magazine, *Hanımlara Mahsûs Gazete,* by Europeans abroad and non-Muslim women in the empire. As the century wound up, Ottoman Greeks and Armenians increasingly joined foreigners in being separated by journalists from Ottoman Muslims, and were portrayed negatively in the short-items section of the magazine more often than they were portrayed in neutral or admiring terms. For example, short items about foundlings allow a fairly regular story line—a helpless Greek or Armenian infant is found either in deplorable state or dead, having been abandoned on the steps of a Greek or Armenian church.[42] While *Hanımlara Mahsûs Gazete* made frequent reference to its benefactions to the Istanbul orphanage, poorhouse, and handicrafts school for orphan girls, there were no notices of Muslim or Turkish foundlings comparable to those for Greeks or Armenians.

Further, multiple births to Muslim mothers were reported as *bereket-i tenasül* (abundance or blessing of reproduction), a title with a decidedly positive air, as when the wife of İsmail ibn Şa'ban gave birth to triplets, two boys and girl all in fine health and "among the living."[43] A Canadian multiple birth was reported in similarly glowing terms, fitting into a generally positive view of Canada as the nation with such admirable attributes as the lowest divorce rate.[44] The birth announcement also contained an editorial comment that showed a kinship with Canada in its ethnic split as well, commenting that French Canadians maintained their position among the British by achieving a high birth rate. Births to minority Ottoman women often carried a far different inflection, as with the report of a deformed baby on the island of Patras, with the deformities described in painful detail, or when the editors reported with horror the murder of a child on the island of Rhodes.[45]

The largely Christian minority and European neighborhood of Galata, along with quaysides in the city of Istanbul, were the sites of shocking baby events as well, and criminal behavior. In 1903, a "despicable mother" (*denî valide*) was reported to have abandoned her baby in a waiting room for the steam ferry.[46] A year later, a short item titled "Birth in the Streets" described a woman who was walking in the streets of Galata when she felt her first labor pains and took refuge in a tavern, where she gave birth.[47] Female breaches of propriety were not limited to family matters, though, as proven by the long-running career of a gypsy pickpocket (*yankesici*) operating at ferry stops.[48] The net effect of these weekly iterations of foreign or non-Muslim Ottoman women's depravity and criminality was to make suspect and alien the whole question of women's visible presence in the streets.

Ridicule was used almost as much as condemnation to demote foreigners from their supposed preeminence, as when editors reported divorce as well as criminal and civil actions in European and American courts. In 1904, *Hanımlara Mahsûs Gazete* reported "A Lawsuit in Paris":

> Lately in a Paris court, a lawsuit was heard between a husband and wife. The basis for the lawsuit was that a husband had insulted his wife during a quarrel by calling her a camel. . . . [I]t is a grave insult among the French for one person to call another a camel.
>
> During the hearing, it was decided that the husband, being in error, had to pay a one-lira penalty. At that point, when the plaintiff did not hide her pleasure in the presence of the court, the husband addressed the judge, saying, "I have been sentenced to pay a one-lira fine for calling a madame a camel. I wonder, if I called a camel 'Madame,' would I be condemned to pay another fine?" When the judge answered, "You wouldn't," the condemned husband addressed his wife, "Adieu, Madame!" and so saying, he left the courtroom.[49]

When seen against the densely peopled background of Ottoman Muslim propriety in relentlessly moralistic *adab* essays for Muslim women and exemplary tales of female *eslâf-i İslâm* (predecessors in Islamic history), such brief reports of freakishness, impropriety, viciousness, criminality, and silliness attributed to non-Muslim women take on more weight than their brevity would seem to imply. They attest as well to how thoroughly such loaded demarcations had penetrated Ottoman life, in that these distinctions of contempt and condemnation were ubiquitous in even the most trivial sections of the women's illustrated press. When taken in concert with impropriety and criminality reported among European women, coverage of minority Ottoman women's misdeeds betrays a depth to fissures of ethnic identity within Ottomanism at the turn of the century.

## Linking Personal and Public Virtues

As women became increasingly active in the production of knowledge and culture in the public sphere through formal education and popular magazines towards the end of the century, they both mirrored and recast the issues at stake in creating an intrinsically Ottoman modernity. As the bases of civic legitimacy shifted under all subjects of the sultan in an era of growing ethnonationalism within the empire and on its borders, women in the Turkish-language press increasingly identified themselves as Muslim, and conflated Ottoman patriotism with modern Muslim proprieties. This latter point is starkly revealed as writers and responsive readers participated in the breakdown of Ottomanism—a consciously multiconfessional national identity—into Muslim and Turkish nationalisms in response to Greek, Balkan, and then Armenian ethnonationalist ideologies articulated with increasing force throughout the century. Writers throughout the press used anthropological and social Darwinist analyses to guide their readers to view both western modernity and westernized modernity among Greek, Balkan, and Armenian nationalities, with considerable skepticism. Writers and readers joined to select from both western practices and from Islamic and Asian practices to create an intrinsically Muslim, nonwestern modernity, which they linked increasingly to patriotism writ large and in the minutiae of daily life. More, they increasingly chose for their needs a broad range of beliefs and practices present within Islam as a sociopolitical compound, and refitted their choices to forward an Ottoman modernizing project. In a sense they used such western ideas as social Darwinism and the human and mechanical technologies of industrial capital as tools to sculpt a series of modern female images out of their Ottoman heritage: educated mothers, scientific housewives, partners in nuclear households, schoolteachers, journalists, skilled workers. They set these images against a backdrop of non-Ottoman and non-Muslim women in poses ranging from the heroic (French police doctors), through the ridiculous (silly plaintiffs), to the criminal (pickpockets and mothers abandoning their babies). These female productions of print culture, then, literally brought modernity home, where readers took it as their own, and made of it individual compounds of choice, rejection, and subversion, which imply far more complex relations of Ottomans to the modern world than our current histories of conquest, decline, and revolution can convey.

## Notes

1. *Hanımlara Mahsûs Gazete,* no. 326 (19 Ağustos 1317/17 Cemaziyelevvel 1319/1 September 1901).

2. KDB: *İnsaniyet,* no. 1 (1299/1881–82): 9–16.

3. Mehmet Rauf, "Büyük Bir Kadın: İngiliz Kraliçesi," *Mehâsin,* no. 1 (Eylül 1324/September 1908): 5–12; Mustafa Refik, "İngiltere'nin en Meşhur Aşçısı," *Mehâsin,* no. 3 (Teşrin-i Sani 1324/November 1908): 191–99; Bintürreşat Übeyde, "Amerika Nisvâni," *Mehâsin,* no. 5 (Kanûn-i Sani 1324/January 1909): 352–56; Cenap Şahabettin, "Rasime-i Hoşamedi: Madame Sarah Bernhardt," *Mehâsin,* no. 3 (Teşrin-i Sani 1324/November 1908): 147–49; Tahsin Nahit, "Musahabe-i Edebiye: Edmond ve Rosemonde Rostand," *Mehâsin,* no. 5 (Kanûn-i Sani 1324/January 1909): 298–303; Tahsin Nahit, "Musahabe-i Edebiye: Kontes Matyü Dunway," *Mehâsin,* no. 6 (Şubat 1324/February 1909): 389–95.

4. *Hanımlara Mahsûs Gazete,* no. 152 (26 Şubat 1313/17 Şevval 1315/10 March 1898): 4.

5. *Hanımlara Mahsûs Gazete,* no. 500 (24 Şubat 1320/2 Muharrem 1323/9 March 1905): 6.

6. *Hanımlara Mahsûs Gazete,* no. 326 (19 Ağustos 1317/17 Cemaziyelevvel 1319/1 September 1901): 5.

7. *Hanımlara Mahsûs Gazete,* no. 507 (22 Safer 1323/14 Nisan 1321/27 April 1905): 2.

8. Ibid.

9. *Hanımlara Mahsûs Gazete,* no. 9 (29 Teşrin-i Sani 1323/6 Zilkade 1325/12 December 1907): 6.

10. *Hanımlara Mahsûs Gazete,* no. 30 (25 Eylül 1319/16 Recep 1321/8 November 1903): 693.

11. The press provided extensive coverage of charitable organizations and individual activities, and *Hanımlara Mahsûs Gazete* itself ran frequent clothing drives for orphans, as well as collecting monies for the dowries of orphaned girls. The increasing civic responsibility given to women was attested to by opposition thinkers as well, as in Ahmet Rıza's *Vazife ve Mes'uliyet,* a series published in

Cairo in at the turn of the century, divided into advice for princes, soldiers, and women.

12. For an elaboration of how censorship operated in the Hamidian sphere to promote high rates of publication, see my dissertation, "Unimagined Communities: State, Press, and Gender in the Hamidian Era," Princeton University, Department of Near Eastern Studies, June 1996.

13. Jürgen Habermas, *The Structural Transformation of the Public Sphere,* trans. Thomas Berger, with the assistance of Frederick Lawrence (Cambridge: MIT Press, 1989), introduction.

14. See Leslie Peirce *The Imperial Harem: Women and Sovereignty in the Ottoman Empire* (New York: Oxford University Press, 1993), for a discussion of households as units of authority and power, and the architectural and mental uses of thresholds and interior spaces to designate access to authority and power.

15. The grande dame of these magazines was *Hanımlara Mahsûs Gazete* (*The Ladies' Own Gazette*), which thrived for fourteen years (1895–1909), and published its own supplements for girls and a separate gazette for children. It was financially successful enough to found its own printing press and circulated throughout the empire and into Europe and Russia. While it clearly had official protection at the outset, it is unclear whether it succeeded on this count or because it earned a living for its staff.

16. A term derived from *allafranca* and used to describe Westernized things or people.

17. See, for example, Patrick Williams and Laura Chrisman, eds. *Colonial Discourse and Post-Colonial Theory: A Reader* (New York: Columbia University Press, 1994), 21–124, 191–268.

18. See Charles Issawi, *The Economic History of Turkey 1800–1914* (Chicago: University of Chicago Press, 1980); Reşat Kasaba, *The Ottoman Empire and the World Economy: The Nineteenth Century* (Albany: State University of New York Press, 1988); Roger Owen, *The Middle East in the World Economy 1800–1914* (New York: Methuen Press, 1982); Şevket Pamuk *The Ottoman Empire and European Capitalism, 1820–1913: Trade, Investment, and Production* (Cambridge: Cambridge University Press, 1987); Zafer Toprak, *Türkiye'de "Milli İktisat," 1908–1918* (Ankara: Yurt Yayınları, 1982).

19. *Hanımlara Mahsûs Gazete,* no. 5 (1 Nisan 1320/27 Muharrem 1322/14 April 1905): 71.

20. See Halide Edib on her childhood reading of an illustrated geography of Africa in *Memoires* (New York, 1929), 89–91. Also see "Patagonian Women," *Hanımlara Mahsûs Gazete,* no. 490 (15 Şevval 1322/9 Kanûn-i Evvel 1320/22 December 1904). Other examples in *Hanımlara Mahsûs Gazete* are "The Chinese," no. 166 (11 Haziran 1314/3 Safer 1316/23 June 1898); "The New Japan," no. 492 (29 Şevval 1322/23 Kanûn-i Evvel 1320/5 January 1905); "Siamese Women," no.

326 (19 Ağustos 1317/17 Cemaziyelevvel 1319/1 September 1901); and short notices throughout the gazette about European women winning academic prizes and achieving success in the arts and in various professions, as *Hanımlara Mahsûs Gazete,* no. 500 (2 Muharrem 1322/24 Şubat 1320/9 March 1905).

21. Zeynep Çelik, *The Remaking of Istanbul: Portrait of an Ottoman City in the Nineteenth Century* (Seattle and London: The University of Washington Press, 1986); Steven Rosenthal, *The Politics of Dependency: Urban Reform in Istanbul* (Westport, Conn.: Greenwood Press, 1980), 3–28.

22. Gülistan İsmet, "Korsa kullanmayınız," *Hanımlara Mahsûs Gazete,* no. 357 (4 Nisan 1318/8 Muharrem 1320/17 April 1902): 1–2; "Mütenevvia: Çin kadınlarının Ayağı," *Hanımlara Mahsûs Gazete,* no. 25 (19 Ağustos 1320/17 Cemaziyelevvel 1322/1 September 1904): 391.

23. "Felemenk Kadınları," *Hanımlara Mahsûs Gazete,* no. 9 (29 Nisan 1320/ 25 Safer 1322/5 May 1904): 131.

24. Several treatments of Japanese and Ottoman modernization can be found in Dankwart Rustow and Robert Ward, eds., *Political Modernization of Japan and Turkey* (Princeton: Princeton University Press, 1964). See also Renée Worringer, "Japan as Archetype: Arab Nationalist Considerations as Reflected in the Press, 1887–1920," paper presented at the Middle East Studies Association Annual Conference, Washington, D.C., December 7, 1996.

25. "Japonya Kadınları," *Hanımlara Mahsûs Gazete,* no. 337 (25 Teşrin-i Evvel 1317/25 Recep 1319/31 October 1901): 5–6.

26. Ibid.

27. Ibid. For a discussion of Egyptian intellectuals adopting western critiques of Muslim culture in an effort to modernize, see Leila Ahmed, *Women and Gender in Islam* (New Haven: Yale University Press, 1992), 161ff; and Beth Baron, *The Women's Awakening in Egypt: Culture, Society, and the Press* (New Haven: Yale University Press, 1994), 4–6.

28. For other articles on Japan, see "Japonyalılar," *Hanımlara Mahsûs Gazete,* no. 5 (1 Nisan 1320/27 Muharrem 1322/14 April 1904): 69–71; "Japonyalılara Dair-1," *Hanımlara Mahsûs Gazete,* no. 10 (6 Mayıs 1320/4 Rebiyülevvel 1322/ 21 May 1904): 148–49; "Japonyalılara Dair-2," *Hanımlara Mahsûs Gazete,* no. 11 (13 Mayıs 1320/10 Rebiyülevvel 1322/27 May 1904): 163–64; "Japonyalılara Dair-3," *Hanımlara Mahsûs Gazete,* no. 12 (20 Mayıs 1320/17 Rebiyülevvel 1322/5 June 1904): 180–81; "Japonya'da İnas Darülfünunu," *Hanımlara Mahsûs Gazete,* no. 522 (9 Cemaziyelahir 1323/28 Temmuz 1321/10 August 1905): 3.

29. Bahtiyar, "Kinetoskop nedir?" *Hanımlara Mahsûs Gazete,* no. 22 (2 Teşrin-i Sani 1311/22 Cemaziyelevvel 1313/15 November 1905): 2.

30. "Havadis-i Nisa'iye," *Hanımlara Mahsûs Gazete,* no. 28 (11 Eylül 1319/2 Receb 1321/24 September 1903): 650–51. See also "A New Invention in America," *Hanımlara Mahsûs Gazete,* no. 151 (19 Şubat 1313/10 Şevval 1315/3 March 1898): 4; Ahmet Faruki, "İksir-i Melahat" (Elixir of Beauty Invented by an

American Girl), *Hanımlara Mahsûs Gazete,* no. 490 (15 Şevval 1322/9 Kanûn-i Sani 1320/22 December 1904): 3.

31. Leipzig, 1900. A best-seller in Europe, this book went through nine editions and numerous translations, such as *De la debilidad cerebral fisiológico, o el sentido débil fisiológico de la mujer* (Quito 1902) and *L'inferioritá mentale della donna* (Turin 1904). The Ottoman respondent rebutted Möbius' claims by asserting that more girls than boys won prizes in the Ottoman state schools and by pointing out the variety and number of inventions patented by American women. *Hanımlara Mahsûs Gazete,* no. 338 (8 Teşrin-i Sani 1317/11 Şubat 1319/21 November 1901): 3.

32. "Havadis-i Nisa'iye," *Hanımlara Mahsûs Gazete,* no. 28 (11 Eylül 1319/ 2 Receb 1321/24 September 1903): 650–51.

33. A. Rasime, "Fransa'da yeni bir muvaffakiyet-i nisvâniye," *Hanımlara Mahsûs Gazete,* no. 191 (3 Kanûn-i Evvel 1314/1 Şaban 1316/15 December 1898): 2–3.

34. See Fatma Müge Göçek, "Ethnic Segmentation, Western Education, and Political Outcomes: Nineteenth-Century Ottoman Society," *Poetics Today* 14:3 (Fall 1993).

35. Rasime, "Fransa'da yeni bir muvaffakiyet-i nisvâniye."

36. Ibid., 3.

37. *Hanımlara Mahsûs Gazete,* no. 47 (29 Kanûn-i Sani 1319/24 Zilkade 1321/11 February 1904): 1107; *Hanımlara Mahsûs Gazete,* no. 495 (13 Kanûn-i Sani 1320/ 20 Zilkade 1322/26 January 1905): 8.

38. *Hanımlara Mahsûs Gazete,* no. 4 (1 Mart 1320/29 Zilhicce 1321/17 March 1904): 2.

39. *Adab* refers to literature or behavior; as a literary genre, *adab* or *edeb* essays were used to outline proper civic, public, and private behaviors in Muslim societies. Makbûle Leman, "Bir Hikâye: Tashih," *Hanımlara Mahsûs Gazete,* no. 14 (5 Teşrin-i Evvel 1311/28 Rebiyülevvel 1313/17 October 1895): 2–4; Makbûle Leman, "İmtihan," *Hanımlara Mahsûs Gazete,* no. 84 (17 Teşrin-i Evvel 1312/22 Cemaziyelevvel 1314/29 September 1896): 1–3; Emine Semiye, "Muʿallime" *Hanım Kizlara Mahsûs Gazete,* no. 58 (8 Nisan 1315/20 April 1899): 8.

40. Makbûle Leman, "Bir Hikâye: Tashih," *Hanımlara Mahsûs Gazete,* no. 14 (5 Teşrin-i Evvel 1311/28 Rebiyülevvel 1313/17 October 1895): 2–4.

41. Hamiyet Zehra, "Kadınlarda Vazife!" *Hanımlara Mahsûs Gazete,* no. 25 (13 Teşrin-i Sani 1311/8 Cemaziyelahir 1313/27 November 1895): 2–3.

42. *Hanımlara Mahsûs Gazete,* nos. 28 (11 Eylül 1319/2 Recep 1321/24 September 1903) to 30 (25 Eylül 1319/16 Recep 1321/8 October 1903) and 42 (25 Kanûn-i Evvel 1319/17 Şevval 1321/7 January 1904): 2.

43. *Hanımlara Mahsûs Gazete,* no. 1 (4 Mart 1320/29 Zilhicce 1321/17 March 1904): 2.

44. *Hanımlara Mahsûs Gazete,* no. 34 (24 Teşrin-i Sani 1319/16 Şaban 1321/5 November 1903): 2.

45. *Hanımlara Mahsûs Gazete,* no. 5 (5 Nisan 1319/18 Muharrem 1321/16 April 1903): 2.

46. *Hanımlara Mahsûs Gazete,* no. 3 (20 Mart 1319/4 Muharram 1321/2 April 1903): 53.

47. "Yol'da vazı-ı haml," *Hanımlara Mahsûs Gazete,* no. 23 (5 Ağustos 1320/16 Cemaziyelahir 1322/25 August 1904): 354.

48. *Hanımlara Mahsûs Gazete,* no. 4 (27 Mart 1319/11 Muharrem 1321/9 April 1903): 2.

49. *Hanımlara Mahsûs Gazete,* no. 1 (4 Mart 1320/29 Zilhicce 1321/17 March 1904): 2.

10

# "Nothing Romantic about It!"

## A Critique of Orientalist Representation in the Installations of Houria Niati

*Salah Hassan*

Houria Niati is an Algerian-born, London-based contemporary artist whose work presents an interesting and dynamic interplay of gender representation and creativity as informed by her experience of working and living in the West. Executed in a postmodernist conceptual mode, Niati's work confronts colonialist and Orientalist imagery under which Algerian and other Middle Eastern women were the object of a controlling western gaze. In a series of installations, executed in the late 1980s and early 1990s, Niati addressed the subject matter of Orientalist paintings, such as Delacroix's *The Women of Algiers* and popular imagery circulated in the form of postcards during the French occupation of Algeria. The "subject" of these Orientalist images is multifold: on one level, they are colorful, detailed representations of ordinary Muslim and North African women, but on another level they are the product of a western male visual system that "objectifies" the Algerian and North African women from a position of a colonial power.

As recent critical approaches to art history reveal, works of art are part of a visual system of representation in which the relationship between the "subject" and "object" is determined within a socially constructed field of vision. Following this line of interrogation within feminist discourse, the relationship between the "viewer" and the "viewed" emerges as explicitly or implicitly gendered. In a western male-dominated field of visual production, it is the men who have historically controlled the "gaze," consequently giving men power over women's representation, and hence their external identities. Within such a system, women of Middle Eastern and African descent suffer double jeopardy as the marginalized "other" when shared elements of gender and race are juxtaposed and foregrounded.

The issues of marginalization, otherness, and the gendered visual field area by now recognized by scholars of visual culture and comfortably accepted in mainstream intellectual debate. In the art world, as well, the theme of men looking at women, and women turning the gaze back upon men, has been explored. But rarely has one artist used her work to critique the politically repressive role of the colonial and gendered gaze, which, in Africa, the Middle East, and Asia, combined to dehumanize the subject nation, and thus to intellectualize and disapprove it, while humanizing the colonial power, thus asserting the superior strength, rationality, and justice of the European nations. The gendering of roles thus served political aims, and representation was a powerful tool for assigning the colonized and the colonizer to their respective gender positions.

Niati's work exposes the relationship between colonial hegemony and gender. Moreover, she takes colonial imagery as her starting point and repossesses her own image and the representation of her women compatriots. In more ways than one, her works deconstruct and critique the hegemonic gaze that sought to objectify and fetishize North African women, and in so doing, she subverts the power system that establishes them as "other" and "marginal." Niati is engaged in constructing new visual systems of representation and thus establishes herself as an active author who is no longer the displaced and subdued object of a hegemonic (foreign and male) gaze. Instead, she has become a centrally located active creator who calls that gaze into question.

From an equally important perspective, the life and works of Houria Niati are exemplary of the little-known journeys of African and other nonwestern artists into western centers of modernism: London, Paris, and other western metropolises. As I have argued elsewhere, African artists have been at the forefront of modernism as well as postmodernism.[1] Like other African artists in her predicament, Niati's work appears prima facie indistinguishable from that of her western colleagues, yet a more careful look reveals her work as reflective of her experiences and expressive of her problematic relationship with western modernism and the western world in which she lives. Hence, her work can only be analyzed and understood within the context of the "other's" response to colonialism and postcolonial conditions and resistance to western hegemonic practices.

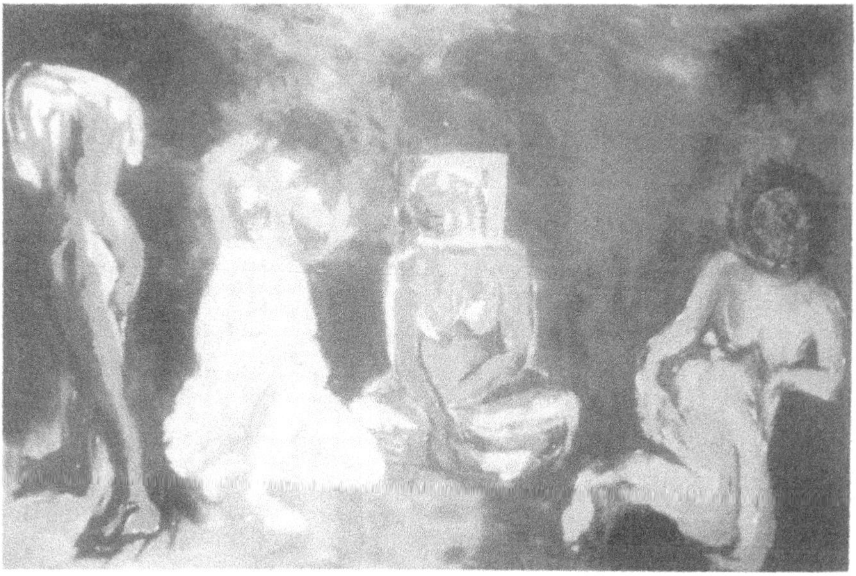

**Fig. 10.1.** Houria Niati, *No to the Torture* (detail) 1983–1996. Mixed media installation

In this essay, I focus primarily on two of Niati's recent installations. The first entitled *No to the Torture* (fig. 10.1), is a commentary on the nineteenth-century Orientalist French painter Eugene Delacroix's *The Women of Algiers.* The other, entitled *Nothing Romantic about Bringing Water from the Fountain* (figs. 10.2–4), continues in her exploration of similar Orientalist images and constructs of Algerian women in popular photographs and postcards from the French colonial period in Algeria. A study of these photographs and postcards has recently been made by the Algerian writer Malek Alloula in *The Colonial Harem.*[2]

The two installations are discussed here within the context of the Orientalist tradition, which Niati's work criticizes, and in relation to colonialism and postcolonial circumstances. This, it is hoped, will shed some light on the untold and complex experiences of African artists in their confrontation with the West and with themselves as well. Hence, Houria Niati's work is best read with her biography as the subtext, which, I believe, motivates and renders her visual artistic expressions even more meaningful. In other words, Niati's installations are autobiographical, in the sense that literary critics would call auto/text or auto/fiction. Niati's work is significant in relation to the Algerians' discourse on their own culture, that

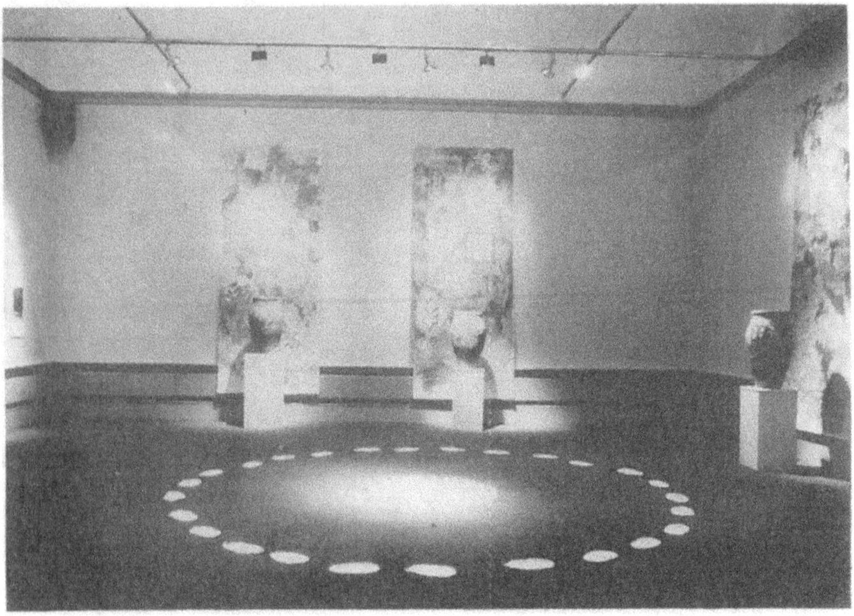

**Fig. 10.2.** Houria Niati, *Nothing Romantic about Bringing Water from the Fountain,* 1991. Mixed media installation

is, Algerians' views and evaluations of their culture and other concepts central to their critical value judgments. In this respect, Niati is participating in a larger intellectual and creative effort initiated by her Algerian compatriots, especially women, who have been engaged in a critical and self-critical discourse about the West, their own past, and present society and culture.

Born in 1948 in Khemis Miliana, a small town near Algiers, Houria Niati earned a diploma in community work specializing in visual arts and music. She has been living and working in London since 1979 where she studied at the Camden Art Center and Croydon College of Art. Like many other Algerians of her generation, Niati lived part of her childhood under the French occupation toward the end of the war for independence in the late 1950s and early 1960s. The French occupation of Algeria, which lasted over a century, ended with Algerian independence in 1960 after a heroic armed and mass political resistance led by the F.L.N. (the National Front for Liberation) and in which over one million Algerians were killed by the brutal efforts of the French to end the resistance. She witnessed the cruelties of the French and the heroic resistance of her people. At age twelve, Niati

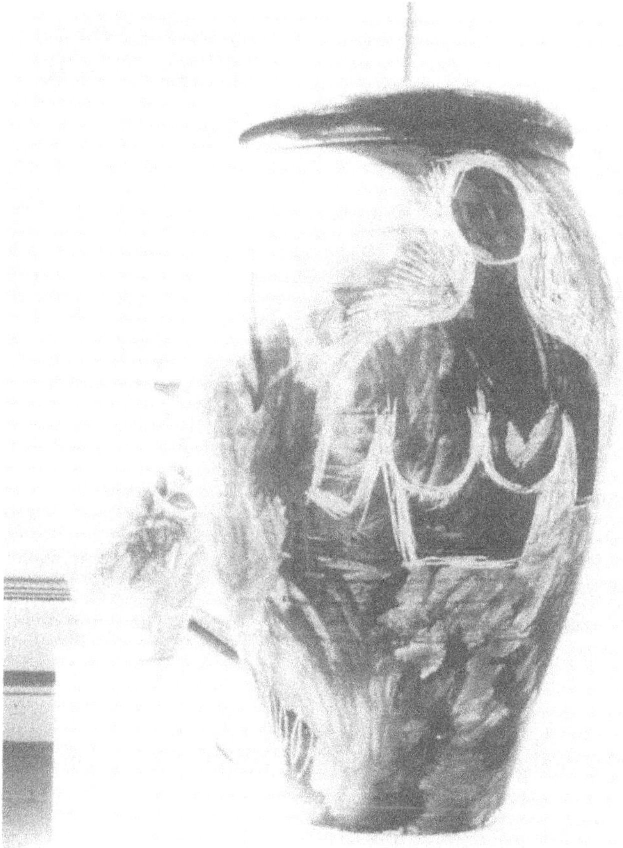

**Fig. 10.3.** Houria Niati, *Nothing Romantic about Bringing Water from the Fountain,* 1991. Mixed media installation

experienced that terror first hand when she was jailed briefly for writing anticolonial graffiti and participating in a demonstration against the French occupation. Niati still recalls being isolated in a prison cell and the real fear that, as a child, she felt of torture or death. Moving to London at the age of thirty in the late 1970s to study art, Niati found herself again confronting the West, but on different terms; this time with respect to images made by westerners of her country and people, especially women—fictionalized, exoticized, and constructed in western paintings or in photographs from the nineteenth and early part of the twentieth centuries.

In understanding Niati's experience, one must avoid the risk of oversimplifying the colonial experience. The West in itself, transformed by the

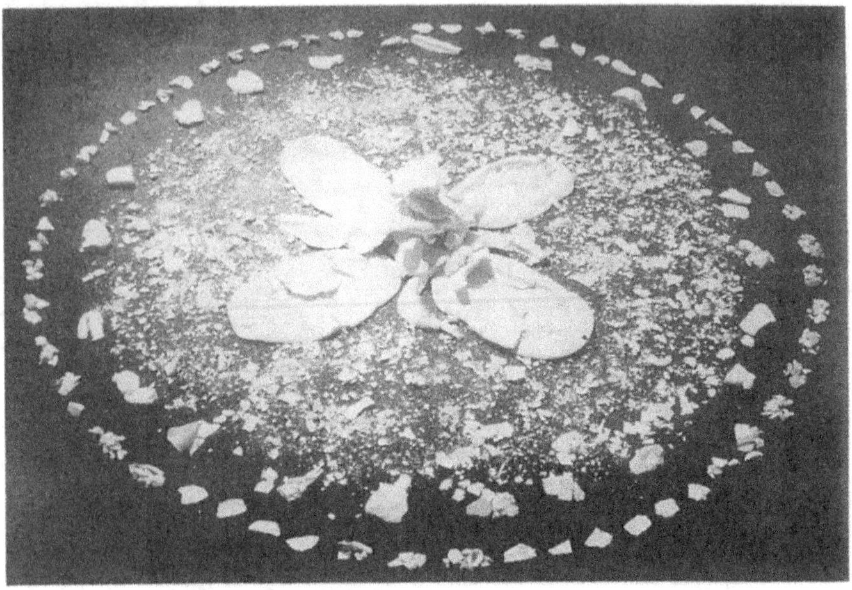

**Fig. 10.4.** Houria Niati, *Nothing Romantic about Bringing Water from the Fountain,* 1991. Mixed media installation

colonial experience, accorded Niati, an emigré, the expatriate status, and provided her a second home among a community of liberal intellectuals and artists in London. It is an irony of the colonial experience that the western metropolis, such as London or Paris, becomes a safe haven for political radicals and avant-garde artists from ex-colonialized territories, despite past colonial expression. One may go so far as to suggest that this setting provided them a more receptive audience to their artistic production, and in some cases more enthusiastic to their work than what could be expected from people in their homeland. Such ambivalences and contradictions of the colonial experience are essential and fascinating aspects of being an emigré in a colonial metropole. Niati's new experience in the West, plus her complex background as a woman, a Muslim Algerian of Arabic and Berber heritage, are reflected in her style and in the multiple references in her work. These multiple references serve as an essential point of departure in understanding Niati's installations.

The multiple references, the sources of design, the motifs, and the distinct techniques Niati has developed in her work are complex and merit deep consideration. Niati's attachment to her cultural and artistic heritage grew deeper and, ironically, were strengthened by her European experience. This becomes evident in her visual vocabulary. Niati likened the silhouette-like figures in her paintings to those of ancient Egyptian hieroglyphs, and the techniques of the scratching that marks the surfaces of her work to those of the ancient cave painting of Tassilli-n-ʿAjjir in the southern part of Algeria. Asserting her pan-African vision, Niati employs motifs and designs from wider African artistic traditions expressed in the mask-like figures and recognizably West African decorative elements that occupy her canvases. She also attributes similar designs to the magical world of folk tales and legends she grew accustomed to as part of her childhood. Niati admits to the influence of postimpressionism, surrealism, and various twentieth-century European artists, more specifically Cy Twombly, in her artistic development. However, she asserts her Algerian and African identity, as well as her right, like her Western colleagues, of looking at artistic traditions other than her own and using what she likes. As she often comments on her experience in Europe, "I speak with a French accent, and in Europe some got confused about how to classify me, but I am not French, I am Algerian and an African." It is clear that over the years Niati has successfully developed her distinctive style and visual language, derived from multiple sources, to explore issues related to her culture, her own existential circumstances, and the world at large. Even while she reworks images and motifs from the past, Niati works in a postmodernist mode that shows she is not the product of a static tradition but at the forefront of a rapidly changing, innovative global art movement.

Niati often employs vivid, raw colors painted directly over her canvases without sketching. A daring artist by nature, Niati works spontaneously exploring as well as developing her concepts as the work progresses. She normally paints in layers starting with bright colors and following with darker ones. The layers are then worked into shapes and forms that are again painted with fresh brush strokes and solid painted shapes, giving the work a pastel-like texture, the trademark of Niati's style. Such remarkable spontaneity reflects Niati's original and uninhibited nature born out of her instinctive knowledge and strengthened by her constant struggle and need for adaptation to new environments and places.

Niati's installations consist of a series of paintings and mixed media works with a vibrant environment of sound and color, accompanied by poetry and songs by the artist herself. As a trained singer in the Andalusian-Shaʿbi and Rai musical traditions (publicized in the west through the music of Cheb Khalid, the Algerian singer), Niati accompanies her exhibitions with a musical performance in which she sings traditional Algerian songs and reads English translations of her own poetry (ironically, composed in French, see appendix for an example).

Through the live performances that accompany Niati's installations, she attempts to communicate her work to the audience and maximize its effect. In these performances, Niati brings together the visual and verbal expressive elements of her culture and makes them relevant to contemporary issues and concerns. She also uses synthesizers, sound recordings, and special light effects to create a theater-like atmosphere. Hence, Niati's installations become vibrant, magical environments of sound, body movement, and color.

Created in 1982–83, *No to the Torture* (fig. 10.1), is based on Delacroix's well-known painting *Women of Algiers* (1834), depicting idealized and stereotyped images of Algerian women. This installation was first exhibited in the Cartwright Hall Museum, in Bradford, England, in 1990. It is composed of five paintings, drawings, sound tracks, and photos in addition to Niati's own performance of songs and dance at the opening—the content and form of which is integral to the installation. In the 1990s exhibition, Niati included a series of earlier paintings in pastels and mixed media accomplished in 1988, and entitled *Commentary on the Women of Algiers by Delacroix.* Five paintings from the same installation, in addition to three new paintings Niati had finished in 1993, are part of a traveling exhibition that recently toured the United States.[3] Hence, Delacroix is a theme that Niati has explored for some time and in a variety of contexts.

In *Bringing Water from the Fountain,* which was exhibited for the first time in 1991 at the Harris Museum, in Preston, England, a sound track of female voices and of water accompanies several painted huge jars (fig. 10.3).[4] Niati installed plaster molds of her bare feet in a circle placed on the center of the gallery's floor (fig. 10.4) and surrounded them with a series of paintings on canvas and paper hung on the wall of the gallery (fig. 10.2). Also on the walls were a series of old photographs in the tradition of the French colonial postcards depicting Algerian women carrying jars and burdens on their heads and shoulders.

Niati's (re)presentations of Orientalist painting and colonial-era photography are critical readings of stereotypes of nonwestern women, in particular North African women. The images that she uses belong to the genres and media that work with other forms of western visual representation to represent the "other": the travel images of North Africa by David Roberts, the documentary photographs of Francis Frith, and the modernist genre as represented by Matisse and Picasso, all assumed a standpoint from which westerners observed and recorded scores and people who were nonwestern and thus visually interesting. The themes of Niati's installations are in dialogue with these western conventions and images of nonwestern people and are rendered more meaningful when read in these contexts. It has been argued that "Orientalist pictures carry meaning through their relation to other pictures and conventions in the Western tradition."[5] This is to say that representations of eastern women, and in particular Muslim women, fascinated western audiences who had keen appetite for such images, precisely because they are different. But in this case, such naive seeing did not necessarily imply understanding. Indeed, the representation of the "strange" dress and appearance of Muslim women served, if anything, to artificially exoticize and fetishize them, while at the same time suggesting an illusory veracity.

In paintings, drawings, or photographs, Orientalist images were accepted by western audiences as authentic ethnographic documentation of their subjects. Among westerners, these images have long been endowed with unquestionable documentary power and regarded as objective and factual representations of their subject matter. Recent scholarship, however, has argued to the contrary. Orientalism, according to Edward Said, has never been a product of a sincere dialogue between western culture and others. Instead, it is a discourse in service of western hegemonic practices and an ideology that has served to rationalize and advance western imperialism in conquering and exploiting the "other" geographically and intellectually. Orientalism, as Said explains, "depends for its strategy on this flexible positional superiority, which put the Westerner in a whole series of possible relationships with the Orient without ever losing him the relative upper hand."[6] Said has articulated eloquently that Orientalism, despite its seemingly coherent content, has been a distorted ideology and private fantasy of its occidental creators.[7]

Delacroix's *The Women of Algiers,* which constitutes a point of departure and contestation for Niati's installation, was a landmark in the Orientalist tradition of European painting that was followed by many modernist European disciples working in the Orientalist genre decades into the twentieth century. Many accepted these European images as eyewitness accounts of Algerian and North African women behind the veil and in the harem. But the ethnographic authority of Delacroix's representation is questionable in light of its particular history as an image. *The Women of Algiers* was a product of a three-day visit to the port of Algiers on June

25–28, 1832, during the stop of a ship aboard which Delacroix was traveling. His visit was part of a French government diplomatic mission headed for Morocco to seek its cooperation in the conquest of Algeria. He was invited by the Comte Charles de Mornay, the ambassador who headed the delegation to Morocco, to commemorate the trip in sketches and watercolors.[8] Such facts established Delacroix's position as part of the western colonial hegemonic structure at the beginning of what was to become the tragic and ill-fated venture of the French in Algeria. During his brief stay, Delacroix was allowed into the women's section of the palace of the harbor-master of the Dey of Algiers, to whom he was introduced by the French chief engineer of the harbor. Delacroix was quoted to have cried out loud: "It is splendid! It's like in the time of Homer! Women in the women's quarters, looking after their children, spinning or weaving wonderful stuffs! This is my idea of woman!"[9]

Delacroix's painting, which depicts Algerian women as exotic odalisques in a harem, was the product of a visit of a few hours, at best. Paradoxical to this fact was Delacroix's detailed depiction of the women's cloth and jewelry, palace interior, and architecture, which was used to enhance the ethnographic claim of the work, as if the veracity of the details confirmed the truth and objectivity of the representation as a whole. Delacroix had little first-hand acquaintance with the lives and customs of Algerian women; as a man and a foreigner, it is highly doubtful that he would have seen anything beyond the women's reception room where they entertained female visitors and as on this rare occasion, the occasional man. His knowledge of North African women and their quarters was undoubtedly mediated by European travel accounts, which were increasingly abundant and with which he was well acquainted.[10] For visual details, he followed the conventions, iconographic concerns, and detailed descriptions of costumes found in the drawings and water color paintings that illustrated travel books.

Even more than Delacroix's painting, the French postcards of colonial Algeria have been viewed as photodocumentaries and endowed with ethnographic authority, however surrealistic or pornographic some of them may seem by today's standards (fig. 10.5). Assumingly unmediated and noninterpretive, these photographs seem to claim a greater truth than painting. Perhaps, it is because of the mechanical and thus supposedly more objective eye of the camera itself or the clarity of the photographic medium in which it is seemingly impossible to hide anything. However, as Susan Sontag argued, "the authority of the photograph will always depend on the

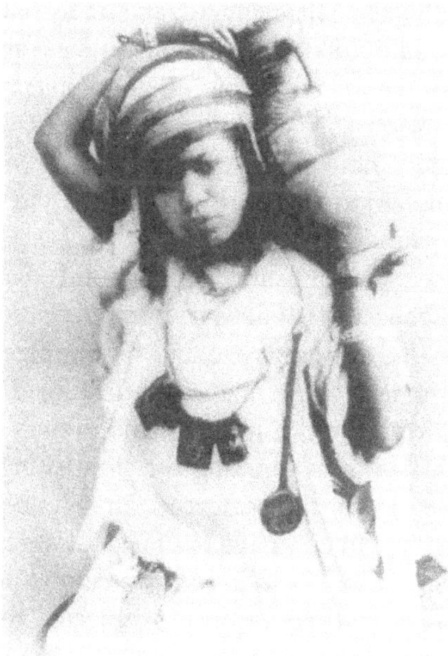

**Fig. 10.5.** Postcard, North Africa (Algeria?), late 19th or early 20th c.

subject, . . . all claims on behalf of photography as art must emphasize the subjectivity of seeing."[11] Their ethnographic claim had gone to the extreme of viewing Algerians, specially women's bodies and lives, as objects subjected to classification according to the title of some of the postcard series, *Scènes et Types.* In those photographs we find Algerian women's bodies eroticized, sexualized, and classified accordingly. Photographs such as figure 10.5 and others are among many from that tradition that have formed, according to Niati, the basis for Niati's installation *Bringing Water from the Fountain.* The origin of these postcards can be traced to the late-nineteenth-century commercial ventures by certain French entrepreneurial families.[12] For decades, these postcards served as a popular means of correspondence between the French settlers of Algeria and their families, relatives, and acquaintances in France. The profit-seeking basis of the postcards and the sensationalist images they depicted clearly contradict their documentary claim and establishes them within a western system of stereotypical representation of the "other." One must distinguish between popular imagery of postcards and the more intentionally documentary photographs intended for albums, scholarly books, and ethnographic books. Even such documentary photographs were not outside the realm of, and rarely have they risen beyond, such stereotypical representations. Recent studies and exhibitions have shown how photographs taken during ethnographic expeditions were far from sacrosanct or objective. Many anthropologists have staged photographs when their camera did not see what they needed. Many anthropologists have used their camera not necessarily to capture the world they claim to have studied but in many ways to create it.[13]

Both Delacroix's painting and the postcards were part of a visual tradition built on preconceived notions that served to establish visual models and conventions for the western gaze and its ultimate violent expression, colonialism.[14] For France, these images rationalized the larger imperial venture; coinciding with the beginning of the French invasion of Algeria, as in the case of Delacroix's painting, or flourishing during the French occupation, as in the case of the postcards. They helped establish the view of the native as an "untamed" natural object of western benevolence as well as western desire. The Algerian was visually exposed as an object of the gaze, and at the same time an object subjected to western economic, political, and even sexual power. These images take on greater importance when contextualized within the events and debates of the French colonial period in Algeria because Delacroix's painting and the postcards were motivated by a strong desire to reveal that which, by its virtue of being private, was most tantalizing. These images violated the privacy of Algerian families by entering that forbidden zone, the *harem.* Paintings such as Delacroix's that expose women to the public eye were instrumental to the unveiling project; the postcard popularized it and ultimately made unveiled women objects of entertainment for the French middle class.

One must recall here the very ceremonial act of unveiling women by the military French government in Algeria in 1958. Such acts, as Franz Fanon explained, despite the condescending claim of liberating Algerian women from the repression of their own patriarchy, were really intended to weaken the original structure of the Algerian society and hence to destroy its capacity for resistance.[15] To achieve that goal, women had to be conquered, and unveiled.[16] Fanon states, "The officials of the French administration in Algeria, committed to destroying the people's originality, and under instructions to bring about the disintegration, at whatever cost, of forms of existence likely to evoke national reality directly or indirectly, were to concentrate their efforts on the wearing of the veil, which was looked upon at this juncture as a symbol of the status of the Algerian woman."[17] The veil was a long-standing tradition concerning the separation of the sexes according to the norms of Islam. The veil was also part of a mechanism of resistance within the Algerian resistance movement. As Franz Fanon reminds us, the veil could be abandoned as the Algerian did in the course of revolutionary action, but could also be used as a disguise, an outer facade with which to confuse the colonial viewer and, hence, a source of power. The act of veiling oneself was used creatively during the war of resistance to meet new demands created by the struggle, as dramatized by Ponto Corvo in his film *The Battle of Algiers,* a cinematic reading of Fanon's ideas about the Algerian revolution. In *The Battle of Algiers,* most memorable are the scenes of three Algerian women removing their veil, cutting their hair, and applying lipstick to look westernized. They easily pass through the checkpoints carrying empty baskets to be used later for concealing bombs and manipulating the flirtatious French soldiers. Once in the French quarter, they successfully carry out bombing missions in a French café, a milk bar, and a dance club. Disguised as veiled women, several F.L.N. leaders change their hiding places and move weapons from one to the other.

Niati has creatively exploited this discourse of the veil in *No to the Torture.* In the painting central to this installation, the artist has stripped the background and setting of Delacroix's painting. The women in Niati's painting are not just unveiled but totally naked, stripped of their decorative clothes and jewelry; their faces are distorted by brutal, prison-like cage bars, and their feet are shackled. Yet the women in Niati's painting are positioned in a manner that directly compares to those of Delacroix's women who, in Orientalist manner, were painted in odalisque-like, submissive postures surrounded by a sumptuously decorated, romantic background. The artist confronts the viewer with her own re-presentation of the *Women of Algiers,* suggesting that Delacroix's painting was the product of his male, Orientalist desire. By removing the veil and depicting the women faceless but naked, Niati takes the act of unveiling, historically the prerogative of the Orientalist's gaze, to its extreme and rendering it ineffective. The bars marking their faces transform them from objects of romance and sensuousness to victims of the colonizing gaze. *No to the Torture,* therefore, demystifies the French idealized version of Algeria, which is the absolute reverse of the French abuse, exploitation, and genocide of more than a million Algerian souls as a price tag for liberation. The women in Niati's painting not only become symbols of repression and torture, but at the same time symbols of defiance and resistance. Niati steps out from the position of object of a westerner's gaze in order to appropriate it for herself, for it is now an Algerian woman who wields the paint brush and commands the view.

The second installation is a tribute to Algerian women's hard work and role in society, having to work, fetch water, and take care of their families and children. Like *No to the Torture,* it deals with the existential circumstances of Houria Niati as an Algerian artist living in the west. In explaining this installation, Niati recalls how disturbed she was upon seeing images, circulated in photographs from the French colonial period, of Algerian rural women carrying water jars on their shoulders. It was in the early 1970s, when she herself was forced to abandon school and work to support her family due to the early and sudden death of her father. As Niati said, "I would like to pay tribute to those women who give their lives for their families. To get water from the sources is a daily hard work. How many miles did they walk and how many jars did they transport through their lives?"[18] From a romantic fantasy she moves us to a reality with a thump, asking us to imagine aching backs and cracked feet. She continued, "Water is a source of life, but also the source of myths and legends. Therefore, I would like to create a dream-like atmosphere for my installation, for it to appear in a half-light. . . . I remember our own folk songs which praise the beauty of the 'girl who brings water from the fountain,' but there is nothing romantic about it."[19]

Niati recalls the first time she confronted Delacroix's work and the feelings of disgust she felt when she first saw the painting at the Louvre in the late seventies.[20] Her attention was drawn to the work by Simone de Beauvoir, the French existentialist philosopher and feminist, with whom Niati had corresponded. De Beauvoir was known for her defense of the Algerian right for self-determination and of women who were involved in the resistance movement during the Algerian Revolution.[21] Thereafter, Niati began to research Orientalist painting and recalls discovering some sketches by Delacroix of a North African woman with a jar on her head, made during his famous trip to North Africa.

As a first impression, one feels that the installation is an angry response to the exploitation of Algerian women during the French colonial rule in Algeria. It depicts the personal experience of living with terror firsthand and in constant fear of oppression and arbitrary reprisal during the war of resistance.[22] Given the experiences of her youth, one can understand Niati's justifiably strong antipathy to the Orientalist and French colonialist images of Algerian women as submissive and exotic sensuous beings. Yet Niati does not stop here, and her anger extends to include the exploitation of women in Algeria today and the feeling of betrayal by the revolution's male-dominated leadership after independence. In light of the Islamic fundamentalist terror and attacks against women in Algeria today, Niati emphasizes the need to be ever more vigilant in the Algerian women's cause. In a recent interview in London, she expressed her concern with the recent political developments in Algeria and the danger of losing rights achieved so far by women due to threat of the fundamentalist movement. Using the visual medium, Niati has thus joined her Algerian and North African women literary compatriots such as Asia Djebar, Ahdaf Soueif, Djamila Sahraoui, and Laila Sebbar in rethinking Orientalism and deconstructing western perceptions of North African women.[23] Indeed, in a novel by Asia Djebar, *Women of Algiers in Their Apartment,* Delacroix is depicted as an intruder and a violator of Algerian women's privacy. Thus Delacroix has become the symbol of the Orientalist gaze, which for artists and writers is an agent of female oppression.

In Algeria today, many women writers have challenged western notions of Algerian women as submissive, domesticated, and obedient creatures.[24] They do not stop at deconstructing the western gaze, but critique their own society as women's oppression continues to take different forms. Like other postcolonial African writers and artists, they confront contemporary issues concerning their own present societies. Colonial issues of oppression, subjugation, and exploitation of women have not disappeared with formal withdrawal of colonial powers. Manifested today in different forms, oppression of women continues to be condoned and supervised by oppressive governments such as the one Algeria. Hence, issues of the power of the gaze and representation as a tool for repression and control still urgently demand our awareness and exposure.

Niati's installations force the viewer to confront western images of Algerian women as private fantasies of their European creators and consumers. In confronting women's oppression, Niati does not remain in the past or limit herself to her own society, but extends her concerns and reaches out to women on a global level. In the process of her work, Niati redefines Algerian women's oppression as the particular oppressor(s) transform. Niati continues to challenge patriarchy and the Islamic fundamentalist's rigid interpretation of the Qur'an and other primary Islamic texts in today's Algeria. Niati tries to address these concerns by combining her multiple talents in creating colorful, sensational, and exuberant multimedia installations. In the end, Niati uses the genres of installation and conceptual art, redefining them in her own image in order to create in a new, totally unrecognizable fashion to those who claim to have invented it. Niati's work does not stop at questioning—she has actively pursued an alternative path and has produced an array of exemplary works expressive of her authentic voice and creative imagination.

## Appendices I and II
## Statements of the Artist: Houria Niati

### I. There is Nothing Romantic about Bringing Water from the Fountain

I begin a story which could never exist
In the obscure meandering
Returning with fantastic
Repetition to some civilizations
The strength of pages
Which turn with a multicolored rhythm
Of the prodigious
Inventions
The stories are told but
They do not explode
Because they fuse
Silently to the oppressed spirits
And are engulfed by a cavernous defeat
Which loses itself and is forgotten
Why do the Travelers look for
total accomplishment
of the absolutely unreal or
Provisional separation
Bursting in the veins
Like non-fatal poison
Evidence is not Truth
Because the vision can change
So why idolize
The bodies without feeling
Which swollen by unconscious dissatisfaction
refuse to rebel
And accept the invigorating
Neutrality of the objects
Too much wanted and misunderstood
Traps opening
Like enormous mouths
But the pleasures are transient
The immobility is latent

Aggression and trembling Agony
In the night obscured by
The Ignorance and great
Beauty of the passing sirens
Belonging to the hereditary Power
Of the Man who holds the keys
Of Destiny
The immobility is the strength
Fragile and compassionate
Of the Mothers columns of the descendences
Messengers from the womb
Of the obligatory reproductions
The immobility is the serenity
Contagious the silence in a
World where the explosion of
Revolution blocked by
The walls built by
Possessive hands
The immobility is the repressed dream
Of the impossible escape
To far horizons
That disappear into the thickness
Of the endless night
Not thinking is to accept
The conditions with no conditions
Not thinking is to burst out laughing
Like a bomb
Obscured by the night
By the incredible misadventure
Of limited freedom
No matter what the silence
In the illuminated darkness
Accepting the pleasures of the dark of night
And rejecting the immaculate morning
Who are you women of the mountains
Nymphs of allures who
Amaze the hardest hearts
Do you really exist
Have you really felt
The eyes of this Artist on your bodies
Who bravely
Wanted to capture

This ecstasy
Not only the
Repression and Exploitation
Who are you Women who submit
To sensual passion
In the shadowy houses
With half opened windows
Looking into interior courtyards
Women fatal and mysterious
Powerful in their innocence
Out of the ordinary out of time
But who shut their eyes to
The magical thread of
Racial multiplicity
They are the dream
of a fragile mystery
Which has traveled
Desperately
Searching for peace
And newness
Deformed Orientalist
In the beginning of a destruction
Inevitable but positive
*London, 1982*
(Translation of a poem in French by Houria Niati)

**II.** ***No to the Torture***

I offer to myself the World in a fantasmagoric
Effort of critical transformation
What is it
It is the outcome of the mysterious delirium
That contracts my fingers
On the multicolored pastels
Which trace the words and the shapes
That burst on the paper like a retarded fusion
Of pschydermic frustrations
Of the transcendental relations
The ramifications degenerate themselves
The stories are no longer listened to
The tales are not anymore tackled

In a warm and reconfronting impetus
We do not listen we look at
We accept with infected eyes
Swollen by the resignation and the demission
The ski-lift does not go down
The lifts will never go up
The minds are stagnant like the mirrors
At the bottom of the mountains stunted
The reasons have no more strength to exist
The spring is icy the winter is crumpled

The autumn remains abandoned
The summer does not anymore suffice to itself
We do not know we shut the doors
We go down in the immaculate foundation
Of the fundamental inexperience
Why counting the days when nothing
Will release
Even the last judgment will not happen
Even the weekly crisis will manifest itself
Into a deluge
Of smashed glass on the lost tapestries
In the labyrinth of the infertile towers
The gardens will disperse in the frontiers
And the arcades will come to life
Of fervor of grief
Of unexpected change
The trees will rebel
In an electronic storm which will burn
The antecedents and will reach
The hallucinogenic roots
The bluish fishes
Will extend in the impenetrable light
Of external mysteries
The elements float in the disintegrated
Matters
The walkers meet the walls
Doorless and openingless
The walkers do not dream
They walk on the concrete
And their eyes collide the spy cells
Which pick up their movements

The bodies are not fondled
They are the geometric abstraction
Of the infiltration through the shutters
And the frightened colors
Do not shine
However the days are neither shorter
Nor longer
They are no more Time's consistency
Which draw the marks on our forehead
And which furrow into our skin thousands
Of little dried rivers
Each time they are the morbid dream
Of the unbroken convoys
On the lunar and spatial passages
The dramas lend like a multitude
Of voracious flowers unexpected
The roses are incredible fishes
The fishes walk like humans
Humans with despair fly
And the birds wait for the End
Delirium Delirium
Delirium
*London 1982*
(Translation of a poem in French by Houria Niati)

## NOTES

This paper was first presented at the Tenth Triennial Symposium on African Art, sponsored by the Arts Council of the African Studies Association (ACASA), April 19–23, 1995, New York City, as part of the session "African Artists and the West: A Counter Penetration?" An earlier, short version of this paper was published as "The Installations of Houria Niati," in *NKA: Journal of Contemporary African Art* 1.3 (Fall/Winter 1995): 50–55.

1. Salah Hasan, "The Modernist Experience in African Art: Visual Expressions of the Self and Cross Cultural Aesthetic," *NKA: Journal of Contemporary African Art* 1.2 (Spring/Summer 1995).

2. Malek Alloula, *The Colonial Harem,* trans. Myna Godzich and Wlad Godzich (Minneapolis: University of Minnesota Press, 1986).

3. The exhibition *Forces of Change: Artists of the Arab World,* was initiated at the National Museum of Women in the Arts, February-April 1994, and toured various cities in the United States. See Salwa Mikdadi Nashashibi, ed., *Forces of*

*Change: Artists of the Arab World* (Washington, D.C.: National Museum of Women in the Arts, 1994).

4. *Four X 4: Installation by Sixteen Artists in Four Galleries*, with catalogue foreword by exhibition curator Eddie Chambers (Bristol, 1991). The show was slightly modified and exhibited at the Zora Neale Hurston Museum in 1995; see *New Visions: Recent Works by Six African Artists* (Eatonville, Fla.: Zora Neale Hurston Museum, 1995).

5. Todd B. Porterfield, "Western Views of Oriental Women in Modern Painting and Photography," in *Forces of Change,* ed. Nashashibi, 59–71.

6. Edward Said, *Orientalism* (New York: Pantheon, 1978), 7.

7. Said, *Orientalism.*

8. Yvonne Deslandres, *Delacroix: A Pictorial Biography,* trans. Jonathan Griffin (New York: Viking Press, 1963).

9. Deslandres, *Delacroix,* 66.

10. Deslandres, *Delacroix.*

11. See Susan Sontag, "On Photography," in *Illuminations: Women Writing on Photography from the 1850s to the Present,* ed. Liz Heron and Val Williams (Durham, N.C.: Duke University Press, 1996), 233.

12. Barbara Harlow, "Introduction," in Alloula, *The Colonial Harem,* ix–xxii.

13. See recent publications on ethnographic photography such as *Picturing Paradise: Colonial Photographs of Samoa, 1875–1925* (New York: The Metropolitan Museum of Art, 1996), and Laura Kendall et al., *Drawing Shadows to Stone: The Photography of the Jesup North Pacific Expedition, 1897–1902* (New York: Museum of Natural History, 1997).

14. Alloula, *The Colonial Harem.*

15. See Frantz Fanon, *A Dying Colonialism* (New York: Grove Press, 1965).

16. Such an attitude was not unique to the French. The British did the same in East Africa in relation to female circumcision and India in relation to the tradition of widow sacrifice or *suttee.* The overt program was to liberate women from their male counterpart's oppression and patriarchy, but the larger political goal was the colonial objective of destroying the original structure of the society in order to weaken its ability for resistance. Thus women were used as pawns in a game, in which their welfare and freedom were not the ultimate aims.

17. See Fanon, *A Dying Colonialism,* 37–38.

18. See Juliet Highet, "Houria Niati," in *Four X 4.*

19. Quoted in Highet, "Houria Niati."

20. Interview with the artist, August 1993, London. See also Juliet Highet, "Painter of Dreams," *New African,* December 1984, p. 33, and Houria Niati, Commentary Exhibition Brochure, Cartwright Hall Museum, Bradford, 1990.

21. See Simone de Beauvoir and Gisele Halimi, *Djamila Boupacha: The Story of Torture of a Young Algerian Girl Which Shocked Liberal French Opinion,* trans. Peter Green (London: A. Deutsch and Weidenfeld and Nicholson, 1962).

This is an account of the case of a young Algerian resistance fighter and victim of torture, which became a rallying case for antiwar groups in France.

22. Niati was traumatized even more by the death of her father when she was sixteen years old. A landscape painter himself and with whose work Niati later exhibited her own work, he died tragically and unexpectedly in the prime of his age.

23. For example, see Asia Djebar, *Women of Algiers in Their Apartment* (Charlottesville and London: University Press of Virginia, 1992); Ahdaf Soueif, *In the Eye of the Sun* (London: Bloomsbury, 1992); and Djamilah Sahraoui's documentary film, *The Other Half of Allah's Heaven* (1996).

24. In several contemporary Algerian literary works, Orientalist images, especially Delacroix's *Women of Algiers*, have become a metaphor for the western gaze. Asia Djebar's novel, *Women of Algiers in Their Apartment*, takes its title from Delacroix's work. In the novel, Delacroix is represented as a thief, spy, and an intruder. His painting is, for Djebar, both a depiction of and an agent of the oppression of Algerian women.

# Bibliography

This is not an exhaustive bibliography; nor does it contain all of the works cited in this volume. The books and articles listed below are intended to steer readers toward works, primarily but not exclusively in English, related to the essays in this volume, particularly those sources that are either fundamental, unusual, or simply recent.

## General Studies and Edited Collections


ʿAbd ar-Raziq, Ahmad. *La femme au temps des mamlouks en Egypt.* Cairo: Institut français d'archéologie orientale du Caire, 1973.

Ahmed, Leila. *Women and Gender in Islam: Historical Roots of a Modern Debate.* New Haven and London: Yale University Press, 1992

Beck, Lois and Nicki Keddie, eds. *Women in the Muslim World.* Cambridge, Mass.: Harvard University Press, 1978.

Göçek, Fatma Müge and Shiva Balaghi, eds. *Reconstructing Gender in the Middle East: Tradition, Identity, and Power.* New York: Columbia University Press, 1995.

Hambly, Gavin, ed. *Women in the Medieval Islamic World: Power, Patronage, Piety.* New York: St. Martin's Press, 1998.

Helly, Dorothy O. and Susan M. Reverby, eds. *Gendered Domains: Rethinking Public and Private in Women's History.* Essays from the 7th Berkshire Conference on the History of Women. Ithaca, N.Y.: Cornell University Press, 1992.

al-Hibri, Azizah, ed. *Women and Islam.* Oxford: Pergamon Press, 1982.

al-Hibshi, Abd Allah. *Mujam al-Nisa al-Yamaniyat.* Sanaa: Dar al-Hikma al-Yamaniya, 1988.

Keddie, Nikki and Beth Baron, eds. *Women in Middle Eastern History: Shifting Boundaries in Sex and Gender.* New Haven: Yale University Press, 1991.

Kimball, Michelle and Barbara R. von Schlegell. *Muslim Women throughout the World: A Bibliography.* Boulder, Colo.: Lynne Rienner Publishers, 1997.

Misra, Rekha. *Women in Mughal India (1526–1748 A.D.).* Delhi: Munshiram Manoharlal, 1967.

Nashat, Guity, ed. *Women and Revolution in Iran.* Boulder, Colo.: Westview Press, 1983.

Rosaldo, Michelle and Louise Lamphere, eds. *Woman, Culture, and Society.* Stanford, Calif.: Stanford University Press, 1974.

al-Saʿdawi, Nawal. *The Hidden Face of Eve: Women in the Arab World,* trans. S. Hetata. London: Zed Press, 1980.

Scott, Joan. *Gender and the Politics of History.* New York: Columbia University Press, 1988.

Spellberg, Denise. *Politics, Gender and the Islamic Past: The Legacy of ʿAʾisha Bint abi Bakr.* New York: Columbia University Press, 1994.

Tucker, Judith, ed. *Arab Women: Old Boundaries, New Frontiers.* Bloomington: Indiana University Press, 1993.

Tucker, Judith. "Gender and Islamic History," pp. 37–74, in *Islamic and European Expansion, The Forging of a Global Order,* ed. Michael Adas. Philadelphia: Temple University Press, 1993.

———. *Women in Nineteenth-Century Egypt.* Cambridge: Cambridge University Press, 1985.

Utas, Bo, ed. *Women in Islamic Societies: Social and Historical Perspectives.* London: Curazon Press, 1983.

Viguera, María. *La mujer en al-Andalus.* Seville: Editoriales Andaluzas Unidas, 1989.

Zilfi, Madeline C., ed. *Women in the Ottoman Empire: Middle Eastern Women in the Early Modern Era.* Leiden: E. J. Brill, 1997.

Walther, Wiebke. *Women in Islam from Medieval to Modern Times.* Princeton, N.J.: Markus Wiener Publishers, 1995.

## Representation and Patronage

ʿAbd ar-Raziq, Ahmad. "Trois fondations feminines dans Egypte mamlouke." *Revue des études islamiques* 41 (1973): 95–126.

Alloula, Malek. *The Colonial Harem,* trans. M. and W. Godzicht. Minneapolis: University of Minnesota Press, c. 1986.

Atıl, Esin, ed. "Islamic Women as Rulers and Patrons." *Asian Art* (special issue: *Patronage by Women in Islamic Art*) 6.2 (1993): 3–12.

Bates, Ülkü. "The Architectural Patronage of Ottoman Women," *Asian Art* 6/2 (1993), 50-65.

———. "Women as Patrons of Architecture in Turkey," pp. 245–60, in *Women in the Muslim World,* ed. L. Beck and N. Keddie. Cambridge, Mass.: Harvard University Press, 1978.

Denny, Walter. "Women in Islamic Art," pp. 147–80, in *Women, Religion, and Social Change,* ed. Yvonne Haddad and E. Findly. Albany: State University of New York Press, 1985.

Findly, Ellison Banks. "The Capture of Maryam-uz-Zamani's Ship: Mughal Women and European Traders," *Journal of the American Oriental Society* 108.2 (1988): 227–38.

———. "Nur Jahan's Embroidery Trade and Flowers of the Taj Mahal." *Asian Art and Culture* 9.2 (1996): 7–25.

———. "The Pleasure of Women: Nur Jahan and Mughal Painting." *Asian Art* 6.2 (1993): 66–86.

Golombek, Lisa. "Timur's Gardens: The Feminine Perspective," pp. 29–36, in *The Mughal Garden: Interpretation, Conservation and Implications,* ed. Mahmood Hussain, Abdul Rehman, and James L. Wescoat, Jr. Lahore: Ferozsons, 1996.

Harithy, Howayda. "Female Patronage of Mamluk Architecture in Cairo." *Harvard Middle Eastern and Islamic Review* 1.2 (1994)" 152–74.

Humphreys, R. Stephen. "Women as Architectural Patrons of Religious Architecture in Ayyubid Damascus." *Muqarnas* 11 (1994): 35–54.

Lewis, Reina. *Gendering Orientalism: Race, Femininity and Representation.* London: Routledge, 1995.

Marefat, Roya. "Timurid Women: Patronage and Power." *Asian Art* 6.2 (1993): 28–49.

Micklewright, Nancy. "Women's Dress in Nineteenth Century Istanbul: Mirror of a Changing Society." Ph.D. diss., University of Pennsylvania, 1986.

———. "Tracing the Transformation of Women's Dress in Nineteenth Century Istanbul." *Dress* 13 (1987): 33–42.

Porterfield, Todd B. "Western Views of Oriental Women in Modern Painting and Photography," pp. 59–71, in *Forces of Change: Artists of the Arab World,* ed. Salwa Mikdadi Nashashibi. Washington, D.C.: National Museum of Women in the Arts, 1994.

Renda, Günsel. *9000 Years of The Anatolian Woman.* Istanbul: Ministry of Culture, 1993.

Sadek, Noha. "In the Queen of Sheba's Footsteps: Women Patrons in Rasulid Yemen." *Asian Art* 6.2 (1993): 14–27.

———. "Rasulid Women: Power and Patronage." *Proceedings of the 22nd Seminar for Arabian Studies* 19 (1989): 121–36.

Singer, Amy. "The *Mülknāmes* of Hürrem Sultan's Waqf in Jerusalem," *Muqarnas* 14 (1997): 96–102.

Stillman, Yedida and Nancy Micklewright. "Costume in the Middle East." *Middle East Studies Association Bulletin* 26.1 (1992): 13–38.

Thys-Şenocak, Lucienne. "The Yeni Valide Mosque Complex of Eminönü," *Muqarnas* 15 (1998): 58–70.

Willis, Janice D. "Female Patronage in Indian Buddhism," in *The Powers of Art: Patronage in Indian Culture,* ed. Barbara Stoler Miller. Delhi: Oxford University Press, 1992.

———. "Nuns and Benefactresses: The Role of Women in the Development of Buddhism," in *Women, Religion, and Social Change,* ed. Yvonne Yazbeck Haddad and Ellison Banks Findly. Albany: State University of New York Press, 1985.

## Property, Law, and Codes of Behavior

Abbott, Nabia. "Women and the State in Early Islam." *Journal of Near Eastern Studies* 1 (1942): 106–27.

Arnaldez, Roger. "Status juridique et sociologique de la femme en Islam." *Cahier de Civilisation Médiévale* 20 (1977): 131–43.

Baer, Gabriel. "Woman and Waqf: An Analysis of the Istanbul *Tahrir* of 1546." *Asian and African Studies: Journal of the Israel Orient Society* 17.1–2 (1983): 9–28.

Deniz, Kandiyoti, ed. *Women, Islam and the State.* London: Macmillan, 1991.

Doy, ʿAbdur Rahman. *Woman in Shariʿah.* London: Ta-Ha Publishers, 1989.

Esposito, John. *Women in Muslim Family Law.* Syracuse: Syracuse University Press, 1982.

Gerber, Haim. "Social and Economic Position of Women in an Ottoman City, Bursa, 1600–1700." *International Journal of Middle Eastern Studies* 12 (1980): 231–44.

Goldziher, Ignaz. "Women in the Hadith Literature," 2:366–68, in *Muslim Studies,* 2 vols., ed. S. M. Stern. London: Allen and Unwin, 1971.

Lutfi, Huda. "Al-Sakhāwī's *Kitāb al-Nisāʾ* as a Source for the Social and Economic History of Muslim Women during the Fifteenth Century A.D." *The Muslim World* 71 (1981): 104–24.

———. "Manners and Customs of Fourteenth-Century Cairene Women: Female Anarchy versus Male Sharʿi Order in Muslim Prescriptive Treatises," pp. 99–121, in *Women in Middle Eastern History,* ed. Nikki Keddie and B. Baron. New Haven: Yale University Press, 1991.

Madelung, Wilfred. "Shiʿi Attitudes toward Women as Reflected in Fiqh," pp. 74–75 in *Society and the Sexes in Medieval Islam,* ed. A. L. al-Sayyid-Marsot. Malibu, Calif.: Undena Publications, 1979.

Marcus, Abraham. "Men, Women, and Property: Dealers in Real Estate in Eighteenth-Century Aleppo." *Journal of the Economic and Social History of the Orient* 26 (1983): 137–63.

Mernissi, Fatima. *Beyond the Veil: Male-Female Dynamics in Modern Muslim Society,* rev. ed. Bloomington, Ind.: Indiana University Press, 1987.

———. *The Veil and the Male Elite: A Feminist Interpretation of Women's Rights in Islam,* trans. M. Lakeland. Reading, Mass.: Addison Wesley Publ. Co., 1991.

Petry, Carl F. "Class Solidarity versus Gender Gain: Women as Custodians of Property in Later Medieval Egypt," pp. 122–42, in *Women in Middle Eastern History,* ed. Nikki Keddie and B. Baron. New Haven: Yale University Press, 1991.

Quataert, Donald. "Ottoman Women, Households and Textile Manufacturing, 1800–1914," pp. 161–76, in *Women in Middle Eastern History,* ed. Nikki Keddie and B. Baron. New Haven: Yale University Press, 1991.

Shatzmiller, Maya. "Aspects of Women's Participation in the Economic Life of Later Medieval Islam: Occupations and Mentalities." *Arabica* 35 (1988): 36–58.

———. "Women and Property Rights in al-Andalus and the Maghrib: Social Patterns and Legal Discourses." *Islamic Law and Society* 23 (1995): 219–57.

Smith, Jane. "The Experience of Muslim Women: Considerations of Power and Authority," pp. 91–97, in *The Islamic Impact,* ed. Yvonne Yazbeck Haddad, Byron Haines, and Ellison Findly. Syracuse: Syracuse University Press, 1984.

Sonbol, Amira. *Women, the Family and Divorce Laws in Islamic History.* Syracuse: Syracuse University Press, 1996.

Stowasser, Barbara. "The Status of Women in Early Islam," pp. 11–43, in *Muslim Women,* ed. F. Hussein. London: Croom Helm, 1984.

———. *Women in the Qur'an: Traditions and Interpretation.* New York: Oxford University Press, 1994.

Szuppe, Maria. "La participation des femmes de la famille royale à l'exercice du pouvoir en Iran safavide au XVIe siècle." *Studia Iranica* 23 (1994): 211–57; 24 (1995): 61–122.

Viguera, María. "*Aṣluḥu li'ma'ālī,* On the Social Status of Andalusi Women," pp. 709–24, in *The Legacy of Muslim Spain,* ed. Salma Jayyusi. Leiden: E.J. Brill, 1994.

## Women, Sexuality, and Family Status

Ávila, María Luisa. "La estructura de la familia en al-Andalus," pp. 33–37, in *Casas y Palacios de al-Andalus,* ed. Julio Navarro Palazón. Barcelona-Madrid: Lunwerg Editores, 1995.

Boudhiba, Abdelwahab. *Sexuality in Islam,* trans. A. Sheridan. London: Routledge and Kegan Paul, 1985.

Duben, Alan, and Cem Behar. *Istanbul Households: Marriage, Family and Fertility 1880–1940.* Cambridge: Cambridge University Press, 1991.

Farah, Madelain. *Marriage and Sexuality in Islam: A Translation of al-Ghazali's Book on the Etiquette of Marriage.* Salt Lake City: University of Utah Press, 1984.

Haeri, Shahla. *Law of Desire: Temporary Marriage in Shi'i Iran.* Syracuse: Syracuse University Press, 1989.

Las, Kishori S. *The Mughal Harem.* New Delhi: Aditya Prakashan, 1988.

Marmon, Shaun. "Concubinage, Islamic," 3:527–29, in *Dictionary of the Middle Ages,* ed. J. Strayer et al. New York: Scribner, 1982–89.

Musallam, Basim. *Sex and Society in Islam: Birth Control before the Nineteenth Century.* Cambridge: Cambridge University Press, 1983.

Peirce, Leslie. *The Imperial Harem: Women and Sovereignty in the Ottoman Empire.* New York and Oxford: Oxford University Press, 1993.

Reinhart, Kevin. "Impurity/No Danger." *History of Religions* 30 (1990): 1–23.

Shatzmiller, Maya. "Marriage, Family, and the Faith: Women's Conversion to Islam." *Journal of Family History* 21.3 (1996): 235–67.

Stern, Gertrude, H. *Marriage in Early Islam.* London: The Royal Asiatic Society, 1939.

## Women and Religion

Clancy-Smith, Julia. "The House of Zainab: Female Authority and Saintly Succession in Colonial Algeria," pp. 254–74, in *Women in Middle Eastern History,* ed. Nikki Keddie and B. Baron. New Haven: Yale University Press, 1991.

Elias, Jamal. "Female and Feminine in Islamic Mysticism." *The Muslim World* 78 (1988): 209–24.

Horner, I. B. *Women Under Primitive Buddhism: Laywomen and Almswomen.* London: Routledge, 1930.

Jaine, Padmanabh S. *Gender and Salvation: Jaina Debates on the Spiritual Liberation of Women.* Berkeley: University of California Press, 1991.

McAuliffe, Jane. "Chosen of All Women: Mary and Fatima in Qur'anic Exegesis." *Islamochristiana* 7 (1981): 19–28.

Merguerian, Gayane Karen and Afsaneh Najmabadi. "Zulaykha and Yusuf: Whose 'Best Story'?" *International Journal of Middle East Studies* 29 (1997): 485–508.

Paul, Diana Y. *Women in Buddhism: Images of the Feminine in Mahayana Tradition.* Berkeley: Asian Humanities Press, 1979.

Schimmel, Annemarie. "Women in Mystical Islam." *Women's International Forum* 5.2 (1982): 145–51.

Smith, Jane and Yvonne Haddad. "The Virgin Mary in Islamic Tradition and Commentary." *The Muslim World* 79.3–4 (1989): 161–87.

Smith, Margaret. *Rabi'a the Mystic and Her Fellow Saints in Islam.* Cambridge: Cambridge University Press, 1928.

## Biography and Case Studies

Abbott, Nabia. *'A'ishah: The Beloved of Mohammad.* Chicago: University of Chicago Press, 1942.

———. *Two Queens of Baghdad: The Mother and Wife of Harun al-Rashid.* Chicago: University of Chicago Press, 1946.

'Abddallah Inan, *Nihayat al-Andalus.* Cairo: Maktaba al-Madani, 1987.

Bint al-Shāṭī' (pen name of 'Ā'isha 'Abd al-Raḥmān). *Tarākim sayyidāt bayt al-nubuwwa* (Biographies of the Ladies of the House of the Prophet). Beirut, 1984.

Butenschon, Andrea. *The Life of a Mogul Princess, Jahanara Begum, Daughter of Shahjahan.* London, 1931.

Findly, Ellison Banks. *Nur Jahan: Empress of Mughal India (1611–1627).* New York: Oxford University Press, 1993.

Gholsorkhi, Shohreh. "Pari Khan Khanum: A Masterful Safavid Princess," *Iranian Studies* 28 (1995): 143–56.

Habib, Irfan. "The Family of Nur Jahan During Jahangir's Reign," 1: 74–95 in *Medieval India, A Miscellany.* Bombay: Asia Publishing House, 1969.

al-Hamdani, Husain F. "The Life and Times of Queen Saiyidah Arwa the Sulayhid of the Yemen." *Journal of the Royal Central Asian Society* 18 (1931): 505–17.

Haykal, Muḥammad Ḥusayn. *The Life of Muhammad,* trans. Ismai'īl Ragi A. al-Faruqi. Indianapolis, 1976; originally *Ḥayāt Muhammad,* 1935. (Discusses the Prophet's wives.)

al-Imad, Leila. "Women and Religion in the Fatimid Caliphate: The Case of al-Sayyidah al-Hurrah, Queen of Yemen," pp. 137–44, in *Intellectual Studies on Islam: Essays Written in Honor of Martin B. Dickson,* ed. Michael Mazzaoui and Vera Moreen. Salt Lake City: University of Utah Press, 1990.

Lammens, Henri. *Fatima et les filles de Mahomet.* Rome: Scripta Pontificii Institut Biblici, 1912.

Mernissi, Fatima. *The Forgotten Queens of Islam.* Cambridge: Polity Press, 1992.

Roded, Ruth. *Women in Islamic Biographical Collections: From Ibn Sa'd to Who's Who.* Boulder, Colo.: Lynne Rienner Publishers, 1994.

Rossabi, Morris. "Khubilai Khan and the Women in His Family," pp. 153–80, in *Studia Sino-Mongolica: Festshrift für Herbert Franke,* ed. W. Bauer. Wiesbaden, 1979.

Rossi, Ettore. "La Sultana *Nūr Bānū* (Cecelia Venier-Baffo) moglie di Selim II (1566-1574) e madre di Murad III (1574–1595)." *Oriente moderno* 33.11 (1953): 433–41.

## Anthropological and Historical Studies

Antoun, Richard T. "On the Modesty of Women in Arab Muslim Villages: A Study in the Accommodation of Traditions." *American Anthopologist* 70 (1968): 671–97.

Berkey, Jonathan, P. *The Transmission of Knowledge in Medieval Cairo: A Social History of Islamic Education.* Princeton: Princeton University Press, 1992.

Cohen, Judith R. "The Role of Women Musicians in Medieval Spain." MA thesis, Université de Montréal, 1980, (Ann Arbor: University Microfilms 1319039).

Croutier, Alev Lytle. *Harem: The World Behind the Veil.* New York: Abbeville, 1989.

Davis, Fanny. *The Ottoman Lady: A Social History from 1718 to 1918.* Westport, Conn.: Greenwood Press, 1986.

Davis, Susan. *Patience and Power: Women's Lives in a Moroccan Village.* Cambridge, Mass.: Schenkman, 1983.

Fernea, Elizabeth. *Guests of the Sheik: An Ethnography of an Iraqi Village.* Garden City, N.Y.: Doubleday, 1965.

Friedl, Erika. *Women of Deh Koh: Lives in an Iranian Village.* Washington, D.C.: Smithsonian Institution Press, 1989.

Frierson, Elizabeth. "Unimagined Communities: Women and Education in the Late Ottoman Empire, 1876–1909," *Critical Matrix* 9.2 (1995): 55–90.

Goitein, S. D. *A Mediterranean Society,* vols. 1–6. Berkeley and Los Angeles: University of California Press, 1967–93.

Hanımefendi, Leyla (Saz). *The Imperial Harem of the Sultans: Daily Life at the Çirağan Palace during the Nineteenth Century.* Istanbul: PEVA Publications, 1995.

Marcus, Julie. *A World of Difference: Islam and Gender Hierarchy in Turkey.* London and Atlantic Highlands, N.J.: Zed, 1992.

Melman, Billie. *Women's Orients: English Women and the Middle East, 1718–1918.* Ann Arbor: University of Michigan Press, 1992.

Tugay, Emine Foat. *Three Centuries. Family Chronicles of Turkey and Egypt.* London: Oxford University Press, 1963.

## Women's Writing and Speech

Abu-Lughod, Lila. *Veiled Sentiments: Honor and Poetry in a Bedouin Society.* Berkeley and Los Angeles: University of California Press, 1986.

Badran, Margot and Miriam Cooke, eds. *Opening the Gates: A Century of Arab Women's Writing*. Bloomington: Indiana University Press, 1990.

Baron, Beth. *The Women's Awakening in Egypt: Culture, Society, and the Press*. New Haven: Yale University Press, 1994.

Edib, Halide. *Memoires of Halide Edib*. New York: The Century Company, 1926.

Farmaian, Sattareh Farman with Dona Munker. *Daughter of Persia*. New York: Doubleday, 1992.

Fernea, Elizabeth and B. Bezirgan, eds. *Middle Eastern Women Speak*. Austin: University of Texas, 1977.

Frierson, Elizabeth. "*Hanımlara Mahsûs Gazete:* State, Press, and Gender in the Late-Ottoman Empire, 1895–1909." Ph.D. diss., Princeton University, 1996.

Malti-Douglas, Fedwa. *Woman's Body Woman's Word: Gender and Discourse in Arabo-Islamic Writing*. Princeton: Princeton University Press, c. 1991.

Mernissi, Fatima. *Dreams of Trepass: Tales of a Harem Girlhood*. Reading, Mass.: Addison-Wesley, 1994.

Shaarawi, Huda. *Harem Years: The Memoirs of an Egyptian Feminist,* trans. M. Badran. New York: The Feminist Press, 1987.

Zeyneb Hanoum. *A Turkish Woman's European Impressions,* ed. Grace Ellison. Philadelphia: J. B. Lippincott Company, 1913.

# About the Authors

**D. Fairchild Ruggles** is visiting assistant professor in the Department of Near Eastern Studies, Cornell University. Her book, *Gardens, Landscape, and Vision in the Palaces of Islamic Spain* appeared in 2000. In addition to publications in *Ars Orientalis, Muqarnas, Islamic Studies, Al-Andalus,* and *Gesta,* she was co-editor of "Site and Sight in the Garden," a theme issue of *Journal of Garden History* 14.1 (1994).

**Yasser Tabbaa** has taught at MIT and the University of Michigan, Ann Arbor. He wrote *Constructions of Power and Piety in Medieval Aleppo* (1997) and has articles in *Ars Orientalis, Muqarnas,* and *Journal of Garden History* as well as contribution to museum catalogues. His next book, *The Transformations of Islamic Art,* is forthcoming from the University of Washington Press.

**Ethel Sara Wolper** is assistant professor in the Department of History, University of New Hampshire, where she teaches courses in history, art history, and religious studies. She has published in *Muqarnas* and is preparing a book on dervish monuments in pre-Ottoman Anatolia.

**Leslie Peirce** is associate professor in the Departments of History and Near Eastern Studies, University of California at Berkeley. She regularly teaches courses on women and gender in the Islamic world and her book *The Imperial Harem: Women and Sovereignty in the Ottoman Empire* (1993) won the Turkish Studies Association biennial prize for best book. She is currently writing a book on Ottoman law and society.

**Lucienne Thys-Şenocak** is assistant professor in the Department of History, Koç University (Istanbul), where she teaches history and art history. She has published in *Muqarnas* and is editing a collection of studies on women in the Ottoman world.

**Ellison Banks Findly** is professor in the Department of Religion and International Studies Program, Trinity College. Her books include *Women, Religion and Social Change,* co-edited with Yvonne Haddad (State University of New York Press, 1985), and *Nur Jahan: Empress of Mughal India (1611–1627)* (1993).

**Kishwar Rizvi** is an architect and holds her doctorate from the History, Theory and Criticism Program of the Department of Architecture, MIT. Her essay in this volume won a 1999 award for excellence from The Association for Middle Eastern Women's Studies.

**Nancy Micklewright** teaches the history of photography and Islamic art at the University of Victoria (Canada). She has published in the *Middle East Studies Association Bulletin, Muqarnas,* and *Dress,* and has contributed to edited works on aspects of Ottoman history. She recently completed a book on the photographic albums of Annie Lady Brassey in the Huntington Library (forthcoming).

**Elizabeth Brown Frierson** is assistant professor in the Department of History, University of Cincinnati. Her article, "Unimagined Communities: Educational Reform and Civic Identity among Late-Ottoman Women," published in *Critical Matrix,* won the Turkish Studies Association biennial prize for best article in 1977.

**Salah M. Hassan** is assistant professor in the Africana Studies and Research Center, Cornell University, where he is editor of *NKA: Journal of Contemporary African Art.* His publications include *Art and Islamic Literacy among the Hausa of Northern Nigeria* (1992) and, with Okwui Enwezor, *New Visions: Recent Works by Six African Artists* (1995).

# Index

*Note:* Buildings are listed by name, not city.

www.ingramcontent.com/pod-product-compliance
Lightning Source LLC
LaVergne TN
LVHW011957040926
847296LV00030B/342